Instructor's Edition for

A Writer's Journey

Instructor's Edition for

A Writer's Journey
SECOND EDITION

GEOFFREY PLATT
Orange County Community College

D. C. Heath and Company
Lexington, Massachusetts   Toronto

Address editorial correspondence to:

D. C. Heath and Company
125 Spring Street
Lexington, MA 02173

Acquisitions Editor: Paul A. Smith
Developmental Editor: Linda M. Bieze
Production Editor: Celena Sun
Designer: Kenneth Hollman
Photo Researcher: Martha Shethar
Production Coordinator: Charles Dutton
Permissions Editor: Margaret Roll

Cover Photo: Bowman Lake, Glacier National Park, Montana/Wiley/Wales: ProFiles West

Photo credits: p. 1 Werner Muller/Peter Arnold, Inc.
p. 113 Michael Nichols/Magnum Photos
p. 225 Frank Siteman/The Picture Cube

Published simultaneously in Canada.

Printed in the United States of America.

International Standard Book Number: 0-669-35143-1

10 9 8 7 6 5 4 3 2 1

To the Instructor

In response to comments and suggestions from students and instructors who have used the First Edition of *A Writer's Journey*, as well as my own experiences and reviews commissioned by D. C. Heath, this Second Edition incorporates several changes while still preserving the basic commitment to process writing theory and collaborative learning of the earlier version.

The main change is that Chapter Four in the original version, "Using Your Reader's Needs to Organize Your Writing," has now evolved into two separate chapters—Chapter Four: "Using Your Reader's Needs to Organize Paragraphs" and Chapter Five: "Organizing the Whole Paper to Meet Your Reader's Needs." Also, at the end of each chapter in Part One, "Discovering and Organizing Ideas for Your Readers," an Editing Activity directs the student to a particular chapter in Part Two, "Editing and Proofreading," as well as to the chapter on sentence combining, to develop skills used in the editing of final drafts. You will also find additional professional writing samples, writing activities, and punctuation activities in Chapter 13. Finally, there is a short research assignment in the form of a documented essay, in addition to the material on the full research paper in Part III, "Research." The *Instructor's Guide* has also been revised and expanded.

The text was originally intended for students in pre-freshman composition college courses, but many instructors, including me, have found it effective in some freshman composition courses as well.

This book addresses the need of beginning writers to communicate effectively, not just to polish their grammar and editing skills. It recognizes their need to discover their ideas and to express them effectively as students, as workers, as people who lead examined lives, and as citizens of a democracy.

Certain assumptions guided the writing of this text. I believe, as do many others these days, that writing is recursive, that inexperienced writers need to rewrite extensively, not as punishment, but as a way to discover what it is they want to say and how to say it. Therefore, the book offers extensive opportunities to write and rewrite.

My own teaching experience, as well as my reading, has convinced me of the value of collaborative learning and of the need for writers to get feedback from as many readers as possible. So there are many activities that suggest ways for students to get help from their peers, for them to feel that they are part of a community of writers, not lone individuals trying to please the expert in the classroom who gives out grades.

I also share the assumptions of process writing theory, which holds that developing writers grow by examining what they do when they write rather than by imitating the writing of professionals or by following preset rhetorical modes.

Following process theory, the writing activities in this highly active text begin with the discovery of ideas and with the whole paper, rather than with editing. In fact, I think premature editing causes a great many students to find writing an intimidating task. Therefore, this book's first chapter deals with ways of getting started, using free writing, asking questions, clustering, and getting help from others. Students are encouraged to take chances, to get ideas down on paper without worrying about form or editing just yet.

Chapter 2 focuses on developing a main idea, a contract with readers that will guide the writer in deciding what to include and exclude. Students learn that in rewriting they can clarify, modify, and even radically change this contract.

Chapter 3 helps students move beyond writing generalizations to writing details that are concrete and specific enough to meet the needs of readers.

Chapter 4 focuses on the writer's need to be aware of the questions that a reader has in reading a piece of writing. This chapter helps writers develop their ideas in paragraphs and organize their material in response to an awareness of readers' needs.

Chapter 5 helps students to further develop and to apply organizational skills learned in the previous chapter to the whole essay.

Chapter 6 guides students writers in developing an awareness of how different readers have different needs and shows beginning writers how to use their sense of who their readers are to organize their material.

Chapter 7 has a unique emphasis: students learn to create coherence by anticipating responses from readers to individual ideas and sentences.

Chapters 2 through 7 end with an activity in which students are asked to exchange papers. Each of these activities reinforces concepts from previous chapters while adding new elements from the chapter just completed.

In fact, the reader's needs are a principal concern throughout the text. This concern can be seen not only in the first section, but also in the explanations of grammar and editing in Chapters 8 through 14. The activities in this handbook section, in keeping with the overall emphasis of the book on writing as a whole rather than as separate steps, stress corrections in the context of paragraphs from student writing rather than isolated exercises made up of disconnected sentences. Each grammar chapter ends with a full-length writing activity.

Chapter 15 deals with research methods in a particularly active way. The students are asked to do their own writing before doing research, so they are not put in the position of collecting information about a topic they have not thought about or made a commitment to. There are activities on creating a bibliography, documenting, taking notes, and so on, rather than just a presentation of forms and rules.

After the first chapter, instructors will find the text points to the interaction between the sections that deal with organization and development and those that are mainly concerned with editing. They can also eliminate the collaborative options in any of the exercises according to time constraints and their preference.

Acknowledgments

As in the First Edition, for the theoretical basis of the book, I am indebted to the major figures of modern composition theory—Donald Murray, who emphasized the recursive nature of the writing process, and Peter Elbow, who realized the importance of free writing, which lies in the needs of writers to find out what they want to say. I owe a debt to Gabriele Rico for her exploration of clustering, Kenneth Bruffee for his work that led me to use collaborative learning, Donald Moffet and Janet Emig for their insights into the mental processes involved in writing, and a host of others.

The writing of this book would not have been possible without the guidance and help of Paul Smith, my editor at D. C. Heath, who, like a Zen master, helped me find my own way. Martha Wetherill provided much appreciated help with editing and revising the First Edition, while Linda Bieze was especially helpful in her responses to my frequent questions and in her sage advice on the Second Edition which also benefited from Celena Sun's expert editing. My wife Deanna's ideas, sharp eye, and computer skills made this book so much better then it would have been. Edward Jackowitz, friend and fellow teacher, suffered through multiple drafts of each and every chapter, offering ideas and improvements and showing me what I missed. My thanks, too, go to my son, Justin, who was the willing guinea pig for many of the developing activities. Also, I thank my students, past and present, at Hunter College, Borough of Manhattan Community College, Norwalk Community College, and Orange County Community College, who shared their writing, along with their struggles and triumphs, and helped me better understand the writing process. I owe special thanks to my colleague at O. C. C. C., Ed Godwin, who gave me suggestions, as well as almost daily feedback on how the book was working with his students, and to Susan Herman of North Shore Community College for ideas and advice.

Finally, I also wish to thank the reviewers who provided invaluable assistance throughout the writing process and who made real for me the advice this text offers to students—write, rewrite, and get help from your peers: Leslie Bradley, Pennsylvania State University; Alma Bryant, University of South Florida; David D. Dahnke, North Harris College; Theresa Enos, University of Arizona; Dan Gallagher, Laredo Junior College; Stephen Hahn, William Paterson College of New Jersey; Douglas Hoehn, Community College of Philadelphia; Joyce Kinkead, Utah State University; Cecilia Macheski, LaGuardia Community College; Susan Meisenhelder, California State University—San Bernardino; Tim Miank, Lansing Community College; Glenn Rogers, Morehead State University; Lawrence R. Silverman, Seattle Central Community College; Alberta Smith, Algonquin College; Katharine Stone, Georgia State University; Cynthia Vaughn, Belleville Area College; and Leslie Vitale, Charles Stewart Mott Community College.

G. P.

To the Student

Why Write?

Colleges require courses in writing. In addition, in advanced courses in almost all departments, you have to write essay exams and term papers. In many jobs, you need to write letters, memos, and reports. But writing is more than a practical skill to get you through college and impress employers.

Writing gives you a way to influence others and make your opinions heard. It provides a way to reach others. It leads you to examine what you believe because, in finding ways to reach readers, you look for proof to support your beliefs. This process leads to finding more reasons and thus to making a better case for your position, or it leads you to realize that what you thought was true is not true. It leads you to discover the validity of other opinions. And because communicating effectively in writing requires you to think about your readers' beliefs and attitudes, you develop a richer, less self-centered view of the issues you write about. Writing makes you examine your life more fully than you would otherwise.

But I'm Not Good at It

Virtually no writers are when they start. Writing is like learning to drive, or ride a bike, or swim, or anything else that requires skill. Maybe you're like me. I used to hate writing because I couldn't say the things I wanted to say in the way I wanted to say them, the first time. I assumed I was a failure, lacking a skill other people had been born with. But then I realized that writing is a messy process, that it is recursive—that is, I had to keep going back and changing things. They couldn't be the way I wanted them to be the first time. Writing something over was not a sign of some lack on my part, but rather it was the way I got to accomplish what I wanted. I had to write each chapter in this book several times before any one of them started to say what I wanted it to say. This book will ask you to start out putting ideas down any old way and then organize and polish them later.

Although writing is something you do alone, a little help from your friends can make a difference. So this book contains many activities in which you are asked to exchange papers with other beginning writers who will give you help and advice. If you look at the "Acknowledgments" in "To the Instructor," you'll see that I got lots of help from other people in writing this book. And when I say I couldn't have done it without them, I'm not just observing a convention or being polite. I mean it.

This book will ask you to think a great deal about your readers. That's because writing is much easier if you think about the person or people at the other end, the ones who will read what you write. I only knew what I wanted to say in this introduction when I thought about what you needed to hear. I only knew what order to put the ideas in when I thought about what you needed to read next after I'd said something. And my concern about how best to say it was governed by my desire to have you understand me. So as you work through this book, you'll see that helping your readers understand will help you find what to say and how to say it. You'll see that writing isn't all that difficult if you're not doing it in isolation.

The book has three main parts. The first seven chapters are concerned with the paper as a whole. Chapters 8 through 14 offer help on editing and polishing your writing. And then there is a section on writing a research paper. You'll find the book will ask you to alternate between these two sections so that you can apply your editing skills to what you're learned about the paper as a whole.

I hope this book will make writing a less daunting task, and maybe even an enjoyable one.

Preliminary Activity

Before you start reading the text, take a few minutes to answer these questions in the spaces provided. Your instructor will tell you whether to do this for yourself, exchange answers with another student, or use your answers as part of a class discussion.

1. What do you find easiest about writing?
2. What do you find hardest about writing?
3. What was your best experience with writing? Why?
4. What was your worst experience with writing? Why?
5. How do you write? In other words, what do you do first? Next? Last?
6. What do you want to change about your writing? Be specific.

Contents

PART I
Discovering and Organizing Ideas for Your Reader

Chapter 1

"Every Journey of a Thousand Miles Begins with One Step"

The Chinese proverb quoted in the chapter title has much to say to writers. Obviously, when writing, we have to start with a first step, but that is just what many of us writers don't do.

Some of us don't want to take the first step until we know where we're going and what lies along the way. We become so obsessed with outlines and overall plans that we can't take the first step until we know how it fits in with the whole. But to paraphrase E. M. Forster, author of *A Passage to India*, we can't know what we think until we see what we have to say. Therefore, getting started seems impossible.

Others want to hit the perfect stride immediately, instead of discovering it as the result of taking the journey. When they don't get it right at once, they go back and take the first step again and again. Or they are tempted to give up altogether.

Still others have been trained to think at the very beginning about the last step in the journey—the perfect final paper. Their main concern is with spelling, punctuation, and word choice. So the first step doesn't seem good enough. They take it over and over again and grow more and more frustrated.

With all these difficulties, it is not surprising that writing is right up there with public speaking on many people's list of things they dread.

For example, trying to perfect the first sentence, as the first step, can make writing anything an overwhelming task. Here's what happened when one writer decided to send a letter to her college newspaper. She started this way:

> In this letter I will explain why I disagree with your support of the college's purchase of the land in front of the main gate to build another parking lot.

"No," the writer said to herself, "the letter will show what I feel. I don't have to say what it will do at the beginning." So she balled up the piece of paper and started over:

> Yesterday, I read a stupid editorial in your stupid paper.

"No, that's too slangy, and besides they'll never print it if I call them names."
So she gave it another try:

> In my opinion, I think we don't need to unecessarily spend money
> on a new parking lot.

The writer saw the words *in my opinion, I think* didn't make sense, so she crossed out *I think*. Then she noticed that she had misspelled *unnecessarily*. But then she felt she shouldn't start with a personal note. "Maybe I should give reasons that would speak to other people's interests first."

So the page went into the wastebasket, and the writer sat and sat and grew more and more miserable. It was going to be a long night. And the urge to quit was getting stronger and stronger.

The writer was correct to be concerned about the needs of her readers, about the attitudes of the people who would print or ignore her letter, about her spelling. But worrying about these points before she had any ideas down on paper kept her from writing. It made the writing process far more intimidating than it had to be. These are important parts of writing, but not yet. Writers need to have something to say before they can worry about how they are going to say it.

Writing doesn't have to be a fearful experience. The key is to start with the first step, not with a part of the journey that is some distance ahead on the road. The first step doesn't have to be perfect, or fit into an overall plan, or be smooth and steady, or even point in a particular direction. The important thing is to take the step and then figure out where it's going and improve it later.

The best way to start writing is to start writing, without making any judgments about what is being written. Doing this is known as *free writing* (or *automatic writing*).

What is important now is that you write, that your pen or pencil never leaves the page. If you're stuck, write "I'm stuck." Write "I can't think of anything." Write your name. Write about how you think free writing is silly. Write anything that comes to mind or anything that you feel while writing. But keep on writing.

When you write this way, you no longer stop to judge what you are doing. When you resist the urge to edit at the first step, but save that process for later on, you find you have more to say than you imagined. You begin to get to the heart of what you want to say. You find details to support your generalizations. You may find you really feel the opposite of the way you thought you did. You find better ways to express your ideas than when you sit and think about choosing the right word. You find that the fear of the blank page goes away.

Unfocused Free Writing

Free writing can be either focused or unfocused. Unfocused free writing means that you're writing whatever comes into your head without trying to keep a particular topic or subject in mind. This kind of free writing is useful as an exercise to get rid of that "editor" we have incorporated into ourselves and whose judgments make us feel we can't write or that starting to write is such a difficult task.

Here is an example of one student's unfocused free writing:

> Well, the prof said I had to write for 10 mins about anything. I don't know what to say. I'm stuck, she did say to write that. O.K. I have to say something. This room has no windows, there's not much to see. But this is better than the rooms in the old North building. Those trucks really go tearing down the street. When the windows are open in the warm weather there's so much noise that no one can hear anything. The West building is better, it's modern with air conditioning. What else? Well, speaking of noise, the Fourth of July was terrible as usual. The jerks in my neighborhood turned the streets into a battle zone once again. I'm as patriotic as the next guy, but in a crowded area like the one I live in it's madness for everybody to shoot off 10 million firecrackers. I mean my dog goes crazy. You can't hear your T.V. or stereo. And forget about going outside. They had garbage cans full of boxes of firecrackers and they set them on fire. I was in Joe's car and we couldn't get through some roads. And if you walk you could get killed. My girl friend got her arm burned when some fool 4-year-old set off a rocket. When we yelled at the kid, his parents came over and said "He's just a kid." That's just the point. What kind of parents let a little kid play with explosives? What kind of attitude do they have? Don't they have any common sense? Next year I'm heading for the woods somewhere. O.K. time's up.

As you can see, free writing involves a process of discovery. This student didn't know what he wanted to write about. At first, he couldn't think of anything. Then he started to talk about his surroundings, and finally he hit on something he felt strongly about, firecrackers. Also by starting with uncensored words and thoughts, the author wrote in a conversational tone. He thus avoided the stiffness and stuffiness that people mistakenly believe is necessary when writing in an academic setting. While the writer will ultimately produce writing that is more formal in tone, some of this informal tone will carry over into later drafts, making them lively and easy to read. Of course, sometimes the writer might have ten disconnected thoughts, but that's fine too, because one of them might be the beginning of something he can go on to write about later.

If you are focusing on grammar, you'll notice run-ons, a fragment, and other problems in the piece of free writing. But correcting them is not what the writer cares about right now. All he is doing is getting ideas down, and doing so without having an imaginary editor sitting on his shoulder, telling him he has problems he must correct. Editing is important later, not now. Being prematurely concerned about editing only makes getting started more of a problem than it needs to be.

ACTIVITY 1.1

Take a piece of paper and free write for ten minutes. Your instructor will tell you when time is up. Write about anything that comes into your head—a memory, what you did yesterday, what you see, hear, notice—anything. Just start writing and don't stop until time is up. Your instructor may write along with you.

Some people feel writing is difficult because of the concept we have from movies, TV, and even some books that professional writers create the perfect work as soon as they sit down to write. In the film *Doctor Zhivago*, there is a scene in which the main character enters a room that has filled with snow. He is moved, sits down, and writes a flawless poem. The process may work that way for a few geniuses, but for most writers—and that includes me—the starting point is rough and inelegant. There is also a myth that writing is done in total isolation. But writers share their work with loved ones, friends, editors, and ultimately readers. Writing is sharing and that is sometimes difficult because we fear the judgments of others. But free writing is never judged. There is no such thing as good or bad free writing. If you wrote for ten minutes without stopping and thinking or going back, no negative judgments can be made.

ACTIVITY 1.2

It's time to hear some free writing. Your instructor may read his or her free writing aloud first. Then several members of the class will read theirs.

Some people's free writing may sound like a diary. Others' may describe feelings. Some free writing may present arguments. Others may tell a story. Some may jump around from topic to topic. But all will be first steps. All will contain discoveries of what the writers have in mind, consciously or unconsciously, and what they can write about in greater depth later. All will be ways to overcome fear of the blank page.

It is important in this activity that no comments be made on what people read. Just listen to some examples of free writing. Hear what the process is like and what it produces.

ACTIVITY 1.3

It is helpful for you to keep a journal since free writing becomes easier with practice. Write for ten minutes each day about anything you wish. Write only once a day, but be sure to write every day. Don't do several journal entries all at once. The idea is that you fill a page each and every day, that daily you overcome your fear of the blank page, that you express yourself on paper every day. Your instructor may collect all seven journal entries each week (they, of course, will not be graded), or he or she may just collect a few from time to time.

Because you don't censor free writing, you may write some things you don't want anyone else to read. If you do, fold the page over, or staple or tape it shut. Or write another entry and hand in that one instead. Here is a typical journal entry:

Monday, September 29

Write, write. I have to write every day. Here goes. I'm smoking again. I really know I should give it up. Cigarette smoking is bad for my health. It harms your heart and lungs and all that. I know it's true, but I can't stand all these people telling me what to do. It's like prohibition, that Puritan strain in our country I heard about in my history class. Social pressure to conform gets my back up and I just want to do it to fight that pressure. No, that's not the real reason. I'm just hooked. Let's face it. And if I get sick it won't do anything to defeat the tyranny of the majority. In any case I should stop, but there is another problem. If I stop, I'll eat more and then I'll get fatter and die anyhow. Hey, I've got to get my act together. And while I'm talking about getting my act together, there's that paper I have to write for Prof. Broom. Music That class Oh boy. I have put it off and off. I guess I'd better get started. This is as good a place as any. American music. John Knowles Paine, his Mass sounds like Beethoven or Brahms. We were under the influence of Europe, Germany especially. Ives is the first unique American voice. Is that true? I'll have to read some more. There was the influence of France and Stravinsky which was very strong later on. What makes American classical music sound American? Hard edges. What makes it sound like Benton looks in painting for at least through the 30s, 40s and 50s Copland and all that. Maybe I'll write about how it got to sound American.

A journal not only helps you overcome your fear of the blank page, but as the above example shows, it gives you a chance to express your ideas about personal concerns. Writing about them lets you get other concerns out of the way. Maybe the writer's concern with smoking could become the basis of a paper later. For this reason you should save all your journals for the whole term. In fact, you should keep a portfolio of all the writing you do. You can read through it periodically for ideas that you may want to take further at a later date. In this case, sitting down and doing free writing got the writer started on a project he had been putting off for some time.

Focused Free Writing

Free writing is also helpful when you have to write a letter or an assignment on a given topic, whether it is an in-class essay, a short paper written at home, or a long piece of writing like a research paper. Focused free writing is essentially the same as unfocused free writing in that you just start writing and keep on writing without editing. However, in focused free writing you keep a topic or question in mind. If you digress, that's fine. Just keep coming back to the issue you're writing about.

For example, here is a piece of free writing a student did as a first step when she decided to disagree with a newspaper editorial praising the school's decision to buy land for a new parking lot:

> O.K. that editorial. It made me mad. Why? I take the bus so a new parking lot won't do me any good. I don't care. But that's not it at all. Why am I mad? I don't know. Yes I do. It's the money. There are so many better things that the school could do with it. Like what? Well, how about more staff. Then we'd have smaller classes. What else? More books for the library maybe or they could spend it for activities. A health spa, movies, they could buy movies, or rent them, millions of them, and show them to us cheap. Think of all that money spent on buying the land, tearing down that gas station and ripping the tanks out of the ground. We could use another building. No that would cost more than that old parking lot. Oh I know, pollution—the air would get worse with more cars. Now what do I say? I'm stuck, stuck. I'm lost. Oh there go Jane and Teddy. What does she see in him, his car? Oh yeah cars. Could I say it's unfair to those of us who don't drive in. More cars and maybe they'll cut back on the buses and we'll be out there for hours. It's favoring just one group. That's it. This will just help some we need to spend the money on things that help everyone. On things that are for the good of the school as a whole.

As you look at the piece of free writing above, you can see what happens as the writer discovers that she wants to discuss the needs of nondrivers and the needs of all students, which she comes to feel is the main argument. She discovers these ideas in random order, just as she would in a conversation with a friend, and she even digresses about her friends and the role of cars in courtship. Most writers asked to write about an issue being debated on campus who start trying to write perfect sentences, while getting all the details in the right order, would have a much harder time beginning the letter and would no doubt lose some of the important points.

Now, the student would not hand in this piece of writing as it stands. But a finished paper is not the goal of free writing, at least not yet. The writer is merely at the first step. The focused free writing begins a process of discovery. The writer will discover more by reading over her free writing and sharing it. Then, she can rearrange, expand, cut out inappropriate material, and polish the style later, much later. But for now she has taken the first step and discovered some valuable ideas in doing so.

ACTIVITY 1.4

For ten minutes do focused free writing on one of the following subjects, or one suggested by your instructor, or on a topic you think of. Just keep writing. If you get off the track, come back to the original subject.

Here are some suggestions:

1. A difficult course you're taking
2. Dealing with a serious problem
3. Using a computer
4. How you feel about writing
5. A terrifying experience
6. Your best friend
7. A favorite place
8. Being self-reliant
9. How other people see you
10. A problem or a proposed change

Giving and Receiving Feedback

When you write, it is important to get feedback from others. Readers, or in this case listeners, can show you what is most striking, what ideas and words stand out in your writing. For this process to work effectively, however, listeners have to follow certain guidelines in responding to a piece of free writing.

The first point to keep in mind as a listener is that you are not dealing with a completed work here. Therefore, you can make no judgments. Especially avoid negative judgments. All they do is make the writer feel uncomfortable and create the dangerous illusion that the piece being discussed is in its final stages. It does not help writers to tell them that something does not work. The writer becomes frustrated and engages in premature editing, which can be highly destructive of the writing process.

You should also avoid positive judgments. Don't say, "I like . . ." Rather tell the writer what you remember most strongly, what stood out for you. This gives writers the freedom to decide whether they want to eliminate an idea or to keep it or even expand it, based on the impressions others received from their writing.

Also, because our concern is with what is written now, and what will be written in response to what others say, the writer should not comment. The writer should not say, "What I meant was . . ." or "I'm going to add this or that." Those ideas should be written later, not spoken now.

OK. Let's try it.

ACTIVITY 1.5

1. Form small groups of no more than five people. (Your instructor will determine the size of the groups based on the size of the whole class.) Group members should introduce themselves if necessary.
2. In each group, one writer will read his or her free writing.
3. During the reading the others in the group should just listen. The only reason to interrupt is if the reader is going too fast or if they didn't catch a particular word.
4. When the writer has finished, the listeners should jot down the words and ideas they recall most vividly and what they would like to hear more about.
5. Sometimes, the writer may read the free writing a second time, especially if it was read quickly or if the piece is too long to recall accurately. The audience can write down additional points.
6. All the listeners then tell the writer in turn what they remember most and where they want to hear more. It is important that the responders do not take the piece away from the writer with comments like "That reminds me of the time I took a trip to Mexico." The writer's words alone are the subject of discussion.
7. The writer should record the comments made by those who listened to the piece of free writing.
8. Repeat the process for each of the other members of the small group.

Using Feedback

At this point we are not ready to bring any piece to completion. However, we can take a second step and do another focused free writing based on the first piece and the feedback from others in the group.

Let's take a look at how this process works. When the writer of the letter (page 8) read her piece aloud, her audience told her that they wanted to hear more about the needs of drivers and more about the problems she thought the money could be used to solve. One person suggested telling more about crowded classes and the lack of books. Another wanted to hear more about waiting for the bus. Her audience said they were most struck by her description of what would be involved in tearing down the gas station. Several people weren't sure what the proposal the original editorial favored was all about. So with her readers' responses and questions in mind, the student did a second free write and produced this:

The editorial in last week's paper supporting a proposal by one of the deans to purchase the gas station opposite the main gate of the college and use the land for additional student parking is just plain wrong. Sure, students who drive to campus find that there's not much parking space. Yes, a new lot would make life easier for them. But would all of the students benefit? I don't think so. For one thing, if more students brought their cars not only would there be more pollution but since there'd be fewer passengers maybe the bus company would cut down on the number of runs. As it is, a lot of us are standing around on the corner in all kinds of weather. Right now I have a cold I got last week while standing in the pouring rain waiting for a bus. The parking lot proposal only addresses the needs of students who have more money and can afford a car or whose family can buy them a car. Instead the money should be used for something that would benefit all students. The money could be used to hire more faculty, especially for those giant lecture classes where they don't know your name. Those classes where you can't ask a question. Or if there's not enough for more teachers maybe they could hire student aids or tutors to help out. Or the money could be spent on the library. If there were more books the students could do a better job on their research papers. All students, not just some, would benefit then. Or the college could buy more copying machines or have more student workers so things would go more quickly. That would help everyone. All that money to tear down the gas station and pull out the pumps and dig out the tanks underneath and fill in the holes and pave it over should be used for everyone's good.

In this second free writing, the author is developing a clearer sense of what it is she is going to write about and how she is going to present it. Again, the writer is not yet concerned with style and editing, only with getting started, discovering what is important, finding a tentative direction, recalling more details.

ACTIVITY 1.6

Free write again on the same topic on which you did your first free write. Keep in mind what your audience in the small group had to say. When you start writing, just dig in. *Don't reread the first piece of free writing.*

Now reread both your pieces of free writing—the original one and the one you wrote after receiving feedback. How did your second piece differ from your first? Was the process of writing any different from what happened when you wrote the first one? Discuss the changes with others in your group or in the class as a whole.

Asking Questions to Get Started

Another way to get started writing, without getting tied up looking for the right words or the overall outline, is to ask questions.

Suppose you have to write a paper on gun control. One way to find out what you might want to say is to ask questions of yourself or others. Let's start with a little help from our friends. Here's an illustration of how the process might work:

Student 1	"I have to write about gun control, and I don't know where to start. What do you know about it?"
Student 2	"I read in the paper yesterday about a kid who shot his sister with his father's gun. He found it in a closet and was playing with it."
Student 1	"Yeah, I could be in favor of gun control and tell stories of accidents that happen when people have guns in the house. What do you think? Are you against gun ownership?"
Student 2	"Sure, I mean, if guns are around people will use them. Like husbands and wives. If they have a fight, out comes the gun and boom. That's it. The same thing could happen if two guys have an accident. They get out of their cars. They argue and if one of them, or both, has a gun, things can get really serious."
Student 1	"Oh, I remember I saw on the news that some man shot his son who forgot his keys and was climbing in the window late at night. But what about the other side?"
Student 2	"I guess you could talk about people needing to defend themselves, store owners and people like that."

What is happening in this conversation is very much like what happens in free writing. One idea leads to another, and the writer gets ideas much more quickly than by just sitting and waiting for inspiration or trying to write a topic sentence before deciding on a point to prove. Of course, writers should jot down what they and the other student come up with in the conversation.

ACTIVITY 1.7

1. Pick a topic from the following list, one of your own choosing, or one selected by your instructor:
   a. Teenage parenthood
   b. The value of writing well
   c. Working mothers
   d. Problems with public and/or private transportation
   e. Large families versus small families
   f. The value of required courses
   g. Living at home versus living on campus
2. Ask another student the following questions about your topic:
   a. What do you know about this topic?
   b. What have you heard or read about it?
   c. How do you feel about it?
   d. Why do you feel that way?
   e. Can you think of any arguments people might make if they were on the other side of the issue?
3. Be sure to write down the ideas that develop in the course of your conversation.

ACTIVITY 1.8

Free write for ten minutes using the ideas that developed in your discussion of your topic with the other person.

Using Questions to Get Started

You can also use questions as a starting point when you work alone. Question yourself. For this process to be effective, you must work quickly as you did while doing free writing. While responding to these questions—the same types of questions you would ask of others—don't stop and think for a long time. Jot down ideas. When you can't think of anything else about a particular question, move on to the next one. Think of the situation in which you asked a fellow student for help. When you speak, you have to say something fairly soon, or the other person gets impatient. So you take a chance and say whatever pops into your head. Let's go back to the topic of gun control and see how it works. What follows is a list of one student's questions and some ideas he discovered in responding to his own questions.

1. What does the topic involve?

   It involves laws that forbid private ownership of handguns.

2. What caused this to develop?

I guess the large number of crimes committed with guns and the large number of accidents that happened because people had guns.

3. What are the results?

I don't know. I have to do some reading and find out if fatalities caused by guns decline when they are banned. Or maybe I could say that people feel helpless, unable to protect their lives and property, because there are not enough police officers around, or even if there are many, they can't be everywhere all the time.

4. Can I compare or contrast it with anything else?

It's like any other law that protects people from harming others. Saying you can't have a gun is like saying you can't yell "fire" in a crowded the-ater or drive down the streets at 100 m.p.h. or drive while drunk. The difference is that these things can harm the one who does them as well as others. Well, a gun can harm the owner if someone steals it and uses it in a crime or if a person is trying to defend himself, but the criminal takes the gun away from him and uses it on the owner.

5. What have I heard others say about it?

My uncle says the Constitution guarantees the right to own a gun and that if guns are banned, only criminals will have guns.

6. How do I feel about it?

I don't know. I can see arguments for both sides.

7. What stories can I tell about it?

Well, I saw a piece on the TV news the other night about a couple of guys who were in an accident. They started arguing about whose fault it was and came to blows. The one ran back to his car and got his pistol. He shot the other man and killed him. If he didn't have a gun with him, the reporter said, the worst thing might have been a broken nose or a black eye.

8. How can I describe this?

I guess I'd say if you have a gun or rifle around, there's the urge to use it for some people. But I've grown up with guns in the house. My father taught me how to shoot but also to respect what guns can do. I can't say I can recall any desire to use them in an argument. I know I feel good knowing they're in the house if anyone ever broke in.

If, like this student, you come up with contradictory ideas, you may have the urge to pick a side, eliminate some material, and start to organize. But that is another example of taking a step now that comes farther down the road. Wait until you do some free writing on a topic before you take a stand. You may find that a side for which you have only a few points becomes the side you want to take. Or in doing free writing, you may come upon new ideas that change the direction in which you think you're going. There will be a discussion in Chapter 2 on finding a focus, making a contract, and sticking to it. But that is not yet your concern. You are just generating ideas now.

Here is a piece of free writing that this student did based on the ideas he generated in response to the questions he asked and answered:

> I guess it all depends on where you live. Where I grew up, we always had guns in the house. I was taught to shoot and to be careful around them. Target shooting was fun and since the state prison was just down the road, we all felt good that we had guns in the house. In a big city, there's a lot of crime, so there too people want a gun for protection so they can protect themselves. But things don't always work out the way they are planned. Sometimes, when there's a gun in the house and only one person knows how to use it, young children find it, even if it is well hidden. They play cops and robbers or army or whatever, and the next thing you know they injure or even kill one of their friends or a member of the family. Also if the mother and father have a fight and one of them gets real mad that person may go and get the gun and then someone is in the hospital or dead and the other is in jail. The same thing can happen if neighbors have an argument or people argue because of a traffic accident. I saw a report about such a situation on T.V. the other night. I think in crowded cities where there are millions of people and many people who want guns haven't grown up with them and where they don't get to practice and teach their children about what guns do first hand, we need laws to ban guns. We need these laws like we need laws against drunk driving or speeding. They can save lives. These laws can keep you from going to prison if someone steals your gun and these laws can keep you alive. A criminal could take your gun away from you if he doesn't have one of his own and shoot you with it. The constitution said we could have weapons so we could defend the country if it were in danger. The writers of the constitution didn't intend for people to run around endangering themselves and others.

The free writing reproduced above shows how a writer works with the ideas he gets from answering questions about his topic: some change and grow, other ideas fall away, and new ones appear. The writing process is one of change and growth. This is, of course, not a paper yet, but the writer has taken the first step. Writers are not committed to use every idea that they come up with. Nor do they have to use every word they write. Writers are not locked into keeping words or phrases. Because they are not editing at this point, they haven't made a great investment in their words, so they can let them go easily. A strong attachment to what they have written makes for a great many problems for writers. By using free writing, they will also come to see that they don't have a limited number of words that they might use up, but rather that writing is like building muscles. Writers gain strength by writing. The more they write, the more they find to say, and the more they find out what it is they want to say.

ACTIVITY 1.9

Pick a topic from the list on page 9, one you choose, or one suggested by your instructor. Ask the following questions. If you don't have answers for all of them, don't worry. Some questions are more productive with one type of topic, and some with others.

1. What does the topic involve?
2. What causes are involved?
3. What results does it produce?
4. Can I compare or contrast it with something else?
5. How can I describe it?
6. What stories can I tell about it?
7. How do I feel about it?
8. What have I heard others say about it?

ACTIVITY 1.10

After you've jotted down your answers to the questions, free write for ten minutes using your answers as the starting point for the piece of writing.

Clustering

Another way to get started writing is to do what is known as *clustering*. Let's take as our topic the question of whether teenagers should be punished for crimes in the same way as adults are punished. Write the topic in a circle at the center of a page, and write your ideas in circles that radiate out from the center. (See Figure 1.1.) It is important to do this quickly and not stop to think about each point for a long time. You should work at the same speed you use for free writing. Just let each idea lead you to the next.

Figure 1.1 The Clustering Technique

After you get some ideas written down, more specifics or ideas related to the ones you already have will come to mind. You can write these in, radiating not from the original topic but from the ideas to which they are most closely linked. (See Figure 1.2.) Of course, as you get practice in clustering, you can do both of these steps at the same time.

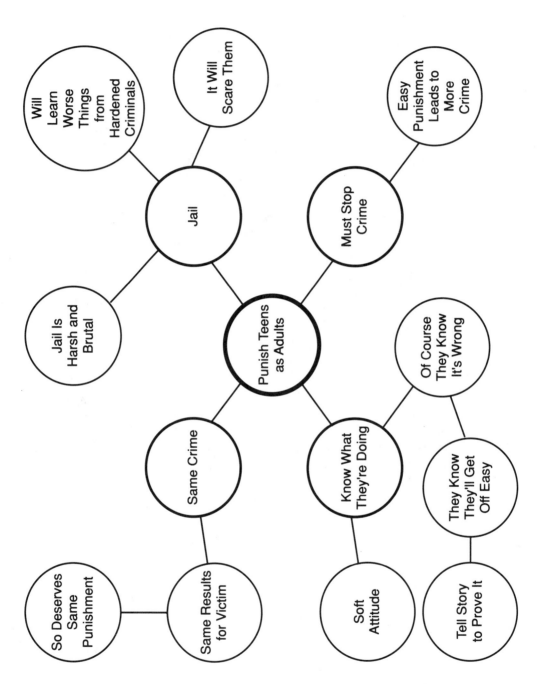

Figure 1.2 The Expanded Cluster

Using the cluster as a starting point, you can then do a free writing that includes some, if not all, of the ideas you came up with. Here's an example:

Let's see. My cluster seems to say that I'm in favor of punishing teens as if they were adults. Crimes committed by teenagers are a growing problem, and we have to find a way to cut down on these crimes. The same crime committed by an adult or a teenager has the same result. If a friend or relative is shot in a holdup the suffering is the same. So the punishment should be the same. I don't think the age of the criminal should mean he should pay more or pay less for what he did.

I don't believe that teens don't know what they're doing when they commit a crime. If they didn't think it was wrong, why do they try to run away if the police show up? In fact, they know they'll get off easy. I saw a movie in which a bunch of kids plan a murder. They talked about the fact that since they were "underage" they couldn't be sent to jail. This happens in real life too. I read in the paper about a kid saying that he knew that he'd get off easy even though he'd killed someone. So not punishing teenagers harshly encourages crime. Anyhow, it really doesn't matter if they know what they're doing when they commit a crime or if they are immature and don't have a sense of responsibility yet. A child learns responsibility by being told NO. You stop a toddler by smacking hands or putting them back in their crib. That's how they learn the limits of what they can do and what they can't do. The same goes for teenagers. They can't learn the limits between fun and games and crime unless they're punished.

I know some people say if you put them in jail with hardened criminals, they'll learn worse things. Maybe, but many will become scared and won't want to go back. And if they're beaten or abused, they deserve it if they did it to someone else. Well, OK. maybe I only mean teenagers who have committed serious crimes that involve injury to others should be punished like adults. Those who steal cars and stuff shouldn't be in jail with murderers.

Here, the writer has used free writing to think out his feelings about the pros and cons of the issue he discovered in clustering. He has moved toward taking a side. He kept some of the ideas developed by clustering and cast others aside. He has discovered new illustrations, like his example of how younger children are taught the difference between right and wrong. He speculates on causes and solutions that came to mind only when he did the free writing.

ACTIVITY 1.11

Construct a cluster for a topic of your choice or a topic that you haven't written on before from the lists in Activity 1.4 or Activity 1.7.

ACTIVITY 1.12

Do ten minutes of free writing based on the ideas you developed in your clustering.

As you begin to write, you can use any of the methods for getting started—free writing, getting feedback, asking questions, clustering—in combination with any or all of the others. For instance, you could cluster and then ask questions of others and/or yourself. The important thing is to get started, to find things to say. You can always change what you've written. I've changed this first chapter in major ways many times. But at this point, don't worry about completing a piece of writing. Just start the journey. Take those all-important first steps.

Chapter 2

Making Contracts with Your Reader

The Importance of a Main Idea

"Yes, but what's the point?"

Often in conversation, you hear these or similar words. A person may be saying various interesting things, but the listener wants to know what they add up to, how they all fit together. In a conversation, unless people are just talking to talk, to fill up time—and even then, many times—there is a kind of contract between the speaker and the listener. The speaker's contract is this: if you listen to the details I'm giving you about my car, or my friend, or my trip, you'll hear something humorous, instructive, informative, or whatever. The implied contract says, "What I have to say is leading somewhere; it has a point." In the same way the person listening is part of a contract. The listener says, "I'm putting all the things you're telling me together. I'm giving you my attention in return for your punch line, suggestion, or insight."

In a movie, book, or TV show, people get impatient with details that don't seem to fit. They wonder why a particular event or detail is included. If they figure out how it ties in, they are pleased. If they don't, they are annoyed. I enjoy comedies in which all the jokes are part of the plot or the main theme. And I dislike ones in which the gags have nothing to do with the show as a whole. When the pieces don't fit together, I lose track of where the plot is going. I feel as if I've been handed a lot of broken pieces, but I don't know how to put them together, or even *if* they go together at all.

The same is true in a writing situation. Both writer and reader look for meaning, for a focus, for a main idea—a thesis, if you want to call it that.

As writers move from free writing or clustering, they need a sense of what all or most of the details they've created add up to. This helps them to decide what to include as they begin to write for an audience. The main idea is a contract for themselves and for their future readers that establishes the reason behind the writing.

And, of course, readers will want a sense of why they are reading the piece of writing. They need to feel that all the information they're getting has a point. They need a contract to help them see how all the parts fit together, how they support one basic message. The contract created by the main idea keeps them from being confused by what they are reading. It keeps them from getting frustrated and, as a result, from losing interest in the piece.

A main idea, whether it is stated directly in words or just implied, is necessary for both writers and readers.

Topics and Main Ideas

In Chapter 1, when you did focused free writing or clustering, or asked questions of yourself and others, you wrote about a particular topic or subject. The examples you saw—gun control, the need for a new parking lot, and punishing teenagers like adults—were all topics. A main idea is a statement about that topic. It's like a one-sentence telegram that summarizes the main thrust of what you wrote.

You must be able to state a main idea in a sentence, whether you include that sentence in your writing or not. You can't make an accurate assertion about a topic in less than a sentence. (See Chapter 8 for more on recognizing sentences.)

For example, the *Yellow Pages* is a topic. If a writer wrote a paragraph full of examples of how hard it is to use, his main idea might be: "Using the *Yellow Pages* can be frustrating." If he wrote a paragraph that showed how easy it is to find information in the *Yellow Pages*, his main idea might be stated this way: "The *Yellow Pages* are easy to use."

A main idea may be stated explicitly in a piece of writing, or it may be implied. In either case, it determines what writers choose to include and exclude as they write.

Look at the following piece of writing on the topic of appreciating Shakespeare's *Hamlet*.

> When I was in high school, I read *Hamlet* in class. It was hard going because the language was difficult for me, and I had to keep looking at the bottom of the page to find out what certain words meant. The teacher helped somewhat by talking about how some of the words had different meanings, and he explained the culture of Elizabethan times. <u>This helped me to understand the play to a certain degree, but it wasn't until I saw it performed on stage that I really appreciated *Hamlet*.</u>
>
> The actors used the same words I had read, but they said them in a way that I could understand better. Often it was a gesture an actor used, or a facial expression, that made me understand that, although the words sounded pleasant, they were meant to be ironic or sarcastic. The actor showed me that Hamlet was frightened but doing his best to hide that fear when he faced the ghost. I knew he was angry when he found out the truth about his mother, but now I felt his outrage and grief at her deceit. My teacher had explained the soliloquy as an expression of Hamlet's despair, but this Hamlet was confused and searching for an answer to an impossible situation. The duel in the last

act was a fight between two real people. They leaped over tables and pushed people out of their way. Their struggle was real. When Hamlet was killed, I felt sad because the actor had made the character so real to me. What he had said and done had more meaning to me because I cared for that person on the stage.

<u>Seeing a play acted out increases the viewer's understanding and involves the viewer to a much higher degree than just reading the words on the pages of a book.</u>

In this piece of writing the author has a clear main idea, stated at the end of the first paragraph. She only came to really appreciate *Hamlet* after seeing it acted. At the very end of the paper, she extends her experience to her readers and revises her main idea, making it more inclusive.

The main idea guided her in deciding what to put into her writing. Everything she says contributes to proving that she came to appreciate and enjoy the play more when she saw it performed. Similarly, readers are not frustrated because there is nothing here that does not support the contract the writer made with them.

Each of the first two paragraphs has a certain degree of independence. In the first, the writer talks more about her experiences in high school, and in the second, she has more to say about what happened when she saw the play. But both contribute to the same main idea—the play became more real for her in the performance.

Here's a shorter piece of writing. The topic is clearly boxing, but the passage lacks a unifying main idea.

Boxing is an exciting sport. It is filled with tension that keeps you on the end of your seat wondering who is going to win. You wonder how much punishment a fighter can take. Of course, sometimes fights are fixed. Or if a fight lasts only 90 seconds, anyone who paid good money to see it will feel cheated. Fighters suffer terrible eye and brain injuries. Sometimes they even die. I sure wouldn't ever want to be a boxer. I don't know why anyone would subject himself to such dangers.

The writer of this passage does not have a clear main idea, so he is frustrated in his attempt to keep the passage focused, and the readers don't know what the writer wants them to come away with after reading it. The writer says boxing is exciting. He says sometimes it's not. He says boxers suffer terrible injuries. He says that he can't understand why anyone would be a boxer.

Of course, all is not lost in this case. The writer could decide that his main idea is that boxing is exciting and then rewrite adding more examples to prove it. In that case he could throw away the negatives, or he could admit the dangers but say they only add to the excitement. Or the writer could rewrite and argue that boxing should be banned because fighters are often seriously injured. Or the writer could make a contract with the reader that states that although boxing is exciting, it is a dangerous, brutal sport that we might be better off without. And there are other possibilities.

Now let's practice recognizing main ideas, contracts with the reader.

ACTIVITY 2.1

In the space provided after each of the following passages, write a sentence that you feel expresses the main idea, the contract the writer has made with his or her reader. Your instructor may ask you to work individually or in small groups. Discuss your answers with others in the group or in class as a whole.

1. Protesting an unfair action by the government can sometimes serve as an excuse to express racial and ethnic hatreds. For example, in 1863, Lincoln's government passed a draft act that permitted anyone who was called to serve to buy a substitute for $300. Naturally, this angered the poor, and in New York City, this anger took the form of violence. However, the violence of the mob was turned not only against the rich and the police. Mobs attacked and burned an orphanage for blacks in the Harlem section of the city. They lynched black men and boys and attacked Jewish and German store owners. There were also attacks on Chinese peddlers.

MAIN IDEA

_____

_____

_____

2. My grandfather always listened to the baseball games on the radio when I was young. I enjoyed the excitement of the games and it was fun to hear Grandpa curse the Yankees, but I had to keep very quiet when the game was on. And three hours was a long time for a five-year-old to sit still. I wanted to be with him and to hear his comments about the players, but he wouldn't let me say anything. If I asked about the significance of a certain play or term, he would get angry and tell me to keep quiet. If I walked in or out of the room, he would grow impatient. As a result, I have grown up with mixed feelings about going to or watching baseball games.

MAIN IDEA

_____

_____

_____

3. When I was fourteen, I got my first job. I was a counselor at a day camp. When we had arts and crafts, I would come home covered with paint and glue. On days when we went on trips, I'd come home half-dead from chasing after six- and seven-year-olds who would wander off despite my threats. The kids showed their affection by punching me in the arms, legs, and back. They liked to throw things like paper airplanes, paper bullets, and spitballs at me. They also had a good time talking back to me and calling me names I'd never heard before.

MAIN IDEA

_____

_____

_____

4. Traditionally, in England and America, when there was any examination of the race to the South Pole in 1911, the winner, the Norwegian Amundsen, was regarded in books and on film as little less than a villain. Scott, the Englishman who lost the race and died with all his party on the way back from the Pole, was glorified.

   Then came Roland Huntford's book on the two explorers and the public television series *The Last Place On Earth*, which was a dramatization of the book. Now, the reader or viewer learned that Scott was opinionated, vain, and foolish. He played favorites, acted insensitively, and ran his expedition like a military dictatorship. He didn't believe the evidence of his eyes that dogs were best for pulling sleds. He spouted nonsense about how noble it was if the men themselves, instead of animals, dragged the heavy loads across the ice. He failed to do proper research, and so he made poor decisions about what kinds of food and clothing to take to Antarctica. The new view is that Scott was responsible for the deaths of those who went with him to the Pole.

   On the other hand, although Amundsen made mistakes and crushed challenges to his authority when necessary, he asked for opinions, expressed more concern for his men, and created a more cheerful atmosphere. More important, he did his homework. His team had proper clothing and food, and they did not exhaust themselves dragging great weights. They reached the Pole first and came back to tell their story. Obviously, Amundsen was the better leader.

MAIN IDEA

_____

_____

_____

Finding Main Ideas in Free Writing

In Chapter 1, you used free writing as a way to get the writing process started. You got help from others by asking them what they remembered most. Now you will use this method as a way of moving toward a contract with your readers and of finding the direction your papers will take.

When writers produce pieces of focused free writing, they generate information. Some of this information seems to point toward one assertion. Other information points in another direction. So, they need to take another step and try to find a main idea in the free writing. This main idea may be a statement of the direction in which most of the information in the free writing is pointing, or it may be a statement about only one fairly small part of the free writing that is particularly interesting to the writers and their audience.

Here is a piece of free writing by Tabitha Alston. Remember, this is free writing and the writer is not concerned with grammar, spelling, punctuation, or organization at this point. She is not yet writing for a reader.

Sports is a very large field consisting of baseball, basketball, track & field and a lot more. One of my cousins is very good at baseball, but I like track & field best. It appeals to me because I always wanted to run. Also, unlike in team sports there is only one individual winner. There's more glamour and glory in being the winner of an event than in being part of a winning team. I always thought it was the easiest thing to excel in track and field, but I found out that it's hard work. I started running when I was about 10 years old. I ran around my block and raced all the kids for short distances like 50–100 yards and there wasn't one kid, guy or girl, young or old, who could beat me. Too bad I've lost touch with some of my friends from those days. When I was around 12 I'd watch the Colgate Women's games on TV and said I wanted to be in them. At the age of 13 I had the chance to run with them. I only ran one meet out of the six which wasn't enough for me to get into the finals. I only got this far because the meets were in one city and I lived in another. I was only able to recruit an adult to take me once. My mother was working and wouldn't hear of my going alone. My mom worked as a secretary for some big company downtown. When I was 14 I ran for my junior h.s. track team and we had Olympic time at the end of the year. I passed the trials and was going into the finals as the fastest in the school but two days before the finals I pulled a muscle in training and so couldn't run. Bye Bye, again to make a career out of running in my first years of high school. I thought the track team was a bunch of fools not good for anything but dirty jokes. I didn't run with them. My last two years were spent in a different school because my family moved. That's when I lost a lot of my friends from the early days. My new school was a place where the going was rough. The coach was so hard I wanted to quit.

What is the main point that Tabitha is making?

_____

_____

_____

When she read her free writing in a small group, her audience said they felt that she was showing that she had a lot of difficulties in succeeding at her favorite sport. And she agreed that this was the contract she wanted to use when she wrote on the topic again.

Figure 2.1 illustrates the process of getting a main idea from free writing.

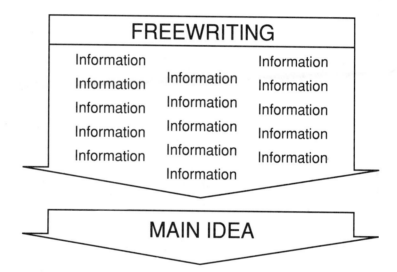

Figure 2.1 Free Writing Leads to a Main Idea

Figure 2.2 shows the pattern of Figure 2.1 applied to Tabitha's piece on running.

FREE WRITING

cousin good at baseball	beat all other kids	h.s. team not serious
I like track and field	lost touch with friends	didn't run with them
always wanted to run	watched Colgate Games	moved
only one winner	missed some meets	where mom worked
glory and glamour	couldn't go alone	new school
thought it was easy	passed trials in jr. high	lost friends
it's not	had injury	coach was hard
started at age 10	couldn't run in finals	wanted to quit

MAIN IDEA

I had lots of difficulties succeeding at my favorite sport.

Figure 2.2 Illustration of Free Writing Leading to a Main Idea

ACTIVITY 2.2

Do ten minutes of focused free writing on one of the following topics, a topic you choose, a topic you wrote about in your journal, or a topic suggested by your instructor. After the ten minutes are up, read over what you have written and decide on a main idea. Write out that main idea in a sentence after your free writing.

If your instructor suggests, read your free write aloud to a small group or the entire class. Don't announce your main idea until others have responded. Then compare their thoughts on what contract you might make with your readers with your own.

Remember, it is possible to go in more than one direction with a particular piece of free writing.

TOPICS

1. The environment and why we should be concerned about it
2. The need for national health care insurance
3. A person, real or fictional, you admire or despise
4. Are video and computer games harmful?
5. A memory
6. Marriage versus living together
7. How do you define success?

Save this free writing and main idea. You will be working with it again later in this chapter.

Turning Information into Evidence

Once you have decided on a main idea, the next step is to look back at your free write and decide which pieces of information support that main idea and which don't. The pieces of information that you keep are now evidence for your contract. They support it, illustrate it, show that it is true. Those pieces of information that are not evidence can be discarded. Because they are the result of free writing and have not been produced as the result of careful thought or editing, and because you have no great investment in them, you can let them go easily.

Figure 2.3 illustrates how discovering a main idea leads to a sifting process in which you keep some information that has been generated in the free writing as evidence and remove any information that does not support that main idea.

Here's Tabitha's free write once again. If you look at this paragraph and the model in Figure 2.3, you'll see that the underlined parts are the evidence she will keep to support her contract—"I had lots of difficulties in succeeding at my favorite sport." The parts that are not underlined are those pieces of information that do not support her main idea, her contract. They are the pieces of information that have been removed in the final part of Figure 2.3.

Sports is a very large field consisting of baseball, basketball, track & field and a lot more. One of my cousins is very good at baseball, but I like track & field best. It appeals to me because I always wanted to run. Also, unlike in team sports there is only one individual winner. There's more glamour and glory in being the winner of an event than in being part of a winning team. I always thought it was the easiest thing to excel in track and field, but I found out that it's hard work. I started running when I was about 10 years old. I ran around my block and raced all the kids for short distances like 50–100 yards and there wasn't one kid, guy or girl, young or old, who could beat me. Too bad I've lost touch with some of my friends from those days. When I was

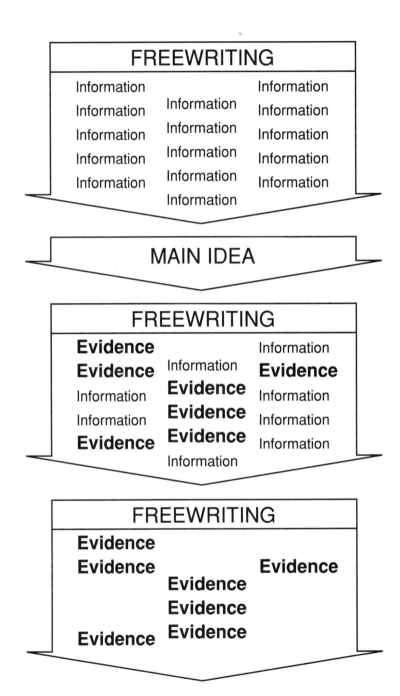

Figure 2.3 The Main Idea Determines the Supporting Evidence

around 12 I'd watch the Colgate Women's games on TV and said I wanted to be in them. At the age of 13 I had the chance to run with them. I only ran one meet out of the six which wasn't enough for me to get into the finals. I only got this far because the meets were in one city and I lived in another. I was only able to recruit an adult to take me once. My mother was working and wouldn't hear of my going alone. My mom worked as a secretary for some big company downtown. When I was 14 I ran for my junior h.s. track team and we had Olympic time at the end of the year. I passed the trials and was going into the finals as the fastest in the school but two days before the finals I pulled a muscle in training and so couldn't run. Bye Bye, again to make a career out of running in my first years of high school. I thought the track team was a bunch of fools not good for anything but dirty jokes. I didn't run with them. My last two years were spent in a different school because my family moved. That's when I lost a lot of my friends from the early days. My new school was a place where the going was rough. The coach was so hard I wanted to quit.

ACTIVITY 2.3

Look at these pieces of free writing followed by main ideas. Decide what information the writer can turn into evidence and what information should be cut in the next draft. Your instructor will indicate whether you should work in small groups or individually. Discuss your answers either in the group or with the whole class.

1. I think I'm beginning to like this writing class. I thought at first I wasn't going to like it, but now I do. I'm glad I had to take it because now I'm beginning to see things I didn't understand before. You know they teach you differently in college than in high school. I hope, I pray, I pass this course. In high school we did a lot of grammar and wrote about stories. My high school was really small in comparison and I had lots of friends. At college, I was lonely at first, but there are really nice people here too. Oh yes, how is it different? Well, here we learn about writing as writing. There we got corrections, but we didn't talk about what went into writing. We talked about what we ended up with, but not how to get started. Boy, it's hot today. I think I'm really getting more confident now.

MAIN IDEA   I like writing better in college than I did in high school.

CHANGES

_____

_____

_____

_____

_____

2. I have to write about a place. What's really special to me is, of course, my home, but what other place? Well, the old railroad station in the center of my town is special. I really like to take railroad trips because I can sit back and not worry about driving. The same is true of buses, but they're not special in the same way. There's not as much room, and you can't get up and walk around. There's something romantic about riding the rails. The terminal is built of red stone and is covered with carvings. The clock tower is the tallest structure in town and has a really grand Gothic looking clock on all four sides. The waiting room is panelled in rich, dark wood and has carved moldings and massive chandeliers. When I heard this building was going to be torn down, I was upset and signed petitions. Realizing I had to do more, I went from door to door getting signatures myself. I'm sure glad we saved the terminal. It is our major landmark.

MAIN IDEA   The railroad terminal is a landmark and deserved to be preserved.

CHANGES

_____

_____

_____

_____

_____

ACTIVITY 2.4

This time, find a main idea in the following pieces of free writing. Then decide what should be deleted because it is not evidence for the main idea you have chosen. Your instructor will indicate whether you will work individually or in small groups. Discuss your main idea and the changes you made when you turned information into evidence.

1. Write about the last book you've read. Well, that was Margaret Atwood's *The Handmaid's Tale*. I really liked that book and I had a lot of good discussions with my friends about it. It wasn't hard to read at all, but it raised important issues. It offered a terrifying vision of the future. For some reason it seems that the birth rate in the U.S. had fallen and there were very few fertile women. I've heard a lot on TV about women who can't have babies, but I don't think it's a national problem. We're talking about fiction here anyhow. A horrible dictatorship has taken over in a backlash reaction to Women's Lib. I guess something like that could happen. Anyway in the book, women are not allowed to have money, hold jobs, travel, etc. Those women who are fertile are forced to act as baby making machines, called handmaids, for childless couples high in the government. I found the idea of this legalized rape really upsetting and was furious at a society that permitted this to happen.

All the rules and restrictions on the handmaids' freedom made me really mad too. I cheered at every rebellious act of Offred, the heroine. Even her name had been taken away. Offred was Of Fred, the man for whom she had to produce a baby. When a handmaid had a baby, it was taken away from her and she was sent to another family. There she got a new name—of and the man's first name. I was boiling. She had nothing of her own but a red dress and a big white hat with wings that acted as blinders. How could people be treated this way? I just couldn't live that way. Well, I guess I'd have to if I lived in that society. But I think I'd show my anger more than she did.

What seems to be the main idea? In what direction is this writer going? State the main idea in a sentence. Remember, you can't make an assertion in less than a sentence. Remember too that the cruelty of the society, the antiutopia, is the topic. The main idea is what the writer is saying about that topic, not your opinion on the topic.

MAIN IDEA

_____

_____

_____

What information would you delete because you've chosen this main idea?

_____

_____

_____

_____

2. I'll write about what happened in class today. We talked about why writers need to be specific. One sentence we looked at was "My father is a good cook." The prof. asked us what good cooking was and there were a lot of different answers. Some people said they thought spicy food was good. Others said they liked plain cooking. When I lived home, my mother thought salt and pepper were what made food spicy. When I came to live in the dorm, I roomed with some guys from India. The first time they cooked, I nearly died. I drank a whole pitcher of water after that meal. Boy, that food was hot. I swore I'd never touch it again. But then a week later, I was begging them to cook again. Now I'm a spice

junkie. So I guess that not only do different folks think different foods are good, but even the same person can like opposite kinds of food at different times of his life.

MAIN IDEA

_____

_____

What information would you leave out? What would you leave in as evidence for your main idea? What might you add as further support for your main idea?

_____

_____

_____

_____

_____

Revising Information to Create Evidence

It is possible to come up with more than one main idea from a particular piece of free writing. And deciding on a given main idea requires changes in the nature of the information that you will use as evidence to support your contract.

Look at the following list of points that were generated when one student free wrote on the topic of diet.

1. I eat three meals a day, no more, no less.
2. I make sure that those meals are nutritionally balanced.
3. I drink eight glasses of water a day.
4. Junk food is a no-no for me.
5. I avoid snacking between meals.
6. I watch my intake of calories, cholesterol, and carbohydrates.

If the writer decides that her main idea is "I watch what I eat," this simple list would support that contract with her reader.

If, however, the writer decides that the main idea is "To stay healthy, I watch what I eat," she has to change the information she employs to fulfill her contract with her reader. Then she must add other statements that show how following these rules leads to good health and/or how not following them can have negative results. Again, if in looking over this list, she is struck by how difficult it is to observe these "dos and don'ts," she must add more facts that prove this point.

ACTIVITY 2.5

Write a sentence that could serve as the main idea for each of the following lists. Remember that a main idea must be stated in the form of a sentence. Your instructor or a student will write four or five suggestions on the board. Check to see if each of the points clearly supports the main idea. Could you say that the point proves the main idea in each case? If it doesn't, change the item so that it ties in with the contract. If you can't make it fit, or if it would take a great many sentences to do so, drop that item from the list.

1. Topic: Scheduling my day
   a. I keep busy.
   b. I break up my day's work.
   c. I schedule "play time" every day.
   d. I spend some time doing physical exercise.
   e. I make lists of what I want to do each day: two hours of studying, one of writing, etc.

2. Topic: Working and attending school full-time
   a. I work four nights a week.
   b. I work five hours each night.
   c. I have several term papers due this month.
   d. I have to read more than a hundred pages by the end of the week.
   e. I need my job to pay for my schooling.
   f. I don't want to get any incompletes.

Finding a Main Idea in a Digression

Writers often pick as their main idea a point that seems to be supported by most of the information contained in their free write. At other times, however, a point that is only touched on briefly in the free writing seems to be the most promising as the basis of a contract with their readers. In that case, writers generate new evidence to support this main idea as they rewrite.

Here is a focused free write on the topic of AIDS by Frances Brea:

AIDS stands for Acquired Immune Deficiency Syndrome a lethal disease that affects the immune system which is the body's protection against disease. What I can't understand is all the lies spread about AIDS, you could get it from a toilet seat or if you touch a victim. It is simply not true. It is only acquired by blood to blood contact or sexual intercourse, oh sorry I sneezed! Anyway you would be surprised that in a hospital I found AIDS victims were the nicest, maybe because they're dying. I don't know, but they appreciate all the care you can give them. As a nurse I found them to be human beings who needed so much care and understanding. I'm stuck. I don't want to write boring facts about AIDS, but then again maybe more people need to hear all the facts. All I want to say is that people shouldn't treat AIDS victims like animals or abandon them. They are like any other victim. They need help. I'm stuck and I think my professor is looking at me and he is probably checking to see if my pen leaves the paper, but no like a noseybody I have to look up to see what's going on, one of my bad points. I hope a cure for AIDS is found. I hope soon. The disease is terrible, these people are susceptible to the smallest colds that can turn into pneumonia. I remember when I was a student at the hospital, I saw when an AIDS patient died. It was awful, he had so many black and blues and it looked like he was lying in a pool of blood. It was just an awful thing to see. And AIDS babies are the worst to see.

After Frances completed her free writing, she read it to several other people and they told her what they remembered most and what they wanted to hear more about. They thought the paper was going in the direction of an examination of the clinical nature of AIDS, but noted that she said she didn't want to talk about that. They also remembered that she spoke about the personality of AIDS patients. Further, they said they wanted to hear more about how AIDS patients are mistreated. Frances decided to write again and to focus this time on the mistreatment of people with AIDS.

Here's Frances's second free write:

AIDS is that terrible fatal disease which has everyone all over the world horrified. I could understand why people have such great fear. It is a highly contagious disease, but people sometimes let ignorance and insensitivity take over. Then it gets to the point where the sick get treated like animals. What I mean by that is that they don't get treated like other patients in hospitals. Of course you must take precautions, wear double gloves, a mask and a gown, but not treat them like nothing. For example, at the hospital I worked in, when an AIDS patient called for help with their bell, the nurse used to come half an hour later, and their food trays are left outside the door. Is it going to kill you to bring in their food and ask how they're feeling? It is a small thing to do, but these small things make these people feel good. That's what people don't understand. I'm not saying that all hospital staff are like that, but a few are and medical workers should know better. I think that the people who should be extra careful are those who deal with needles used by AIDS victims. They need to be careful not to prick themselves. I wonder how this disease really came about, who brought it. I've read many stories, but they are too bizarre to believe.

One was that a monkey brought it. Who knows? Just remember that
AIDS victims are victims. They need serious care, help, and sensitivity.
Yes, fear is great, but just give a little, and remember that it is a human
being you're dealing with, who on top of this dreadful disease doesn't
need to be treated bad.

After this second free writing, Frances saw that she could support the main
idea that AIDS patients need to be treated with sensitivity just like any other
patient. As she looked over this free writing, she saw that everything contributed to proving her main idea except the section near the end on the ori-
gins of the disease. That part would have to go.

Creating a First Draft

As writers move from free writing, they start to think about their readers'
needs. They begin to be more careful about what they put first, second, and so
on. They think about editing—spelling and punctuation. They word their
ideas more carefully so that readers will not be confused. If they have written
extensive details on several major supporting points for their main idea, they
start to break the material into paragraphs. (For more on paragraph organization and boundaries see Chapters 4 and 5.) At this point, writers are not at
the stage of the journey where they will share what they are writing with an
audience, but they are getting close, so they start to be more careful. They use
their knowledge of the editing skills presented in Part II of this text (or refer
to Chapters 8 through 13) for points they may not be sure about.

Frances was now ready to write a first draft, keeping in mind her contract
with the reader. She worded more carefully and created separate paragraphs
for her major points. Here's her first draft:

1   AIDS is that terrible, fatal disease which has everyone all over the
       world horrified, but fear of the disease is no reason to treat the
       victims of this disease in an insensitive manner.
2   In a hospital where I worked, AIDS victims were treated unfairly. I
       observed that they didn't get treated like the other patients. For
       example, I observed that the food trays of these patients were left on
       the floor outside the doors of their rooms. They could have been
       carried inside without endangering anyone.
3   If an AIDS patient rang a call bell, the nurse waited ½ hour to an
       hour to respond to it. And I saw health care professionals go into a
       patient's room and throughout the care not say a word to the person
       with AIDS. The other patients were asked throughout their care how
       they were feeling, how they slept, etc. The AIDS patients weren't.
4   What makes me so angry is that the people who teated the AIDS
       victims this way were professionals who should know better. AIDS is
       only acquired from an exchange of blood or sexual intercourse, not

from talking to people, asking them questions, or handing them some
thing. I'm not saying all health care workers or even most of them do
this, but I've seen a few, and, in my opinion, there shouldn't be any of
this happening in a hospital.

5   I could understand why people have such a great fear of AIDS. It is
a highly contagious and lethal disease, but after precautions are taken
this is no reason to act foolishly and insensitively. These people are
victims, and like any patient they need help, but most of all sensitivity
and understanding from those around them. These victims of a
terrible disease are human beings who on top of their disease don't
need someone to treat them like the lowest thing on earth.

As you see, Frances kept her contract with herself and with her readers.
While various parts of the draft touch on different aspects of the problem,
everything leads the reader to the conclusion that there is no reason AIDS
patients should not be treated with respect and sensitivity. Obviously, this is
not a finished paper; it is only a first draft that still needs editing, proofreading, and expanding. But Frances has taken the next step in moving toward a
completed paper.

Including Conflicting Points

In a piece of writing with a clear main idea, everything contributes to the
main idea. But that doesn't mean you must write a one-sided paper. You can
argue that there is validity to more than one point of view on a particular
issue. Or you can acknowledge another opinion and then show how it is
wrong.

For example, here is a free write on the topic of the right of police officers,
firefighters, and health care workers like nurses, lab personnel, and ambulance attendants to strike:

Can they go on strike? They have an obligation to protect the public, right? A lot of accidents can happen if they go on strike. There
could even be many deaths. Who will protect and help us? If there is a
fire, no one will be there to put it out. Lives may be lost. If there is a
shoot-out or a maniac holds people hostage no one will rescue them.
There will be no law and order. There will be unchecked robbing,
raping, and killing; it would be a real disaster. But if they don't get paid
enough and are worried about supporting themselves and their families, they can't do a good job. If nurses work 72 hour shifts, they can't
do a good job and will make mistakes. So maybe a strike could help the
public in the long run. But what about all the people who would die in
the meantime. It's unamerican not to be able to strike. Then again,
who could take the place of these workers. Who could handle hoses
and other fire truck equipment. Cops go through long hours of train-

ing. Inexperienced hospital workers would make mistakes and kill people by giving them the wrong medicine. Temporary lab workers might misread test results and stuff like that.

This writer clearly saw validity in both sides of the issue. But the majority of the information pointed to the conclusion that these workers should not strike. So he decided that his main idea would be that workers who provide the public with vital services cannot be allowed to strike. But when he rewrote, he didn't have to throw away all the information that supported the other side. He incorporated the other side by saying that, while it is true that these workers need to earn a living and have decent hours and working conditions, they can't have the option to strike because of the amount of suffering and the loss of life that will result if they do so. Obviously, he needed examples and illustrations to back this up. So picking one main idea and using conflicting information will lead to a new main idea and a change in the way the evidence is presented. It will be used not to support another main idea, but instead as part of the line of reasoning that leads the reader to accept the writer's point of view.

Here is what happened when this person rewrote:

1   It is true that all workers, including police and firepersons, as well as health care workers like nurses, lab personnel, and ambulance attendants, need decent salaries and working conditions. It is also true that if their rate of pay causes them to worry a great deal about their finances, they may not be able to do a good job. If they have to work long hours without a break, like nurses who sometimes have 72 hour shifts, they may make life threatening mistakes. However, the cost in human life if these workers go on strike is just too great. They cannot be allowed to strike.

2   The fire department cannot go out on strike, no matter how dissatisfied they are, because if there is a fire, property and lives will be lost. And lives are more important than money and better working conditions. Also temporary volunteers could not operate the equipment they use and might lose their own lives as well as fail to save others.

3   The same is true of police persons. If they were to strike, we would be at the mercy of criminals. Robberies and murders would be unchecked. Again, volunteers would not know how to handle a hostage situation. They might shoot innocent people and be injured themselves. Even with years of training and experience, police officers occasionally make mistakes and are injured and killed, and sometimes they even kill innocent people while trying to apprehend criminals.

4   If health care workers went on strike, sick people in hospitals and those who had been in accidents would suffer more than is necessary and many would die. Short term replacements might mean well, but

most likely they would make mistakes in administering medicine and first aid. They would misread test results if they tried to replace these skilled workers.

5   So police and firepersons, as well as health care personnel, can not go on strike. If management is unresponsive to their just complaints, their unions could take out ads in newspapers. They could try to mobilize the public to write letters to support them, but they can't go as far as striking.

This draft supports the idea that workers who provide vital services deserve decent pay and decent working conditions and that they should strive to obtain them. But it also makes it very clear that the writer believes they should never strike to reach their objectives.

ACTIVITY 2.6

Rewrite the free writing you did in response to Activity 2.2 (page 28), using either the main idea you found, the one suggested by others in your audience, or a totally new one. As you write your first draft, change the information that you have, if possible, so that it supports your main idea. Eliminate any information that was in your free writing that can't be used, even if you modify it, to support your main idea.

Flexible Main Ideas

Although it is true that in a finished piece of writing you must stick to the contract that you make with your reader, at this stage of the writing process, a main idea is not a binding contract. As you write a first draft, your main idea may change as a result of how your piece develops.

There is a reciprocal relationship between the main idea and your evidence. (See Figure 2.4.) And as you saw in the piece on AIDS and the one about workers who provide vital services going on strike, a new main idea leads to new evidence. (See Figure 2.5.)

Let's return to Ms. Alston's developing piece on running track (see page 26). As you recall she decided to use "I had a lot of difficulties succeeding at my favorite sport." Here is a first draft she wrote, keeping in mind her main idea—her contract with her readers.

1   Track and Field is the sport I like the most. At the beginning of my life as a runner, I encountered many problems, but they all were worth it. And in the end, all my hard work paid off.

2   I realized how much I liked to run when I was about ten years old. I would race the kids on my block in 50–100 yard dashes. I thought it

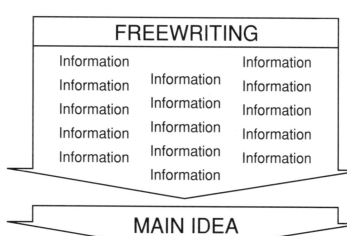

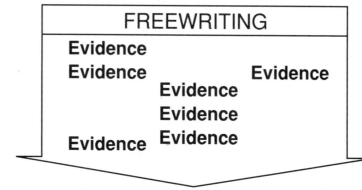

Figure 2.4 Selecting Evidence Can Lead to a New Main Idea

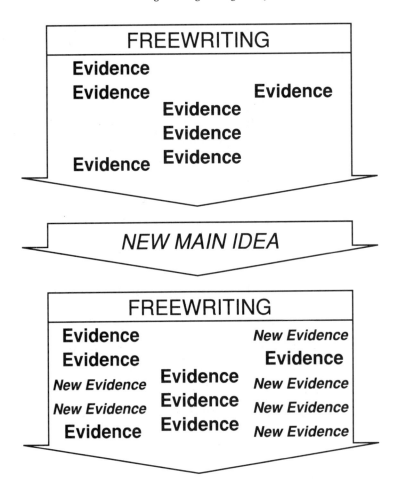

Figure 2.5 A New Main Idea Produces New Evidence

was lots of fun because no one could beat me. At the age of twelve, I finally had the chance to enter the Colgate Women's Games which I always watched on TV, but my career with them didn't last very long. When I signed up, I was required to run in four trial meets to score a certain number of points. Out of the four I was only able to make one meet, and the points I scored were not enough to carry me into the semi-finals. The meets were held in New York and I lived in Connecticut. There was no way on earth that my mother was going to let me go that far without an adult. I was only able to get one to go with me once.

3   At the age of fourteen, I ran for my junior high school track team. Around the end of the year in which I was going to graduate, the school had what was called Olympic Time, and I was in training for the

200 yard dash. During the trial meets, I always came in first, so I just knew it was going to be my race when the finals came around. Two days before the race, while practicing I pulled a muscle and was not able to run in the finals. Bye, bye again to being a running star.

4   During my first two years in high school at Stevenson, I chose not to run with the track team because in watching them, I realized that they were not serious about running. They only cared about dirty jokes.

5   My last two years in high school were spent at Truman because my family moved. The team was serious, but things were hard, so hard I thought about quitting many times. We worked out five days a week and ran on the sixth day. My coach made us do so many things we thought he was crazy. He'd make us do an event over and over until we achieved the times he wanted. He didn't care if it was raining cats and dogs. If we started a workout, we finished it. When it was cold and everyone else was training indoors, he always found some place in the mountains to make us run. Everybody else's training started when school started, but ours started during our free time.

6   But I overcame all the setbacks and all this hard work. It all paid off. I have the proof on my mother's fireplace which is full of my medals and trophies. When my team went to meets, people knew who we were and that we were going to win. I'm proud to say my team and I always made it to the state finals and still hold several state records. I also got to travel to different states with all expenses paid.

As you can see, Tabitha's main idea changed when she wrote the draft based on her free write. She started out to prove she faced many difficulties. With that in mind, she eliminated any information in her free write (page 26) that didn't support her main idea. However, as she wrote, her main idea changed. She realized that she wanted to show that although she suffered setbacks, she did succeed and that all her difficulties didn't keep her down. As she followed through on her first contract with her reader, she developed a new contract.

ACTIVITY 2.7

Using Figure 2.5 as a guide, state Tabitha's new main idea in your own words. Then list the evidence she carried over from her free write (page 26) and the new evidence she generated for her first draft.

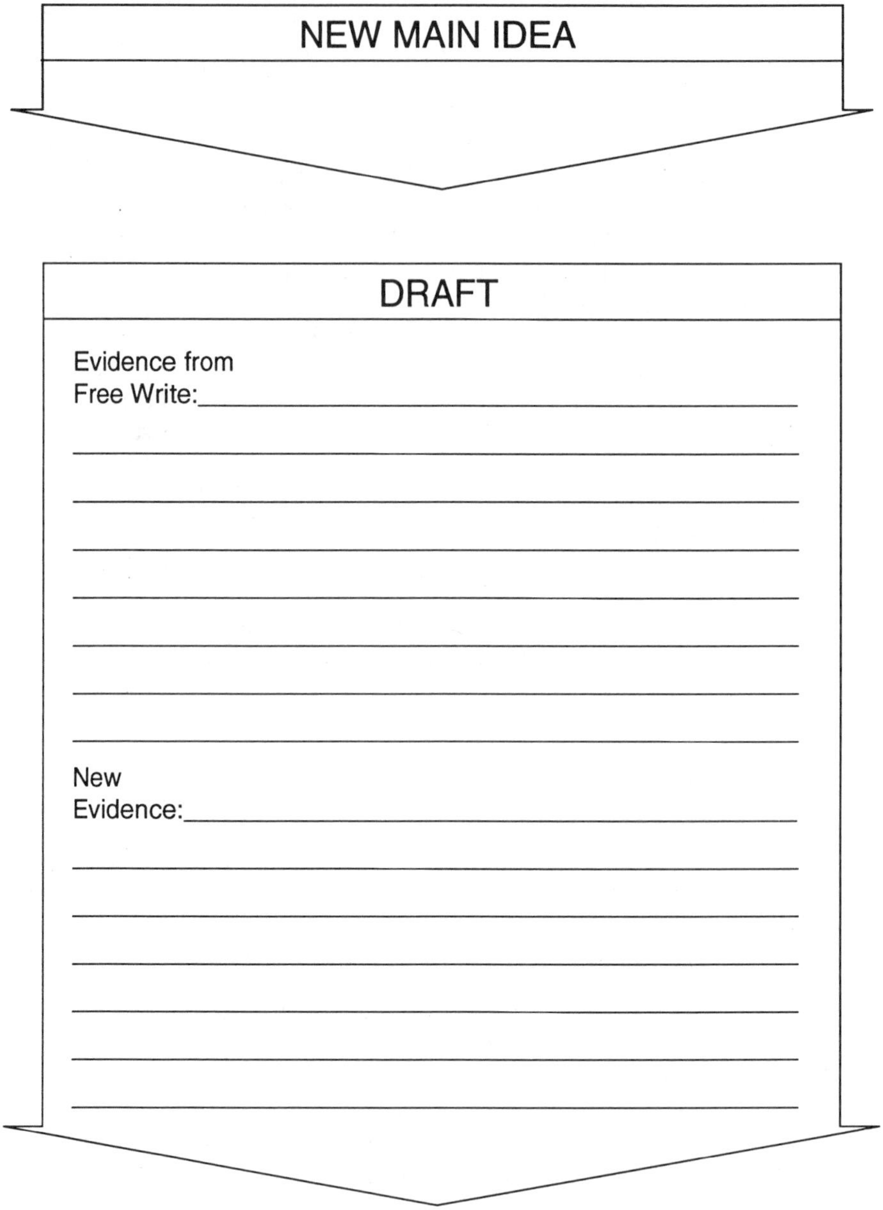

NEW MAIN IDEA

DRAFT

Evidence from
Free Write:_____

_____

_____

_____

_____

_____

_____

_____

New
Evidence:_____

_____

_____

_____

_____

_____

_____

_____

Figure 2.6

ACTIVITY 2.8

1. Reread the piece of writing you wrote in Activity 2.6 and your original main idea statement. If the paper has taken a different direction than you planned when you wrote your first contract with your reader, modify the contract.
2. If your main idea is stated in the paper, underline it. If it is not stated directly but is just implied, skip a line after the end of your piece of writing, and write your main idea in a separate sentence.
3. Put your paper aside and go on to the Editing Activity below.

EDITING ACTIVITY

Before you take your paper any further, it's time to take another step on the writer's journey. You can do this on your own, or your instructor may assign particular activities.

1. Go to Chapter 8, on sentence boundaries. Read over the ideas and do some of the activities on your own, or your instructor may spend some class time on the chapter or assign particular readings and activities.
2. Then turn to Chapter 14 and complete Activity 14.1, combining the short sentences in each grouping into one sentence. Your instructor will tell you whether to work on your own, in groups, or in the setting of the whole class. She or he will also indicate whether you will hand this in, go over it in class, or simply use it for your personal practice.
3. However you work with the materials on sentence boundaries and combining sentences, rewrite your paper, eliminating any fragments or run-ons and improving the sentence level writing.

Activity 8.6 on page 168 offers an additional or alternative writing assignment.

ACTIVITY 2.9

1. Exchange papers with another student. Then, acting as editors, read each other's drafts, checking to see if the writer has a clear main idea and has suppported it. *Do not write on the author's paper.*
2. Instead of discussing the paper with the author, write his or her name on the top of a blank piece of paper and do the following:
   a. Copy the writer's main idea. If the bulk of what has been written contradicts what the main idea stated the paper would be about, write down what you think the main idea is. If there is a clear main idea but some of the information is not evidence for it, indicate which sentences or ideas don't seem to fit.

b.   Indicate whether there are any fragments or run-ons. Tell the writer where they are. Mention in which paragraph and at which line. You might quote the first few words to help the writer find the spot where you see a problem. Then suggest a correction.

c.   Sign your comments and return them with the draft to the author.

3. When you have received your piece of writing and your editor's comments, on another piece of paper state whether your editor was helpful and what if anything you will change as a result of the editorial comments.

4. Rewrite your draft as needed.

5. Your instructor will tell you whether to submit your first version, your editor's comments, and your response along with your final draft, or if you should just hand in the final draft.

In this chapter, you've learned that writers need to make contracts with their readers, and that both writers and readers benefit when the contract, or main idea, is clear. Writers need to know what information to include and exclude; readers need to know what to expect. You've also seen that contracts help writers to find evidence and that evidence helps them to clarify their contracts. You have also begun to edit your writing at the sentence level.

Chapter 3

Developing and Supporting Your Contract

The scene is the office of an executive. In the office is a management consultant who has just spent several days observing the routines of workers at the executive's company. The executive speaks first.

"Well, Mary, did you see what I was talking about?"

"Tim, I saw much that was impressive during the past three days here at Jackson and Jones, but there are some techniques that I could suggest to increase output and efficiency."

"I'm glad we're doing something right. What I meant though was, did you observe the lazy attitude? Did you see the way people just do the minimum and don't really try hard?"

"The staff, it's true, are not working up to their full potential. One cause of that problem is the message they're getting from management."

"Now wait a minute. We are generous when it comes to salaries. Why just a couple of months ago, we commissioned a survey and compared wages in the field. And I don't think we have any dictators among the managers. They care about their workers and try to help them every way they can."

"Management here, Tim, is well-intentioned, but in an old-fashioned paternalistic way."

"What do you mean, Mary?"

"For example, if someone has a problem, he or she is told to turn that problem over to the supervisor and not to worry about it anymore."

"Isn't that a way to help them? Doesn't that make for a low-pressure environment? Do you mean we should be cracking the whip?"

"No, not at all. But being told not to look for solutions on your own does take away initiative. That kind of atmosphere produces people who have no reason to look for better ways to do their jobs. You get workers who follow the rules and never take any chances. Creativity is not rewarded, but rather praise comes as a result of being stuck in a rut. There's no investment on your employees' part in making the company run more efficiently. So production is not what it could be, and workers are bored and see no reason to push the limits that have been set for them."

"Oh, now I see. We have to give them more chances to find creative solutions, to set goals that, I think you're suggesting, may be more ambitious than what we are asking for now. Mary, I think your idea may be the solution to our problem."

In this conversation, the executive didn't understand exactly what the consultant was getting at until he got specific examples. In fact, at several points in the conversation, he misunderstood what she was saying. Since this was a face-to-face discussion, he was able to ask questions, and she was able to explain her points more fully and, in fact, change her presentation of them in response to his questions. Also, in conversation we respond to facial expressions that indicate comprehension, confusion, and impatience. Further, we pick up on body language, such as nodding in agreement or shifting restlessly in the chair and looking around the room in annoyance, that conveys responses to what we say.

In writing, the situation is similar in one way: a kind of dialogue occurs between the writer and the reader. However, there are obviously major differences. The readers are not physically present when writers are putting their thoughts on the page. The readers cannot ask questions. The readers cannot indicate agreement or bewilderment, attention or boredom, to writers while they are deciding what information to present and how to present it.

So the next step on your journey to reaching your readers effectively is to think about what those readers will need to know later, when you are not there and only your writing is. What readers need from you is this: *specific details*.

The Importance of Details

Without concrete illustrations of the points you are making, readers may misunderstand you. They may not be clear about exactly what you want them to understand or believe if they don't get enough examples. Or readers may get the general idea and fill in their own details. Unfortunately, their details may not be ones you had in mind. Then, the readers might come away with a picture that differs from the one you wanted them to have.

For example, saying that children imitate their parents' negative behavior may get my thought across to my readers, but only in a general, abstract way. Telling my readers a story of visiting a friend who behaved violently in the presence of her child, and then writing about a later visit during which I saw the child acting the same way with a doll makes the experience real for my readers. They can visualize the generalization, and there is no ambiguity. The readers may or may not agree with the conclusions I draw from this narrative, but at least we have shared this one illustration of a child imitating her parents' violence. Readers and writer have been brought closer.

Again, if I read that eighteenth-century Paris was filled with foul smells, the statement might make no particular impression on me. On the other hand, I might try to imagine it. But having no particular knowledge of daily life in that time and place, I might visualize an inaccurate or far weaker picture of what conditions were than the writer intended.

Look at the difference between the unsupported generalization that eighteenth-century cities smelled bad and this passage from Patrick Suskind's novel, *Perfume*, translated by John E. Woods*:

> In the period of which we speak, there reigned in the cities a stench barely conceivable to us modern men and women. The streets stank of manure, the courtyards of urine, the stairwells stank of moldering wood and rat droppings, the kitchens of spoiled cabbage and mutton fat; the unaired parlors stank of stale dust, the bedrooms of greasy sheets, damp feather beds, and the pungently sweet aroma of chamber pots. The stench of sulfur rose from the chimneys, the stench of caustic lyes from the tanneries, and from the slaughterhouses came the stench of congealed blood. People stank of sweat and unwashed clothes; from their mouths came the stench of rotting teeth, from their bellies that of onions, and from their bodies, if they were no longer very young, came the stench of rancid cheese and sour milk and tumorous disease. The rivers stank, the marketplaces stank, the churches stank, it stank beneath the bridges and in the palaces. The peasant stank as did the priest, the apprentice as did his master's wife, the whole of the aristocracy stank, even the king himself stank, stank like a rank lion, and the queen like an old goat, summer and winter. For in the eighteenth century there was nothing to hinder bacteria busy at decomposition, and so there was no human activity, either constructive or destructive, no manifestations of germinating or decaying life that was not accompanied by stench.

You cannot be indifferent to the images of this passage as you can be to this simple, unsupported statement: "Paris at that time stank." Even if you don't know exactly what caustic lye or feather beds smell like, you do come away with the main idea Suskind wanted you to get. You have shared the sense, and smell, of the place, and you are convinced. You are disgusted, as the writer intended you to be, because of all the solid, specific details he has given you.

---

*Patrick Suskind, *Perfume*, translated by John E. Woods (New York: Alfred E. Knopf, 1986), 3—4.

Let's practice being more specific. Look at this example of a general statement:

> The food that my friend cooked was not very good at all.

The reader of this sentence wonders what kind of food the writer's friend cooked, perhaps who the friend was, and certainly why the food wasn't good in the writer's opinion. Response to food is highly subjective. What one person likes, another hates. So readers need to know just what bad cooking is in the writer's opinion. If that information is not provided, the readers will reach a conclusion based on their own attitudes toward food, a conclusion that may be very different from the one the writer wanted them to get from the sentence.

The writer needs more than one sentence to make his ideas clear to his readers. He needs to expand. Here is a more effective presentation of the ideas:

> My friend George cooked hamburgers last night, but they were terrible because he used a cheap grade of meat, and so they were very greasy. Also, I like my burgers well done, but even though I mentioned this fact to him, they were very bloody. Also they were heavily salted, and salty food is not something I like very much.

Now we know exactly why the writer thought that the food was not very good. Some of his reasons for feeling that way, like the greasy quality of the meat, may be reasons his readers would agree contribute to burgers, a specific type of food, being not very good. The fact that the burgers were bloody and salty may not in the readers' opinion prove the food was not good, but at least there is no confusion about why the writer felt that way.

ACTIVITY 3.1

Rewrite the following sentences, replacing any vague words with solid, specific details. In some cases, you may want to write more than one sentence. Compare your changes either in small groups or in the setting of the whole class. Your instructor will tell you which method to use.

1. I thought that movie was really very good.
2. I have to replace that chair; it's really in bad shape.
3. Since I've moved, I have a much more difficult time getting to work.
4. Children can get in trouble by imitating what they see on TV.
5. Taking that course really helped me a lot in my other classes.
6. Some diets can be dangerous.
7. There are things that my instructor does that are confusing.
8. I had problems understanding what that writer was saying.

9. That car has many features I wish I had on mine.
10. She's so talented.

Using Details to Give Your Reader Instructions

Another way to become aware of the needs of a reader for specific information is to practice giving instructions on how to do something. To give instructions or to explain a procedure requires an awareness of all the things a reader needs to know. Unfortunately, when writers give instructions, they often take for granted that the reader knows what certain items are, how they work, where to get them, and when to use them. They assume the reader is looking at what they are looking at. But usually this is not the case. And that is why poorly written operation manuals and cookbooks are so frustrating.

Look at these effective instructions on how to make Turkish, also known as Greek or Arabic, coffee:

1   To make Turkish coffee, you must first buy a small, long-handled pot called a *tanaka* in Arabic, an *ibrik* in Greek. These pots come in brass, copper, and enamel, in various sizes—holding from one to five demitasse cups. They are quite inexpensive. You will need either fresh ground Yemen Mocha, Brazilian, or Kenya coffee beans, but you can also use canned stoneground coffee. You will also need sugar and cardamom seeds, as well as small cups. Italian-style demitasse cups are fine; however, if you want to be more traditional, you will use small cylindrical cups without handles that fit into brass, copper, or silver holders.

2   Let's say you're making three cups. First, fill a pot designed to hold three demitasse cups of water three-quarters of the way up with water. Next, add three level teaspoons of coffee and some sugar. Turkish coffee can be served sweet, with three to four spoons of sugar, medium with two spoons, or bitter with only one. Then, stir the coffee and sugar in the water. Next, put the pot on a high flame, and watch the pot closely. When the coffee begins to boil, let the foam that forms on top rise to the rim of the pot. As soon as this happens, remove the pot from the fire. Be careful. If it spills or boils over, you'll have a terrible mess on your stove. Tap the side of the pot with a spoon two or three times until the foam goes back down to the three-quarter point. Then, return the pot to the fire until the coffee boils again and the foam rises to the top.

3   Now, pour the coffee into the cups. As you pour, make your hand tremble a bit. This will force some of the foam, which is highly valued in Middle Eastern cultures, into each of the cups. Finally, add a cardamom seed to each cup. Do not stir the coffee. Instead, wait a few

moments to allow the grounds to settle to the bottom of the cup. Sip until you reach the grounds.

These instructions can be followed because the writer has considered the needs of readers for specific information about unfamiliar terms and processes. In the first paragraph, the writer has listed what items and ingredients the reader will need to make this type of coffee. He has also realized that the reader may want to substitute a type of coffee or cup he or she could obtain more easily.

In the second paragraph, the writer presents the process of making Turkish coffee step by step and anticipates some problems the reader may encounter. In the third, he again explains everything the reader needs to know and, again, includes details that grow out of an awareness of what the reader might do wrong. The needs of the reader led the writer to include more specifics than he may have at first felt to be necessary.

ACTIVITY 3.2

1. Free write about what is involved in one of these processes:
   a. Preparing a dish
   b. Changing a tire
   c. Preparing for a test in a specific subject
   d. Building something
   e. Finishing furniture
   f. Shopping
   g. Performing CPR
   h. Any other process you wish
2. Next, write a draft in which you explain this process step by step to a reader. Think of your reader as someone who is unfamiliar with the process you are describing.
3. Read your draft to a partner or in a small group. Ask your listener(s) to act out the process. Your listener(s) will indicate whether any additional information is necessary to comprehend the process.
4. If there were steps in the process that were not clear, steps for which your audience needed additional information, or if some steps were missing, rewrite and make the process clearer and more complete for your readers.

Adding Details to Make Your Generalizations Real for Your Readers

When you write about larger societal issues, specifics make the difference in reaching your reader. One way to find specifics is to do research and add facts and figures. We will look more closely at this in Chapter 15, when we work on the research paper. For now, let's just work on adding details that come from personal experience, details that we generally recall from reading or watching TV, or fictionalized specifics to illustrate generalizations we know to be true.

The writer's concern is to include specifics that make the assertions in the paper real for the reader. If I say, "We should have trade barriers because cheap foreign goods put Americans out of work," this statement may make sense to readers if they have had a firsthand experience of losing a job because of competition from cheap foreign goods, or a friend or relative has had such an experience, or they have seen a televised report or read an article about the problem recently.

But if none of these situations has occurred, the statement may not be particularly clear to readers. If, however, writers tell a story to illustrate the generalization they have made, they are more likely to convince readers or, at the very least, make them think about the statement in more depth.

Look at the following illustration of the claim that we need trade barriers to protect American workers, and notice how much more you are involved in the issue. It will either convince you in a way the original sentence did not, or if you feel the statement is still not valid, you will be more interested and may even be eager to write a paper that refutes its claims.

1   When I was a boy back in a small town in Georgia, my father owned one of the three shoe stores in town. He sold shoes mainly made right there in town by the local factory, good old Southern Leather Works.

2   Then, one day, a salesman showed Dad how he could buy less expensive imported shoes. Dad was pleased as punch. He could buy more for less. He could sell cheaper. Tom Park's store across the street, which still sold only the local product, couldn't compete. Dad's store expanded; he bought Tom's store and had more business than he ever thought possible.

3   Well, after Tom's store went out of business, the remaining store owner caught on. He wasn't a dumb fellow, so he started selling the cheaper imports too. That slowed down sales a bit, but Dad had the biggest inventory, so he was still doing fine.

4   But after a year or so, no one was buying locally made shoes, in town, in the state, in the whole area. As a result, the local factory closed its doors. Dad's stores lost big money. People were out of work. They bought fewer shoes, less often. Then things generally got worse. People started moving away. Dad had to sell the second store.

5   Dad wasn't blind. He saw what the score was and started selling only high quality, higher priced shoes made across the state line. He built up a decent trade with people from the big city who came up for the summer. They were impressed with the high quality goods that were made here in America, and they bought them, even if they had to pay more. But sales were never what they had been in the first place.

6   I think there's a lesson here. We need to beware of the Trojan horse of cheap, foreign-made goods. And since immediate profits

often blind us to what can happen in the long run, we need help from the federal government. If high tariffs had been placed on those cheap foreign goods, half of my home town would not have lost their jobs. If trade barriers had existed, we wouldn't have suffered those hard times. And if trade barriers had existed, all those people wouldn't have had to move away.

Asking Readers What They Need to Understand Your Writing

As a writer you must try to anticipate what an audience needs, even though that audience is not present while you're writing. In class, however, you can get some practice in finding out what readers need to hear more about.

Here's a draft on the topic of dress codes. The writer's main idea is that he is opposed to dress codes because they are harmful to the students. As you read, think about what additional details you need from this writer.

1　　　Some people say that schools and colleges should have dress codes again. They should have rules and regulations about what students can and cannot wear to class. However, going back to dress codes would be unpopular with students and would cause them to do poorly in school.

2　　　One problem is that the dress codes would create conformity, something that many people in our society dislike. Another problem is that enforced conformity builds hostility. If you're hostile and angry, you won't do well. Also, if the dress code involves wearing uncomfortable clothing, you might not concentrate as well. You couldn't do some things you wanted because you'd have to worry about your clothes. Also, you might want to do something after school and the clothes the school required you to wear might not be appropriate. Or what if you wanted to go out and have some fun? You can't wear the same things everywhere you go. Also, what they make you wear might not be your style. You'd be forced to be someone you're not.

The student read this in a small group. His audience said they'd like to hear more about resentment and discomfort caused by dress codes. They wanted to know what kinds of activities he had in mind when he wrote about worrying about clothes, where the clothes that were required by the dress code might be inappropriate, and how the individual's sense of style would be at odds with the dress code.

The writer kept in mind the points his audience wanted to hear more about as he prepared this second draft:

1　　　In the past, many schools and colleges had dress codes, rules and regulations governing what students could or could not wear to class.

Some people feel that it would be a good idea to reinstate dress codes. But they are wrong.

2   Students who were forced to dress in a particular way might become rebellious. I had a friend who went to public school with me. He had high grades and never got into trouble. But then his parents decided he should go to a private school. At his new school, he had to wear a jacket and tie every day. He hated being forced to dress this way and began to act out his resentment. His grades plummeted, and he started getting into trouble. Since he looked like everyone else, he couldn't declare his identity by wearing a shirt that had a clever saying or a picture of his favorite singer. He felt that the only way to be noticed was to get into fights, destroy the school property, and act up in class.

3   It is hard enough for many younger students to sit still and concentrate. If they are forced to wear, say, a tie and jacket, instead of jeans and a T-shirt, especially in hot weather, they will fidget even more. And, as a result, they will find it more difficult to concentrate on what is going on in the classroom.

4   Having to dress up for school makes engaging in some activities both in and out of school more difficult. If you're wearing a jacket and tie or a blouse and skirt, you don't want to do all the work in bio or chemistry labs. Even if you have a lab coat or smock, you still worry about your clothes. You don't want to mix chemicals or cut up that frog. After classes, younger students can't play games without going home first and changing. Many college students must go to work. Again, if the clothes are not appropriate, they have to waste time changing for work. A student can't work around greasy food in his or her best clothing.

When this student read his second draft to the other students, they had a much clearer sense of his arguments against dress codes.

ACTIVITY 3.3

Read the following passages. Decide which statements need to be developed with specific examples. Draw on your experience and your reading, or create original examples and details to support the generalizations. Your instructor will tell you whether to revise the passages individually or in groups and whether to share the results with a small group or the whole class.

Remember, there is no one right answer. But you want to provide your readers with specifics they can see, feel, touch, hear, and, yes, even smell.

1. When mothers work, both they and their children benefit. The women benefit because they get to be more independent, and independence is a quality many women need to develop. Their children also benefit when their mothers work because they develop the

same qualities of independence. Both women and their children are better off financially when mothers either start working or return to the job force after their children are born.

2. Children suffer when their mothers work full-time. They are influenced by people outside the home, and these influences can be harmful. They become lonely and resentful. These children often have burdens thrust upon them which they are not mature enough to handle. They also get into more trouble and have more accidents than children whose mothers are home.

3. It is a waste of time to vote. Nothing ever changes. The politicians promise all sorts of things, but once they get into office, they don't keep their promises. Even if there is an honest person running for office, he can't make any real changes. Powerful special interest groups always get their way in the long run.

4. People who don't vote are being foolish. They don't care about their communities or their nation. They don't have a say in picking officials who could help them or in removing those who are making policies they disapprove of. They say, "There should be a law against that" or "That is an injustice, and we must change that law." But by not voting, they can make no change in things that affect them.

5. Schools should have dress codes or require that their students wear uniforms. Having such rules would reduce peer pressure which, in turn, would save students and their parents money. Theft would be lessened, and students would not have a reason to ridicule each other's clothing. Dress codes or uniforms might prevent students from getting in trouble or cutting classes because they could easily be identified.

ACTIVITY 3.4

1. Free write, cluster, or use questions to start writing on one of the following topics:
   a. Fast-food restaurants
   b. Taking attendance in college
   c. Fathers getting custody in divorce cases
   d. Women in combat
   e. The situation of the elderly in our society
   f. The benefits and/or dangers of using credit cards
   g. A topic of your choice (Remember to consult your journal entries for topics.)
2. Decide on a main idea and write a first draft. Include stories and examples to support your main idea, to make it real to your readers.
3. Read your draft to the members of a small group of no more than five students. Ask the group what they think the main idea is and what they want to hear more about.
4. Rewrite in response to the feedback that you received, adding more details.
5. Try out your second draft on a larger audience or in a different group.

Adding Details Can Modify Your Main Idea

In Chapter 2, we saw how deciding which evidence to include can lead to a revision of the main idea. The same thing can happen when more specific details are added to a draft.

Quickly review the paper in Chapter 2 (pages 38–39) on whether police officers, firefighters, and health care workers have a right to go on strike. Then read the following revision:

1   It is true that all workers, including police and firepersons, need decent salaries and tolerable working conditions. It is also true that if their rates of pay cause them to worry a great deal about their finances, they may not be able to do a good job. If they have to work long hours without a break, they may make life-threatening mistakes. However, the cost in human life would be too great if these workers were to strike because no one could replace them on short notice. Therefore, these workers cannot be allowed to strike.

2   The fire department cannot go out on strike, no matter how dissatisfied they are, because if there is a fire, property and lives will be lost. And lives are more important than money and better working conditions. Also temporary volunteers could not operate the equipment firefighters use and might lose their lives as well as fail to save others.

3   Recently, while riding on a bus, I passed a school yard where firemen were training. A new recruit was trying to hold on to a hose from which water was pouring out with great force. He could not control the direction of the water. In fact, he couldn't hold on to the hose. He was being thrown about like a cartoon character. A replacement could not direct the water to put out a fire, nor could he perform the other tasks firepersons train long and hard to master. If the regular firefighters went on strike, lives would surely be lost.

4   The same is true of police persons. If they were to strike, we would be at the mercy of criminals. Robberies and murder would go unchecked. Again, volunteers would not know how to handle a hostage situation. They might shoot innocent people and be injured themselves. Even with years of training and experience police officers make mistakes and are injured and killed, and sometimes they even kill innocent people while trying to apprehend criminals.

5   I once saw a show on TV on training procedures for new cops. They searched an abandoned building. At various spots mechanized dummies would pop out of doorways. First, there was a figure with a gun. The rookie cop did not shoot, and the narrator of the film said the officer would have been shot. Next, another figure appeared, and he shot quickly, but this time it was a woman holding a baby. Learning how to react quickly and correctly is the result of much training and

years of experience on the streets. So a replacement couldn't have the knowledge of how to react if he or she had to start working immediately.

6   So police and firepersons cannot go on strike. If management is unresponsive to their complaints, their unions could take out ads in the media. They could try to mobilize the public to write letters to support their cause, but they can't go on strike.

In this version, the writer added more details to show how workers in areas of vital service could not be replaced if they went on strike. The result is a paper with more vivid details, but also one with a slightly different main idea. Instead of just proving the public would suffer if these people went on strike, the writer is anticipating and refuting an objection from readers that someone else could replace these workers. This was touched on in the first version in Chapter 2, but the idea has become more significant now. It is so central to the draft that it is now part of the main idea—"Workers can't go on strike because, since no one can replace them, many people will suffer and die."

Also, since he added so much information about how replacements for police and firefighters could not adequately do the job, the writer decided to drop the section on health care workers. He felt the reader would get the idea and that another category of evidence would be overkill. So adding more specifics led to a change in the categories of workers being discussed in the body of the paper and to yet another change in the main idea.

It may seem more than obvious to say that when you tell a story, you want it to support your main idea. However, as you write, details have a way of taking their own direction. For example, printed below is part of the paper in which the writer was arguing that police and firefighters as well as nurses didn't have the right to go on strike. The writer showed how a fire department strike would result in property destroyed and lives lost. The writer went on to contend that without nurses the suffering of patients in hospitals would increase, and again lives would be lost. Then she wrote this:

> The police shouldn't strike at all because it takes them long enough to answer a call as it is. They are either giving out traffic tickets or catching teenagers who don't pay their fare on public transportation. In one case, there was a young man who was going to commit suicide by jumping off the roof of a building near me. The cops took too long to get there, and so the young man had to be talked down by other people in the neighborhood. The police arrived only after they weren't needed anymore. They should have been there to help this person from the beginning.

What this story illustrates is not that lives will be lost if the police go on strike, but rather, if they go on strike, the public will take care of problems themselves.

Now the writer has two options. She can either replace this story with one that would support the main idea that the public will suffer if workers who provide vital services go on strike, or she can change the main idea. What would you do?

ACTIVITY 3.5

Work on one of the following questions individually, in groups, or in the setting of the whole class, according to your instructor's directions.

1. What would you substitute for the story about how local citizens handled the suicide attempt without the help of police if you wanted to support the existing main idea with an illustration that showed how the public would suffer if the police went on strike? Try to generate an example that was not used in the responses to this issue on page 57.
2. What new main idea would you create, and how would you change the other categories if you wanted to keep the story? Remember, the topic is still whether workers who provide vital services have the right to strike if they are dissatisfied with salaries or working conditions.

ACTIVITY 3.6

Form groups of no more than five students each. Each group will choose a secretary and will pick or be assigned one of the following sayings. Each member will contribute ideas, and the secretary will write down a paragraph that illustrates the motto. Each group will share its version with the whole class. The other members of the class will comment on how well the story supports the generalization. Remember, if the examples do not support the saying, which is in effect the main idea (see Chapter 2), change it to one that *is* supported by the evidence that has been generated.

1. The past is your guide to the future.
2. Less is more.
3. The tree that does not bend often snaps.
4. You have to have to get.
5. Great success is not always planned.
6. Silence can speak loudly.

ACTIVITY 3.7

Revise the paper you rewrote in response to Activity 2.9, or if your instructor suggests, any draft you're written so far. Add more solid, lively details to make your points more real and more vividly alive for your readers. Remember, after you expand, you may need to modify your main idea.

A Professional Writer's Use of Details

Read the following article by Morris Lurie, which appeared in *The New York Times*. Pay special attention to the main idea and how that idea is supported by illustrations and examples.

The Safest City in the World*

1   It is nine o'clock at night in Tokyo, hot and humid, and I am sitting in a park. A small park. Bushes, benches, gravel paths. There are children playing, a few students, lovers, a man with a dog. The park borders on a school of music, and I can hear a soft saxophone, backed by a piano. The air is so still the smoke from my cigarette rises straight up. In the smoggy air, there is only one star.

2   It gets to be 10 o'clock. The children go home, the man with the dog walks away, the students amble off. The park is empty except for mostly me.

3   And then a policeman appears.

4   He is wearing a gun, of course, plus all the other stuff policemen have: nightstick, radio, flashlight, cuffs.

5   He asks for my passport.

6   This has happened to me only once before, in 15 years of traveling, and that was in Spain, Franco Spain, 1965. I don't know where I was exactly, a small town, a village, somewhere between Madrid and Gibraltar, hitching through to Tangier. It was afternoon, a sunny Spanish afternoon, and this policeman came up.

7   He had a gun, of course, and a stick, and he didn't look too bright. Take away the uniform and what you'd have was the village lout, and why he wanted to see my passport—why he demanded it of me standing there in the street—was to impress the locals who were watching, to show them his power. See? I can do this.

8   Authority.

9   Macho force.

10   And I understood that, and I showed him my passport, and he scowled at it, flicking through the pages—I am sure he didn't understand what he was looking at—but despite that, despite understanding the whole little charade, I felt humiliated and belittled, as he had, of course, wanted me to feel.

11   But that was Franco Spain and this is Japan, and Japan is a democracy. More than that, Japan is the safest country in the world, and Tokyo is the safest city.

12   You can sit alone in a park at 10 o'clock at night.

---

*Morris Lurie, "The Safest City in the World," *The New York Times*, November 24, 1979. Copyright ©1979 by The New York Times Company. Reprinted by permission.

13   No muggers.

14   No pickpockets.

15   No violence.

16   No thieves.

17   This is a condition you feel as soon as you arrive, and if you are used to, say, New York, the feeling you have in Tokyo of safety and security—walking down the street with $500 in an unbuttoned pocket—is so liberating as to be almost heady.

18   You can go anywhere.

19   You are never frightened.

20   You are endlessly safe.

21   Or was I being dumb?

22   I sat with a journalist in the Foreign Correspondents Club of Japan, 20 floors up from the surface of Tokyo, above and across from the neon fireworks of Ginza, and he told me, no, that's how it was.

23   An American, this journalist, but here now for 25 years, an old Japan hand, as they say, married to a Japanese too. He knew the place. He knew the Japanese mind.

24   "I could tell you stories," he said. "You leave your wallet in a restaurant, and the next day it's returned. I know one guy, left his in Kyoto, the owner closed the place, came to Tokyo, gave it back to him. Personally. Tracked him down."

25   "Why?" I said.

26   "They still hang people here," he said. "Not as many as they used to, but it happens. Listen, you should see the jails here. They're bad. Stone and iron. You don't get television, you don't get books. You get nothing. You sit there. They don't talk about rehabilitation. This is punishment. In winter, those jails are very cold. At night, you get one blanket. Two of you in the cell? Well, you become friends, you share it. Three?" He shrugged. "And in the morning, they take the blanket away."

27   I looked at a sign for potato chips flashing on and off, yellow discs dancing in the night. Impossible to remember that this city was fire-bombed during the war.

28   "You seen a policeman yet?" the journalist asked me. "Those boys are tough. I've seen them breaking up riots here—those student things a few years back. They don't fool around. It's all very clear. You break the law, you pay."

29   "But police everywhere are tough," I said. "That's what stops crime, surely. What about unemployment, drugs?"

30   "You don't understand," he said. "It's not the police. It's the people. Look. They've got a system here, every part of Japan is broken up into small areas, communities, and every community has got a head. He's responsible. So let's say you rob a bank, here in Tokyo. You go to Kyoto, you go to Osaka. You check into hotel. You don't

make any trouble, you pay your bills. Or even if you stay with friends. O.K. Two days, three, four, and then people want to know what you're doing there, where you're from. They go to the head man, and he goes to the police. All very nice, all very polite. And then the police check their records—and they've got records of everyone—and you get a knock on the door."

31   "I see," I said.

32   "No, you don't, he said. "You don't understand the Japanese mind. Listen, they keep records here from the day you're born. On everyone. Do you know about *eta*? *Eta* means 'unclean.' Slaughterers, anyone connected with killing—that's *eta*. If you're descended from an *eta*, you're *eta* too. Forever. And that means you can't marry, unless it's to another *eta*, certain jobs you can't get, there are places you can't live. Et cetera. Just like in India. O.K. Some years back they decided, no, Japan is a modern nation now, we're going to do away with *eta*. They had big burnings. In public. All the records. I mean, this was stuff going back before Buddhism came here. No more *eta*. But do you know what they did? They kept duplicates. Why? Well, you wouldn't want your daughter to marry one, would you?"

33   He laughed a joyless laugh, the laugh of an old Japan hand.

34   "No," he said, "you break the law here and there's nowhere to go. You want a passport, leave the country? Every passport is good for one trip only. You break the law, no passport. You don't leave."

35   He smiled.

36   "And it works," he said. "See? You can walk down any street. Anytime. This is the safest city in the world."

37   So here I am, 10 o'clock at night, sitting in this little park in the safest city in the world, while the policeman clicks on his flashlight, which he wears strapped to his chest, pointing down—he's not going to waste a good hand holding a nonweapon—as he looks at my passport, and then he gives it back to me, and he nods, and I nod, and I know it's just a formality, it's how things work here, a tiny price to pay, surely, for the peace of mind of sitting here unafraid. So why do I feel as though I have suffered some essential loss?

ACTIVITY 3.8

Answer the following questions about the preceding article:

1. What is the main idea of this article?
2. Why does the author include details about the park at the beginning of the article?
3. What is the purpose of the story about the time he was asked for his passport in Spain?
4. What specific illustrations does the author give to show how safe Tokyo is?

5. What illustrations does the writer offer to show how the Japanese create the atmosphere of safety and security?
6. How are you affected by the other reporter's story about the *eta*?
7. What specifics make you feel the writer's discomfort with the safest city and country in the world?
8. Did the writer's use of specifics lead you to agree with him that the cost of safety in Japan is too high, or do his details lead you to feel we Americans have sacrificed our safety out of a misguided concern for freedom?

ACTIVITY 3.9

Free write on the topic of freedom versus security and what is the proper balance between the two.

ACTIVITY 3.10

1. Form groups of no more than five students.
2. Take turns reading your free write once to the group. During your first reading, the others should just listen.
3. After you have finished reading, the listeners should write down what they recall most strongly.
4. Read your free write to your group a second time.
5. After your second reading, the listeners should write down answers to these questions:
   a. What did they like most?
   b. What do they especially remember? (Here the listeners can use their notes from step 3, modifying them if necessary.)
   c. What do they find to be the main idea of the free writing? Or in what direction do they think it is going?
   d. What do they want to hear more about?
6. Take notes on what each of your listeners has to say. However, do not respond verbally, except to request clarification of the listeners' comments. If you explain or defend what you intended now, you may feel the points have been dealt with, and you may fail to include them in your next draft.
7. Repeat the process for each member of the group.

ACTIVITY 3.11

Write a draft of a paper on freedom versus security based on your free write and the feedback you received from your listeners.

When you've finished, underline your main idea if it is stated in your paper. If it is not stated but implied, skip a line at the end of your draft, and write your main idea in a separate sentence.

EDITING ACTIVITY

Before you take your paper any further, it's time to take another step on the writer's journey. You can either do this on your own or your instructor may assign particular activities.

1. Go to Chapter 9, on editing verb usage. Read over the ideas and do some of the activities on your own, or your instructor may spend some class time or assign particular readings and activities.
2. Then turn to Chapter 14 and complete Activity 14.2, combining the short sentences in each grouping into one sentence. Your instructor will tell you whether to work on your own, in groups, or in the setting of the whole class. She or he will also indicate whether you will hand this in, go over it in class, or simply use it for your personal practice.
3. However you work with the materials on editing verb usage, employ those concepts and what you have already learned about sentence boundaries and combining sentences to improve your paper, by correcting any errors in verb usage, eliminating any fragments or run-ons, and making the sentence level writing better.

ACTIVITY 3.12

1. Exchange the papers you rewrote for Activity 3.11 with another student, someone who was not a member of the group you received feedback from on the first draft. He or she will read your paper, and you will read his or hers. You will act as editors for each other. *Do not write on the author's paper.*
2. Without discussing the paper with the writer, write the name of the person whose paper you read at the top of a piece of paper and do the following:
    a. Copy the writer's main idea. If the bulk of what is written contradicts what the writer said he or she would prove, write down what you think the main idea should be. If there is a clear main idea, but some information is not evidence for it, indicate what sentences or ideas you feel don't fit.
    b. Tell the writer what specific examples you found particularly effective.
    c. Tell the writer where you need or would like more specific details to help you understand what he or she is saying or to make the ideas more vivid and more real for you.
    d. Indicate whether there are any problems with verb usage, fragments, or run-ons. Tell the writer where they are. Mention in which paragraph and at which line. You might quote the first few words to help the writer find the spot where you see a problem. Then suggest a correction.
    e. Sign your analysis of the other writer's draft and return it with the original.
3. When you have received your draft back, along with your editor's comments, on another piece of paper state whether your editor was helpful and what you will change, if anything, as a result of his or her remarks.
4. Rewrite your draft.

5. Your instructor will tell you whether to submit your first version, your editor's comments, and your response along with your second version, or if you should just hand in the final draft of your paper.

At the end of Chapter 9, you'll find an additional or alternative writing assignment.

This chapter has shown you the next steps on the journey—adding details to make your generalizations clear and unconfusing for your reader and, if necessary, revising your contract as your details grow and develop. You have also practiced another step in the editing process.

Chapter 4

Using Your Reader's Needs to Organize Paragraphs

Here's a conversation overheard in a writing class:

Student 1	"You know what drives me crazy?"
Student 2	"What?"
Student 1	"Organizing. Getting things in the right order."
Student 2	"Well, I was always told to make an outline."
Student 1	"Sure, but how do you know what comes first and what comes next?"

Often when I talk to students about what they find most difficult about writing and what they most want to improve in their writing, they frequently express one major concern: how to organize. This step in the writing process, like the beginning step, is often unnecessarily complicated because writers try too soon to take a step that comes later in the process. As you saw in Chapter 1, editing at the beginning is difficult and leads to frustration because you really are not yet ready to edit. You need to find out what it is you have to say first. Deciding on how to organize your ideas in a vacuum is difficult and frustrating too. There is a step that you must take first.

In Chapter 3, you saw how thinking about the needs of readers helps you to be more specific and to give a clearer, more complete picture of what you are writing about. In this chapter, you will see how thinking about your audience, your readers, and what information they need, in what order, and in what form, makes organizing easier.

Paragraphing

One way to make your writing easier for your readers to understand is to break the piece down into fairly short paragraphs. A paragraph is a group of linked sentences that usually develop one main thought. A page that has few paragraph breaks looks intimidating. Many readers feel that writing that goes on for long stretches without white spaces is hard to read. They feel that they are in for a reading experience that is going to be overwhelming. Readers can grasp ideas more easily if those ideas are separated rather than presented in large blocks.

While doing free writing to get started or while writing a journal entry, writers usually don't worry about paragraphing. I don't. In writing this book, I just got my ideas down. I only thought about paragraphs later, when I considered how to make reading easier for my readers, when I started to move from free writing to a first draft.

There is no absolute rule for the right length of a paragraph. Usually, they run from five to ten sentences. But sometimes a single-sentence paragraph can be effective.

I remember reading an article about Japanese business practices. After a fairly long first paragraph that described popular myths about Japanese businessmen, there was a single-sentence paragraph that said something like,

But what they do is good business.

The article then went on to describe, in several more detailed paragraphs, why this statement was correct. The single-sentence paragraph dramatized the main point of the article for an audience who might have shared the misconceptions presented in the first paragraph.

Paragraphs frequently start with a statement of the main idea (called a topic sentence) that the rest of the sentences will develop, but this is not always the case. Sometimes the main idea of a paragraph, just like the main idea of a whole piece of writing, may be in the middle, at the end, or it may be just implied. It may be what the paragraph as a whole adds up to, even though that idea is never directly stated in words within the paragraph.

Look at the following piece of student writing, printed first without paragraph breaks, and then with paragraphs to make reading much easier for you.

    A.   Being a single parent and an older student, I find college difficult in different ways than some of my younger classmates. I feel isolated at times. The younger students have such different interests. They still hang out with their friends and seem to have a great deal of free time, at least to me. They're always talking about the parties they've gone to, the trips they've taken, the shows they've watched, the movies they've seen, and the dates they've been on. I don't have the time to do all the things they do. Also they are much more concerned about clothes and make-up. I can't believe what they spend on what seems to me to be foolish luxuries. They don't seem concerned with rent and food bills or any of the other things that I worry about every day. I worry about my son, Aton. I have to leave him in daycare while I go to class. I had a lot of trouble finding a center that I liked. Some had so many kids that I was sure he wouldn't get personal attention. Some places didn't look all that clean. I placed him with a woman who had a nice home and who only cared for three children. But he came home speaking worse English than I ever heard and repeating the superstitions and religious system of the woman, whose beliefs differed a great deal from mine. I had to get him out of there. Now he is in a better place, I think. But every time I hear about kids being molested, I worry. And that distracts me from my studies. Also when I get home, unlike my younger classmates, I have to cook for Aton, talk with him, play with him, and just generally give him a lot of attention. I don't want to be a stranger to him. I want to share what happened during the day, to comfort him if anything went wrong, and hold him. I don't want him to feel that the people at the daycare center are his real parents. But I have so little time, and there's all that homework. It's hard to be a good mother and a good student at the same time. Of course, I feel proud when I get good grades. I feel more of a sense of accomplishment than some of my fellow students. Many of them are dedicated and care about their work, but I think I'm more desperate to succeed and have a stronger sense of why education is necessary and the cost of failing. All of these things cut me off from my classmates. I care for some of them dearly, and they're great people. But I always feel different.

B.

1   Being a single parent and an older student, I find college difficult in different ways than some of my younger classmates. I feel isolated at times. The younger students have such different interests.

2   They still hang out with their friends and seem to have a great deal of free time, at least to me. They're always talking about the parties they've gone to, the trips they've taken, the shows they've watched, the movies they've seen, and the dates they've been on. I don't have the time to do all the things they do. Also they are much more concerned about clothes and make-up. I can't believe what they spend on what seems to me to be foolish luxuries. They don't seem concerned with rent and food bills or any of the other things that I worry about every day.

3   I worry about my son, Aton. I have to leave him in daycare while I go to class. I had a lot of trouble finding a center that I liked. Some had so many kids that I was sure he wouldn't get personal attention. Some places didn't look all that clean. I placed him with a woman who had a nice home and who only cared for three children. But he came home speaking worse English than I ever heard and repeating the superstitions and religious system of the woman, whose beliefs differed a great deal from mine. I had to get him out of there. Now he is in a better place, I think. But every time I hear about kids being molested, I worry. And that distracts me from my studies.

4   Also when I get home, unlike my younger classmates, I have to cook for Aton, talk with him, play with him, and just generally give him a lot

of attention. I don't want to be a stranger to him. I want to share what happened during the day, to comfort him if anything went wrong, and hold him. I don't want him to feel that the people at the daycare center are his real parents. But I have so little time, and there's all that homework. It's hard to be a good mother and a good student at the same time.

5   Of course, I feel proud when I get good grades. I feel more of a sense of accomplishment than some of my fellow students. Many of them are dedicated and care about their work, but I think I'm more desperate to succeed and have a stronger sense of why education is necessary and the cost of failing.

6   All of these things cut me off from my classmates. I care for some of them dearly, and they're great people. But I always feel different.

As you can see, the writer has created a new paragraph each time she came to a new main idea. The first paragraph gives an overview of what the entire paper is going to be about. The second lists characteristics of the younger students that she doesn't and can't share.

What is the main idea of the third paragraph?

_____

_____

_____

_____

What is the main idea of the fourth paragraph?

_____

_____

_____

_____

What difference between the writer and the other students is the topic of the fifth paragraph?

_____

_____

_____

_____

What is the purpose of the final three-sentence paragraph?

_____

_____

_____

_____

ACTIVITY 4.1

Working individually, in pairs, or in small groups, as your instructor directs, break the following piece of writing into paragraphs to facilitate reading. Underline the topic sentence in each paragraph you create:

It doesn't matter if you are 18 or 35. The first time you live on your own is a startling experience. I was 25 when I got my first apartment. I considered myself a very capable person and so felt I would do just fine on my own. But the first year was an eye-opener. My mother had done everything for me at home. I helped, but I didn't pay much attention. Once I was on my own, I realized very quickly that I didn't know much about cooking. I knew what went into things, but I didn't know how long to cook them or at what temperature. Also I'd reach for a utensil and realize that I'd forgotten to buy it yet. I cooked macaroni but didn't have a colander to drain it in. So first I tried to just tip the pot, but I could see there was still a lot of water left. Next I tried to hold a lid over the pot and tip it, but a great deal of macaroni fell in the sink. Finally, I took a slotted spoon and dipped a spoonful at a time, letting each one drain before putting it into a bowl. After all this, when I put butter on the pasta, it didn't melt. The macaroni was cold. I knew how to work a washing machine, but I didn't know how to sort clothes, how much soap to use, or what couldn't go into the dryer. Once I turned all my underwear blue because I had washed them with a new pair of jeans. Another time I gave myself a rash because I used too much soap. And then there was the time I put a shirt in the dryer and when I took it out, it wouldn't have fit anyone over the age of five. Cleaning, too, was not as easy as I thought. The first time I cleaned the bathroom, I didn't dilute the pine cleaner with water. Even though it was winter, I had to leave the bathroom window open for two days before the smell went away. I dusted all the furniture and then swept the rug with a broom. Then I had to dust all over again. When I waxed the kitchen floor, I started at the end where the door was. After I stood in the corner for half an hour, I gave up, walked over the still slightly damp floor, leaving a trail of footprints and sat down and cried. The next day I waxed it again, this time starting at the end that didn't have a door.

Now that you've practiced breaking large blocks of information into paragraphs, it's time to think about the contents of those individual paragraphs. There are many different ways to organize those paragraphs, and each kind of organization has a different function. What all good paragraphs have in common is that each one has a single main idea, a contract with readers that tells them what to expect in that part of the paper. Each paragraph also provides an explanation of some supporting evidence for that main idea. In a paragraph, where the contract or main idea is actually stated, it is called the *topic sentence*. As you learned in Chapter 2, this topic sentence may come in various places in the paragraph. Or it can be implied; in other words, although it is not written out, all the details clearly show what the main idea is.

Now let's look at three main types of paragraphs—those that appear at the beginning, in the body, and at the end of a paper. You will discover that each of these types of paragraphs, in turn, may be organized differently and may serve different purposes.

Introductory Paragraphs

Before looking at actual paragraphs, let's take a step back on our journey and look at the process of producing the material that will form our paragraphs. Here's a free write one student generated when asked to write an experience he'd love or hate to repeat:

Let's see. What can I write. I guess the worst experience was being in an accident right after I got my license. It wasn't that bad but it was bad enough. I can hear the sound of the car hitting the other car. I hit the back of another car after skidding on a wet road. My stomach still turns when I remember. I came to a hill and I wasn't going all that fast, I didn't think. At the top of the hill I saw there was a string of cars that were all stopped. I slammed on my brakes. It was so terrible, the worst day of my life. My wheels locked and I skidded forward. I turned the steering desperately. But since I was so close, I took off my front left fender and the last car's rear right. I can still hear the sound of the metal tearing right now. I remember thinking "I'm going to die now." I can still feel my heart pounding when I recall the experience. Then I stopped finally. I suffered no physical damage. Then I got out, and the other driver was yelling at me, telling me I was speeding and that I was an idiot. I called the police. I thought about the damage. I wondered how much it would cost to fix. What would my father say? The state trooper came and the other driver started in again about all the terrible things I'd done. The trooper said she could tell that I wasn't speeding by the amount of damage done. Then I pulled into a gas station, afraid to drive. I drove home slowly sickened by the sound of twisted metal scrapping on my tire. I was afraid to go to class or work for several days. I was so shook up that I walked to the nearest store which was more than a mile away and bought cigarettes. And I had quit for half a year. I remember just before the impact I wondered if I'd wake up in a hospital or if it was all over then.

As you recall, after free writing you need to find a main idea in what you have written. This writer decided that his main idea was that the experience he never wanted to repeat was being in an auto accident. Except for the first few sentences, there was nothing he had to eliminate, except perhaps a couple of repetitions. Now, he had to rearrange the details so that related ideas were grouped together. Then, he needed to decide how to break this material down into paragraphs to make it clearer and easier for his readers to understand.

He decided that one paragraph would explain how the accident happened. Another would tell about his feelings while it was going on. And a third paragraph would describe how he felt after the crisis was over. To do this, the writer would have to move a few things around. The information in the free write, of course, didn't completely unfold in this order.

Once he had those units in mind, he knew he would also need a first paragraph to provide his readers an overview of what he was going to write about, or to involve them in some way.

Introductory Paragraphs with the Paper's Main Idea and a Forecast

The easiest way for writers to help their readers is to both state the main idea, the contract for the whole paper, and give a map, a forecast, of where the paper is going to go in an introductory paragraph. Doing this supplies a kind of guide for themselves as well.

Here is what this writer decided to do.

> The worst experience I've ever had was being in an auto accident. It happened near home, in a familiar setting. The terror grew out of the suddenness, the actual experience, and how I felt after. It was certainly an experience I never want to repeat.

This introductory paragraph tells the reader that the paper will contain information about a terrible experience the writer doesn't wish to repeat. It also offers a guide to the reader that the writer will talk about the location of the accident, its suddenness, the actual experience, and what happened afterward. The paragraph also forecasts the order of the paper's major points, and the writer has made a contract not only about his main idea but also about his organizational plan.

ACTIVITY 4.2

Working individually or in groups according to your instructor's directions, read the following and decide what the main idea is, what main categories or divisions you expect the paper to have. Then speculate about what kinds of details the author will include.

> I was born in this country, so I'm not sure what it feels like to be a person in an alien culture, but I certainly know what it feels like to be an outsider. I am six foot, four inches tall now and have always been tall for my age. I felt isolated in grade school from the first day. In high school, I felt out of place at dances. I still feel uncomfortable in social situations.

MAIN IDEA

_____

_____

_____

MAIN SECTIONS

_____

_____

_____

_____

What details do you expect to find in each section?

1. _____

   _____

   _____

   _____

   _____

2. _____

   _____

   _____

   _____

   _____

3. _____

   _____

   _____

   _____

   _____

ACTIVITY 4.3

1. Free write about a best or worst experience.
2. Then, working with a partner or alone, according to your instructor's directions, write out your main idea in a sentence and decide what main sections, what potential paragraphs, you think you'll have.
3. Write a first paragraph that states your main idea and forecasts for your readers the individual ideas that support your contract.
4. Read this introductory paragraph to a different person. Your instructor will explain who your new partner will be.

5. Your new partner will tell you what he or she thinks your main idea is and what your major divisions are going to be.
6. Revise the paragraph if it didn't communicate to your partner what you intended.

Introductory Paragraphs That Offer Background Information

Sometimes writers, instead of forecasting their organization and offering a paper's contract, use the first paragraph to give the reader background information. For example, the writer of the piece on the car accident (pages 72–73) might have begun this way:

> Some people have had experiences they'd like to repeat, like meeting someone special, going on a wonderful vacation, seeing a favorite movie, or hearing a piece of music they love for the first time. Others have experiences they don't want to have again. These might include taking a class they hated, feeling foolish, or being at a loss for words. However, there are some experiences that go beyond pleasant or unpleasant and which can never be forgotten.

This kind of paragraph has a main idea, in this case a topic sentence stating that many people have positive or negative experiences they may or may not wish to repeat. However, it does more. Although it doesn't yet suggest the main idea, the contract, for the whole paper, it does set the stage, establish a common ground with the reader, and create interest about what will follow. As a result, the reader of this introductory paragraph may have a general sense of the paper's topic, may identify with some of the examples, and so may feel involved with what the writer is going to talk about. Such a reader has become interested enough to go on to the next paragraph to see what unforgettable experience will be discussed.

This paragraph might then be followed by one with a main idea and a forecast, like the one on page 74.

ACTIVITY 4.4

1. Write a new first paragraph for your paper about a good or bad experience based on the free write you did in Activity 4.3. The paragraph should set the stage, involve your reader, and motivate him or her to go on to the paragraph you've already written.
2. Form groups as your instructor directs.
3. Read your paragraph aloud to the group.
4. Ask each member what he or she thinks is the topic sentence or main idea.

5. Then ask each person what his or her response was to each sentence. Ask what each one was thinking about as he or she heard each point.
6. Rewrite if your words didn't achieve the effect you wanted.

Introductory Paragraphs That Contain Anecdotes or Stories

Instead of starting with a statement of the main idea, writers, especially journalists, often start with a story that illustrates the main point of the piece they are writing.

Writers do this to involve readers, to arouse their interest by giving them something they can visualize before proceeding with an explanation or a line of argument.

So, for example, before telling you how to make Turkish coffee, the writer might have told you a story about how he discovered that type of coffee, how it perfectly completed a meal, or how he impressed guests with his ability to make it, before moving on to present the process. A writer generating a piece on a public figure, before using order of importance to tell readers about how skillful the official is at handling thorny situations, might begin the piece with a story that shows the subject of the article deftly dealing with a problem. A piece on an archaeological discovery might start, not with the significance of the find in order of importance, but by involving the reader with a description of the actual details of the moment of discovery.

Here is the opening paragraph of a *Reader's Digest* article, by Samuel A. Schreiner, Jr., entitled "How Not to Lose Things."* Prior to giving advice that might seem preachy or unimportant to the readers, the author entertains his readers with illustrations of the kinds of things people lose and the numbers of things lost.

> Poking around in the lost-and-found room at Penn Station in New York City a few years ago, a reporter discovered over 1000 keys, 500 pairs of glasses, 300 umbrellas and half a dozen dentures. There was also an odd-lot variety of items which, at one time, has included a duck, a Chihuahua, a wedding gown, an artificial leg and even a burial urn with ashes.

After involving the readers by entertaining them, and establishing the degree of the problem, the author employs a transition to his advice.

---

*Samuel A. Schreiner, Jr., "How Not to Lose Things," *Reader's Digest*, September, 1988, 55.

Fortunately, we don't have to be losers. Here are five basic skills that can help you remember where you put just about anything.

The author of the piece on the car accident might have begun this way:

The force of the blow shook my whole body. The scraping sound of metal on metal pierced my ears in a way far worse than the sound of fingernails on a blackboard. I wondered if I'd be physically injured to the point that I might never walk again. I braced myself for terrible pain. I thought of all the things I wanted to do but never had.

I was having the worst experience of my life, one that I would never want to repeat. . . .

The writer has made us feel a horrible experience and certainly we are interested in reading on. What would follow would be the paragraph (page 74) that offers the main idea and a forecast. The forecast might change, however. Since he has already described the moment of impact, that part might disappear from the body of the paper.

ACTIVITY 4.5

1. Free write about a different experience you'd like to repeat or you'd hate to repeat. You might try a positive one if you wrote about a negative one last time, or vice versa.
2. Write an introductory paragraph that contains a clearly implied main idea and vivid or dramatic examples.
3. Write a second paragraph that states your main idea explicitly and forecasts the organization of the rest of your paper.

Paragraphs in the Body of the Paper

When you think about giving your readers details in a way that is easy to follow, you are aware that a particular order will be helpful. Just which ordering technique to use will be determined by the nature of the ideas in the paragraph and in the paper as a whole, as well as by your goals.

Sequential Order

When you describe a process to your readers, when you explain to them how to do something, organizing is simple. You have to tell them what the first step is before you can go on to the next. Otherwise they can't follow your instructions. Organizing according to the order in which things happen is called *sequential order,* or *time order.*

If you reread the passage on page 51, which presents a method for making Turkish coffee, and your own response to Activity 3.2, you will see how the reader's need to get information in a particular order governed the writer's decisions and yours about using a specific method of organization. This need for understanding sequential order determines how writers organize whole papers as well as paragraphs.

ACTIVITY 4.6

The writer of the piece on the car accident might have used time order to describe the actual crash.

1. Rearrange the following details in sequential order.
2. Rewrite them as sentences.
3. Then, using those sentences, write a paragraph that has a clear main idea and that follows sequential order.
   a. Bouncing off the back of the other car
   b. Coming to the top of the hill
   c. The sound of metal scraping against metal
   d. Not expecting to see a car in front of him
   e. Coming to a stop with his heart pounding
   f. The brakes locking
   g. Skidding
   h. The other driver accusing him of speeding
   i. Driving in the rain
   j. The arrival of the sympathetic trooper

Spatial Order

If you are including a description in your writing, or if you are writing a piece that is primarily descriptive, your reader's needs can still serve as your guide in organizing, just as they did when you wrote instructions. The only difference is that now, instead of using time order, you will place them in a particular order in space.

Suppose I were trying to describe the room in which I am writing this chapter, and I wrote,

> My computer is on a long desk along with my printer and a white lamp. To my left is a low cabinet with a telephone. To my right is a bookcase. On the cabinet to my left is a pad for taking phone messages and an answering machine. In back of me are more bookcases. The bookcase to my right contains videotapes as well as books. On my desk I have a holder for pens and pencils and a great mess of papers.

I think my readers would have a hard time following my description because of the way I'm jumping around from one part of the room to another. If, instead, I moved in a particular direction, the description would be easier to follow.

I might start with the desk, describe everything on it, and then provide a description of everything to my right. After that, I could talk about what is behind me and finally move on to the furniture and items on my left. I might write this:

> I am sitting at my desk. In front of me is the keyboard, console, and monitor of my computer. On the desk to my right is the printer as well as a white lamp. To the right of the desk is a low bookcase which contains novels and videotapes. Behind me are three tall bookcases which reach almost to the ceiling. They contain more novels, books of poetry, and records. To my left is a low cabinet on top of which are a phone, an answering machine, and a pad for taking messages.

This description was easier for me to write because I had an organizing principle, moving in a clockwise direction, and it should be easier for a reader to visualize my study.

Of course, there is no one order that is best. I might have organized by moving in the opposite direction, going counterclockwise. I might describe a person or what is located along a particular wall by starting at the top and moving to the bottom. The important thing is that there is a logical order to help the writer decide what to describe next and to make it easier for the reader to visualize what is being described. Writing a description in this way is rather like putting into words the movement of a camera in a film. And, imitating camera movement, you might use other variants of this organizing principle. For instance, the movie *West Side Story* opened with a shot of Manhattan seen from the air, then moved to a closer aerial shot of a particular neighborhood. Next, the camera focused on the buildings on one block. As the camera continued to move down, it showed the front of these buildings, and, finally, the street where the members of one of the street gangs stood. There are many possibilities you can try.

Finding a Topic Sentence in a Dominant Impression

There is one more step to writing a descriptive paragraph. You need to have a main idea, a topic sentence, for your paragraph. One solution is to see what dominant impression grows out of the details. For instance, if I were to write about the room in which I am writing now, I might produce these details:

> In front of me on my desk is my keyboard and monitor, next to which is a jumble of pens and pencils, scissors, a jar of rubber cement, pieces of paper—both flat and balled up—and several open books. There is also

a plate with the remains of my lunch and a dirty coffee cup. On the floor next to me are stacks of papers, the drafts of earlier chapters. My dog is sleeping there next to pieces of a rawhide bone she has torn apart.

I have not only given my readers an organized description that moves in a downward progression from the desk to the floor, but I have also clearly created a dominant impression—that the place where I am working is a mess. I might even add a sentence to the beginning or end of my paragraph stating that fact. The sentence might be something like this:

When I write, I am often surrounded by a mess.

ACTIVITY 4.7

1. Free write for ten minutes. Focus on a person or a place you're familiar with, or actually look at a picture, photograph, or illustrated advertisement. Jot down everything you see when you look at or mentally picture your subject.
2. Decide on a dominant impression that can serve as the basis for a topic sentence.
3. Write a paragraph about your subject that supports your topic sentence, organizing the details in spatial order.
4. Read your paragraph to another student. Ask if anything was unclear or confusing, what he or she would like to hear more about, and how the details seem to be organized—left to right, front to back, top to bottom, far to near, or some other way. Did everything contribute to supporting the topic sentence? Write down what the listener has to say.
5. Repeat the process. This time you listen to your partner's description and give feedback about the same points. He or she will take notes on your comments.
6. Rewrite your paragraph based on the feedback you get. If your listener is satisfied, try adding more vivid details to make your description more alive. Remember to include a topic sentence and to use spatial order.

Order of Importance

Sometimes you want to describe a person or a place without using spatial order. For example, I might want my reader to get a dominant impression from my description.

Suppose when I free wrote about the room in which I am writing, the dominant impression of the information I put down on the page was that the room gave off an air of chaos. I might use spatial order, but I might also help the reader share this feeling by presenting the details in order of the degree of messiness. Because readers tend to remember the last thing said most strongly, I'd start with my weakest example first and move on through degrees to my most striking example.

So I might write first about the bookcases. I'd tell my reader how they are overcrowded and some books are piled on top of others that are standing upright. More extreme is the condition of my desk. Mountains of papers are everywhere. They surround my computer keyboard, and a visitor might wonder how I can possibly work in such an environment. Finally, most upsetting to a neat person might be the papers that are piled on the floor next to my chair, like a barricade that would even block the path of a guest.

You can see that my sense of how readers might react determines the order in which I present information to them.

Here is another example of using this organization technique to convey a dominant impression: If I determined, based on my free writing, that I wanted to tell my readers that the room reflected my interests, I could again use order of importance.

I might talk first about the videotapes and how they reflect my love of film. Then, I'd talk about my collection of recordings and my even greater love of music. Finally, I'd write about the books I read and the computer at which I write because I want my readers to have most clear in their memory that I spend most of my time as an English instructor in a world of books and writing.

ACTIVITY 4.8

1. Do a ten-minute focused free write on another person, place, photograph, picture, or illustrated advertisement. Or your instructor may suggest using the same one you wrote about in the last activity.
2. Decide on the point you want your description to make.
3. Write a paragraph using some of the details you've generated. This time, however, arrange them in order of importance, not spatial order.
4. Read your paragraph to another student. Ask what topic sentence or main idea he or she hears, where he or she wants to hear more, and if the details are in an order that builds to the most important point.
5. Take notes on what your partner says.
6. Repeat the feedback process with the other person's paragraph.
7. Rewrite your paragraph, rearranging the details as necessary. Change the main idea if your details did not convey the impression you wanted to make. If the main idea and the organization have been successful, heighten the impression by adding more solid, concrete details that support the main point. Place them so they contribute to the overall effect of order of importance.

Comparison/Contrast Order

As you saw in Chapter 1, one way of getting started is to ask what your topic can be compared to or contrasted with. Comparison/contrast is also a way to expand your writing, organize your thoughts, and make what you have to say clearer for your reader.

Does Figure 4.1 show a large box or a small one?

Figure 4.1 Is the Shaded Box Small or Large?

You might answer that the box is a fairly small one. However, if you look at Figure 4.2, which contains the same box along with a smaller one, you would now describe it as being fairly large.

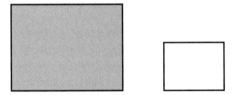

Figure 4.2 Is the Shaded Box Small or Large?

And this picture in Figure 4.3 might lead you to still another conclusion.

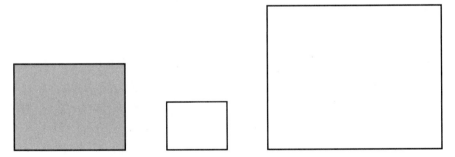

Figure 4.3 Is the Shaded Box Small or Large?

So it is clear that placing one object next to another clarifies what the first object is by showing what it isn't, that it is not like the second object. The same is true in writing. By showing readers what something is *not,* writers clarify what it *is*.

Here is one way to write a paragraph that illustrates the point:

> When I lived in the city, I lived in an apartment. The super fixed anything that went wrong with the wiring, the plumbing, or the windows. I simply walked out my door and threw my garbage down the incinerator. Of course, my neighbors blasted their music and I heard cars and sirens all night, and so I didn't always sleep well. Now that I live in a house in a semirural area, I have to fix everything myself or pay someone to come in and do it, and I have to drag out the garbage. However, it is quiet and I can sleep all night. I guess it's a trade off. There are advantages and disadvantages to living in both places.

In this type of paragraph all the traits of the one place, in this case an apartment in the city, or object, say a type of car, or side of an issue are listed first. Then the writer discusses the same traits in the other. The writer makes sure to touch on all of the same elements; otherwise, the reader is left wondering about differences. For example, if the writer talked about the noise associated with city living but not the quiet of the country, the reader might be confused. The reader might *guess* it's quiet in the second area. Then again, he or she might think the writer intended to suggest there were contrasting noises—of animals, insects, and so on—or something entirely different.

The other way to organize comparison/contrast is to go back and forth between the details about each place in this manner:

> When I lived in the city, I lived in an apartment. When anything needed fixing, the super did it whether it was plumbing, wiring, or windows. Now that I live in a house in a rural area, I have to do all these things myself or pay someone to do them. In the city I just threw my garbage down the incinerator. Now I have to drag out the cans myself. Back in the city, I often couldn't sleep because of noisy neighbors or cars and sirens. Today I have quiet surroundings. I guess it's a trade off. There are advantages and disadvantages to living in both places.

Neither way to organize is better. You do need to be aware that with the first method you need to make sure you are touching on the same points in each half. With the second method, you need to signal to the reader when you are switching. In the second example, the writer needed to use more signals like "Now," "Back in the city," and "Today" so the reader wouldn't be at a loss about which place he was writing about at any point in the paragraph.

ACTIVITY 4.9

1. Pick one of the following two-item topics, or find two things to compare from your journal entries. Do a focused free write, comparing and contrasting the items that you have chosen.
   a. One type of food and another type of food
   b. High school and college
   c. A movie and the book it was based on
   d. Why one course is hard or easy compared to another one
   e. The benefits or dangers of exercising or not exercising
   f. The beliefs of one culture about a particular subject and the beliefs of another culture about the same subject.
   g. Why small-town or suburban life is preferable to big-city life
2. Decide on a main idea, and write a paragraph comparing and contrasting one aspect of your topic.
3. Exchange papers with another student.
4. On a separate piece of paper, he or she will write down the paragraph's main idea, what details were most striking, where he or she would like to hear more, and how you could better develop or organize your comparison/contrast.
5. At the same time, you do the same for your partner's paragraph.
6. When you receive your paragraph and the editor's comments back, rewrite, employing any of your editor's helpful ideas or according to your own insights.

Concluding Paragraphs

At the end of a paper, both readers and writers often feel the need for a paragraph that brings what has been read or written to closure. There are several ways to end a paper.

Conclusions That Offer Summaries

One way to end a paper is to remind your readers where they have been, and to remind yourself too. This kind of conclusion reminds the reader of the main idea and the important supporting points, and helps the writer check on whether he or she has kept the contract and met the reader's needs for well-developed information.

ACTIVITY 4.10

Read the following concluding paragraph. What do you think was the main idea and what were the major paragraphs in the paper?

> So you see that I really enjoyed my trip to Maine. The biking was a pleasure because of the terrain and the scenery. The water was a joy, clean and cool. And, the Fourth of July display was really something special. I hope to go back many more times.

MAIN IDEA

_____

_____

_____

MAJOR POINTS

_____

_____

_____

_____

_____

_____

_____

_____

Conclusions That Go Beyond Summaries

Sometimes writers do more in a conclusion than just summarize what they have said. At the end of a paper that, for example, shows what is wrong with a particular situation—such as the grading system in a particular class—a writer may go beyond a repetition of the problems and call for a change or suggest an improvement. This paragraph is an example of such a conclusion:

Thus you can see that the current pass/fail system does not motivate poor students to work as hard as they might. It discourages good students from learning as much as they can. Further, it does not show employers, schools the students may want to transfer to, or grad schools what any of the students' capabilities are. It is time for a change. We need letter grades that show what we have learned and accomplished.

ACTIVITY 4.11

Reread the concluding paragraph quoted above. What was the writer's main idea? Is it presented in a topic sentence? What were the main categories she explored? Which part of the paragraph offers something new that might not have been discussed in the body of the paper?

MAIN IDEA

_____

_____

_____

MAIN CATEGORIES

_____

_____

_____

_____

_____

_____

_____

NEW IDEA

_____

_____

_____

Not Using Concluding Paragraphs

Sometimes, as in a paper like the one on how to make Turkish coffee, there is no need for a concluding paragraph. The writer has explained the process and when the final step has been discussed, the piece of writing is finished.

ACTIVITY 4.12

1. Do an unfocused free write.
2. Discover a topic in your writing.
3. Free write again on that topic.
4. Decide on a main idea and the major sections (paragraphs) of a paper on your topic.
5. Without actually writing the paper, write a final paragraph.
6. Exchange paragraphs with another student.
7. After reading the conclusions, each writer tells the other what the main idea of the paper was and what the main sections were. Each should also note if the conclusion makes any proposals or suggestions that were probably not part of the body of the paper.

EDITING ACTIVITY

1. After reading Chapter 10 on pronoun usage and doing Activity 14.3 according to your instructor's directions, exchange with another student one or several of the paragraphs you wrote in response to the activities in this chapter.
2. After reading the passage(s), each of you will make notes and discuss any editing of sentence boundaries, verb usage, and pronoun usage that seems to be necessary in each other's writing.
3. Revise your writing if necessary.

An alternative or additional writing assignment at the end of Chapter 10 asks you to work on an entire paper.

ACTIVITY 4.13

1. Look at the above cartoon and discuss it with another student.
2. Free write about the cartoon, getting down as many details as possible.
3. Write a topic sentence that summarizes the cartoon's message.
4. Write a paragraph that reveals to your reader how the message is presented by the cartoon. Use an organizing principle you learned in this chapter to arrange your details.
5. Reread your paragraph, checking to see that everything supports your topic sentence and that you've included all the details you need, in an appropriate order. Proofread to correct any errors in the sentence level writing.
6. Rewrite if necessary.

In this chapter, you have seen how using paragraphs helps your readers and have explored various ways of organizing paragraphs. In the Editing Activity, you have mastered another step in the editing process.

Chapter 5

Organizing the Whole Paper to Meet Your Reader's Needs

As you saw in the last chapter, introductory paragraphs, conclusions, and body paragraphs exist not in isolation but as part of a whole paper or essay. Many of the same organizational principles for paragraphs that you learned in the last chapter also apply to the paper as a whole. In fact, you can think of the whole paper as a long paragraph constructed of other paragraphs. Like a paragraph, the paper as a whole has a main idea or contract. Its sections, instead of sentences, are body paragraphs that contain the solid, concrete details that fulfill the contract in a vivid and real way for your readers.

Sequential Order

In the last chapter, you saw how time or sequential order helps a reader follow a process or a series of events through a paragraph. Now let's look at how time order can help a reader in an extended piece of writing. If a writer wants to tell about a feeling he had at several times in the past, it makes sense for him to present this information in sequential order, not only in individual paragraphs, but in the paper as a whole. In the following paper, you will see how one writer uses time order to do this and to show his readers that a change occurred as he experienced a similar feeling a second time. That idea too demands that he use sequential order for the overall organization, so that the essay will clearly present his ideas to an audience.

Here's the writer's draft:

1   Through the course of a person's life he or she may have experiences of alienation. The feeling of not belonging, of being treated like an outsider, can be overwhelming. I remember two times in my life when I felt this way; both times the cause was my height. The first was just plain terrible. The second helped me deal with these feelings.

2   The first time I felt excluded was my very first day of school. I was excited because I was going to a new place where I would meet new people. But when I got to the school yard, I felt out of place because everyone was so small and I was so tall. I tried to make conversation with some of the other children, but most of them seemed to be afraid of me. Those who were not afraid, laughed at me and made fun of me

calling me the "Jolly Green Giant," "Andre the Giant," and other similar names. I didn't feel comfortable enough to talk to the teachers, and my mother had already left, so there was no one I could turn to. I felt alone and rejected. When it was recess, I had no one to play with and just sat on a bench and waited for time to pass. After the day was over, I went home and cried over how mean people were.

3   Another event occurred during my middle school years. This experience turned out to be less negative than the first one, but was upsetting while it was going on. During the middle of the year the faculty organized a dance. At first, I thought I wouldn't find a date, but I did. At the dance, Joanne and I had a lot of fun talking and dancing apart to fast songs.

4   Then a slow song came on. The top of her head only came up to my chest. I felt even more embarrassed when I noticed that all the other couples were all about the same height. I ran out of the gym and stood out in the parking lot, not knowing what to do. I felt much the same way I had that first day in the school yard. I was sure the rest of my life was going to follow the same pattern and that my height would always cause problems for me.

5   But then my date came outside and asked what was wrong. When I told her I felt out of place being so tall, she told me it didn't bother her and that she was having a good time. I felt better and realized I was excluding myself, that other people didn't see the problem I saw.

6   I first learned the pain of being excluded from others, but then I learned from another that I was the source of my own sense of being an outsider at a later date. I've also learned never to treat anyone else in a way that makes them feel that they don't belong.

As you can see, this paper is organized by sequential order according to this pattern:

Paragraph 1	Gives background, forecasts the order of the main sections, and presents the contract.
Paragraph 2	Describes the first upsetting experience the writer had involving his height and shows the results of that experience.
Paragraph 3	Moves forward in time to a second experience and shows that it didn't seem as bad as the first one.
Paragraph 4	Moves forward in time, showing how the situation became upsetting.
Paragraph 5	Moves forward in time, showing a happy ending.
Paragraph 6	Concludes, sums up the second experience, and then goes further, from the writer's present perspective.

ACTIVITY 5.1

1. Free write about an event that occurred when you were younger.
2. Decide on a main idea and what paragraphs (main sections) you'll use to present your details. Write a draft. The paragraphs should be arranged in terms of time order. The results of the event, or the lesson you learned, should follow the paragraphs that narrate the event(s). This conclusion comes at the end because it contains afterthoughts that followed the actual occurrence.
3. Create a descriptive outline of the paper—like the one above for the draft on being tall—demonstrating how each paragraph functions within the overall structure.
4. Exchange drafts with another student. Each person will read the other's paper twice. Then each will write to the other student, telling him or her:
   a. What the main idea was
   b. Where the reader needs to hear more
   c. What the reader remembers most strongly
   d. What, if anything, was confusing or out of order
   e. How each paragraph functions in terms of the paper's overall structure
5. Take notes on the advice you get, and compare your descriptive outline with the one prepared by your editor.
6. Revise your draft in response to the feedback and your own insights.
7. Don't forget to edit before you submit your second draft to your instructor.

Spatial Order

Like sequential order, spatial order can guide the organization of both a paragraph and an entire paper. That is, you can write an extended description using spatial order throughout much of the body of the essay. For example, a paper in which you describe the ideal house you'd like to live in might describe the outside, moving from top to bottom. Another part of the paper might contain a description of the arrangement of furniture and other items in the living room, moving from right to left. A bedroom might be described in terms of what is to the one side of the bed and what is on the other side. In each case, the writer would use some form of spatial order. (Spatial, or space, order was described in the last chapter on pages 79–80, where you learned about applying this organizing principle to an individual paragraph.)

In the last chapter, you learned that when writing a descriptive paragraph, you could use a dominant impression as the basis for a topic sentence to help you decide what details to include and how to arrange them according to spatial order. And, of course, that topic sentence would help the reader to see why he or she was being presented with the particular details that were arranged spatially in the paragraph. The same is true of a whole paper or essay. You can be guided in your choices when it comes to turning information into evidence if you have a clear main idea, or contract, such as "This house is ideal for me," or "I would never want to live in a ranch-style home."

And, of course, your readers benefit from a clear main idea, or contract, that gives meaning to those details that are offered to them in spatial order.

ACTIVITY 5.2

1. Free write about your ideal apartment, house, classroom, store, mall, car, or similar place or object.
2. Decide on a main idea that contains a dominant impression or a value judgment about what you are describing.
3. Write a draft of the descriptive paper. In an introductory paragraph, give the main idea and forecast the main divisions. (Or generate a first paragraph that tells a story or gives a general overview of the issue, followed by a paragraph that contains your contract and forecasts your organization.) Arrange the body paragraphs according to spatial order. The form of your conclusion, if you provide one, is up to you.
4. Form groups. Your instructor will tell you how many students will be in each group.
5. Read your paper aloud twice to your group.
6. Each group member will tell you what main idea he or she hears, where more details would be helpful, what is most striking, what the spatial order was, and whether anything was confusing. Take notes on what each person says.
7. Repeat the process for each writer in the group.
8. Revise your paper in response to the comments you received. Then edit and proofread your draft.

Order of Importance

In the next chapter, you will see that order of importance is affected by the beliefs of your audience when you are addressing an argument to readers who either agree or disagree with your position. However, for the moment, just consider writing a whole paper that reflects what *you* feel is the order of importance.

Here is a paper one student generated about what qualities are important in a part-time job for a college student:

1   It is necessary for many college students to have a job. The job, if it is to be useful, must have certain qualities. It, ideally, would not be unpleasant. It should provide the money the student needs. More significantly, however, it must not interfere with his or her course load.

2   The perfect job would be in the field the student plans to work after graduation, but this is not always possible. If the person likes dealing with the public, it would involve contact with many people. If the student doesn't, working at filing, stacking, or loading might be better. Yet, since what the student does will most likely be temporary, this is not the most significant factor. A person can do something less than ideal as a means to a goal.

3   Obviously, the job a student has must provide the money he or she needs for books, pleasure—for going out occasionally—rent, if he or she has this expense, as well as for meals and gas or carfare. Thus working on campus, say in the library, may not pay well enough. The same may be true of working in a fast-food place or a retail store. Construction work or a part-time office internship may be better choices if they are possibilities. But money is not the most important consideration.

4   Jobs that leave the student exhausted because of the physical exertion that is involved or which require having to work all weekend and many hours during the week are simply not acceptable. Jobs that leave the student with no time or energy to do his or her papers, read, or study are self-defeating. It is better to cut things a bit close financially or to do without frequent dining out, buying CDs, or going to the movies weekly than to have more money and be unable to succeed academically.

This paper is organized according to the plan that follows:

Paragraph 1   Presents the contract, forecasts the order, and indicates that the paper will be organized according to order of importance.

Paragraph 2   Presents evidence for the least important category, that the job be enjoyable.

Paragraph 3   Presents evidence for the next most important quality, that the job provides money.

Paragraph 4   Presents evidence that the most important consideration is that the job not interfere with the student's academic career.

ACTIVITY 5.3

1. Free write on an issue about which you can advise your readers.
2. Decide on a main idea, organize related details, and determine the order of importance.
3. Write a draft.
4. Exchange papers with another student.
5. After reading your partner's draft, write to that person, and he or she will write to you, stating what the main idea is, what details are most vivid, where the paper needs more support and whether it seems to be organized effectively according to order of importance. To accomplish the final step, each of you can sketch a descriptive outline of the paper, showing how each paragraph functions and how order of importance determines the order of the paragraphs in the whole paper.
6. Rewrite your draft, using your editor's notes and your own insights. Spend some time editing your word use and grammar, as well as the paper as a whole.

Comparison/Contrast Order

In the last chapter, you saw that comparing and contrasting make clearer what something is by placing it next to something else. You also saw that there are two ways to organize comparison/contrast paragraphs: (1) all the information about one person, place, time, concept, or whatever first, and then all of the information about the other; or (2) one quality of A and a related quality of B. Then another quality of A and the corresponding quality in B, and so on. You also recall that whatever issues you touch on in discussing one person, place, idea, book, and so on, must be explored when you discuss the other.

The same comparison/contrast strategies used for paragraphs can be employed to make an essay, a whole paper, clear and logical for your readers.

Suppose a student were to write a paper on why she likes living in a large city. She could simply tell her readers all the things she likes about life there, but she would make her paper more effective if she contrasted what she likes in the city with what she doesn't like about living in a small town.

Here's a piece of writing that illustrates the point:

1   I prefer living in a big city to living in a small town.

2   If I lived in a small town and wanted to see a current film, I would have to wait until it showed up at the one movie house in town. I spent one summer with some relatives in a small town upstate where the one movie house within thirty miles showed the same film for the two months I was there. And, my relatives in central Missouri have to travel for almost an hour to see a film. I can see all the current Hollywood films as well as a wide selection of interesting foreign and art films. And most of them are just a short subway or bus ride away.

3   When it comes to cultural events, a small town has limited resources. In most towns, there is no museum. The only plays are those put on by the local amateur acting troupe. Readings by novelists and poets are nonexistent. And major dance companies, orchestras, and opera companies rarely visit. In a major city, like the one I live in, I can see professionally mounted plays, concerts, ballets and modern dance programs, and operas practically any day of the week. And just last week, I heard John Irving reading from his newest work in progress. Major exhibitions of works by various famous painters are constantly available in the museums, and works by new artists are there for the viewing in the various galleries downtown.

4   In a small town, shopping is difficult. To get anything you need from clothes to food you have to get in your car and drive to a shopping cen-ter, and choices are limited. Here, if I need anything for a meal I can just go to the store on the corner, which is open 24 hours a day. And as far as clothing is concerned, I have a wider range to choose from in the various large department stores located throughout the city.

5   In a small town, everyone is the same. They eat the same food, dress the same, and share common beliefs and attitudes. Living in the big city, I have a choice of Indian, Arabic, Chinese, Japanese, Thai, Russian, Italian food, and many more cuisines, all within walking distance. My choice in clothing is unlimited, and I'm less likely to be judged negatively by others on the basis of what I wear. Finally, I feel that I have become more tolerant, more understanding of people of other backgrounds because I meet such people every day and learn about their customs regularly.

Comparison/contrast gave the writer much more to say, and gave her readers a clearer picture of why she prefers living in a particular environment. But comparison/contrast needs a clear organization so your readers won't be confused.

As described earlier, a comparison/contrast paper can be organized in several ways. If you are comparing A and B, you can write about an aspect of A and then about the same aspect of B. Then write about a second aspect of A, then the same aspect of B, and so on. If you look at the paper above on living in a major city, you will see an example of this second type of organization. (See Figure 5.1.)

The writer presents her favored locale last each time so that readers are more likely to remember its advantages. So order of importance overlaps with comparison/contrast in this model.

The paper could also have been written another way. The writer could have discussed all the disadvantages of the small town first, and then talked about all the advantages of big city life. In other words, she could have written everything she had to say about A before writing about B. (See Figure 5.2.)

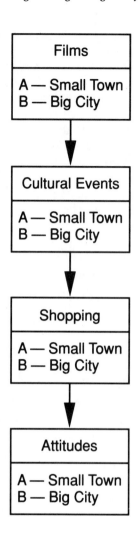

Figure 5.1 Comparison/Contrast Organization Using Order of Importance

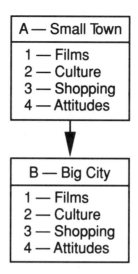

Figure 5.2 An Alternate Combination of Comparison/Contrast and Order of Importance Organization

Again, the reasons for disliking A come first because the writer wants readers to have foremost in their memory the positive features of the big city. This plan, too, combines comparison/contrast and order of importance.

There is no one right way to do it. How would you prefer the paper on big city versus small town living to have been organized? Why?

Whichever method you selected, remember that if you were actually writing the paper, if you mentioned a quality of A, you would have to discuss the same quality when you explored B.

ACTIVITY 5.4

1. Go back to the topic you picked and the paragraph you wrote in response to Activity 4.9 (page 85), or pick one of the following pairs to compare and contrast:
   a. Two sports (either as spectator or participant)
   b. Two types of exercise
   c. Two types of jobs
   d. Two sitcoms, quiz shows, or talk shows
   e. Two cars
   f. Two types of dates
   g. Two buildings
   h. Two types of teachers, doctors, or other professionals
2. Free write on that topic using your paragraph as a starting point. If you select a topic from the list above, start a new ten-minute free write.

3. Decide on a main idea for a comparison/contrast paper, choose one of the two patterns to use in organizing, consider order of importance in arranging your details, and write a draft.
4. Exchange papers with another student.
5. On a separate sheet of paper, write your partner's main idea, what details struck you most forcefully, what you'd like to hear more about, and how the writer could develop a fuller comparison/contrast. Also, make any specific suggestions for editing the paper in terms of sentence boundaries, verbs, pronouns, and the like.
6. Return the paper and your comments.
7. When you get your paper and your editor's comments back, rewrite. Employ your editor's helpful ideas or simply improve the paper according to your own insights.

Papers That Employ More Than One Organizing Principle

Although you may sometimes use one principle of organization exclusively—say, order of importance or time order—more often a paper will use a combination of these principles. If you reread the sample comparison/contrast essay on living in an urban area versus living in a small town (pages 96–97), you'll recognize that the writer used order of importance as well as comparison/contrast to organize her paper. She not only wanted to convince readers that one place was better than the other, she also built her argument to discuss the most important feature last.

She felt that culture was more significant than just cinema, although probably more of her readers would be interested in movies than opera and concerts, that convenience was more significant than pleasure, and that having an open mind to peoples of other cultures was the most valuable result of living in a metropolis. Those beliefs determined the order in which she presented her categories. She started with one that she assumed her readers might be particularly interested in. Then she went to the most personal, possibly the weakest argument for some of her readers, and then used order of increasing importance. She ended with the one she wanted her readers to remember most, and the one she considered most convincing.

Here is a draft of the whole essay one student wrote about a car accident based on his free write and his work on various types of paragraphs in the preceding chapter:

1   There are some experiences that are unpleasant, like bad dates, meeting offensive people, or being frustrated in a store. These are merely annoying. There is another kind of experience that is so truly terrible that the person would gladly face any of these rather than repeat. The one experience that I'd never want to repeat was being in an auto accident. What made it so horrible was the location in which it occurred, the suddenness with which it happened, the sensations at the moment of impact, and my feelings afterward.

2   I was going to class one morning in October last year. As I drove down Route 28 to the main highway that I take to campus, I felt at ease. The road was familiar, and the day was a typical rainy autumn one. Above the sky was gray, and the tree branches were dripping as they arched over the two lane road. To the right and left was the familiar shoulder, narrower than a car width, and beyond it the woods and boulders that I'd passed so often. In front of me rose the small hill, on the other side of whose crest was the stoplight. I was going at my usual speed, expecting to have plenty of time to stop, if I had to, before I was close to the one or two cars that might be stopped at the light at the bottom of the hill. Suddenly, as I reached the crest of the hill, I saw red brake lights. In my calm, uncrowded, comfortable world, there was immediate danger.

3   I didn't have much time. The back of the car in front of me was a few feet away. I slammed on the brakes. But nothing seemed to happen. I kept going at the same speed. So this was hydroplaning. The suddenness of what was happening was terrifying. I thought I was a good driver and had congratulated myself many times before on my quick responses, but they weren't very helpful as my brakes locked. I swerved to the right, but my car hit the one in front anyhow. There just was no time to avoid an impact.

4   Already shaken by the disruption of my safe, familiar world and the suddenness of the appearance of danger, I now was faced with the loud, solid thunk of a ton of metal hitting another ton of metal. The scraping of my car against the other was worse than the sound of fingernails on a blackboard. I was bounced around in the seat and, filled with terror, expecting to feel a violent blow somewhere on my body. I pictured blood, torn flesh, and broken bones.

5   When I came to a stop, my car dented on both sides by the other car on my left and the rocks on the right, I found I was uninjured. I should have felt better, but now I felt even worse. As I got out of my car, I thought in even greater detail what could have happened to me physically. I thought of my parents' anger. I thought how stupid I was not to have started braking as I went up the hill. And then the other driver started screaming about what an idiot I was, how fast I was going, and how I could have killed him. At the moment of impact I had felt fear, but the need to steer kept me going. Now I felt the full horror and was physically ill. I was shaking and had stomach contractions.

6   That was the worst day of my life, but I survived and now I slow down and brake much sooner, no matter where I am or what the weather is like.

ACTIVITY 5.5

1. What is the main idea of the student's paper about his car?

_____

_____

_____

2. What are the main categories or divisions of the paper?

_____

_____

_____

_____

_____

3. What principles did the writer use to organize the essay as a whole?

_____

_____

_____

4. How is each paragraph organized?

Paragraph 1: _____

_____

Paragraph 2: _____

_____

Paragraph 3: _____

_____

Paragraph 4: _____

_____

Paragraph 5: _____

_____

Paragraph 6: _____

_____

ACTIVITY 5.6

1. Go back and reread a draft you wrote in response to one of the activities in Chapters 2 or 3.
2. Analyze it by answering the questions in Activity 5.5, in writing.
3. Rewrite your draft to improve the organization and to help your reader follow what you are saying.
4. Edit the paper, using the skills you've learned about sentences, verbs, pronouns, and so on, since you originally wrote it.

EDITING ACTIVITY

Before you take your paper any further, it's time to take another step on the writer's journey. You can do this on your own or your instructor may assign particular activities.

1. Go to Chapter 11, on editing style, syntax, and diction. Read over the ideas and do some of the activities on your own, or your instructor may spend some class time on the chapter or assign particular readings and activities.
2. Then, turn to Chapter 14 and complete Activity 14.4, combining the short sentences in each grouping into one sentence. Your instructor will tell you whether to work on your own, in groups, or in the setting of the whole class. She or he will also indicate whether you will hand this in, go over it in class, or simply use it for your personal practice.
3. However you work with the materials on editing for style, syntax, and diction, employ those concepts and what you have already learned about sentence boundaries, verbs, and pronouns, as well as combining sentences, to improve your paper by correcting any errors and making the sentence level writing better.

There is an additional or alternative writing assignment at the end of Chapter 11 in Activities 11.8 and 11.9.

Read the following article* about a hoax, then complete Activity 5.7.

1   "This is without doubt the most wonderful moment of my research," marveled retired engineer Pat Delgado last week, as he stood in a wheat field near Sevenoaks, in the British county of Kent. "No human could have done this."

2   Delgado was gazing at a large area where the crops had been mysteriously flattened in a remarkable pattern. A large, nearly perfect circle of plants had been bent down in a clockwise direction. Extending from the circle were other shapes: antennae, a ladder-like strip and a semicircle.

3   The Sevenoaks phenomenon is the latest of hundreds of circular patterns that have appeared in the grainfields of southern England and, in lesser numbers, in the fields of 20 other countries during the past 13 years. And it seemed perfect fodder for Delgado, who now makes a career of investigating and writing about the circles. He has suggested that the circular patterns are created by a "superior intelligence"—most likely extraterrestrial—and has co-authored a book called *Circular Evidence* with another believer, Colin Andrews. It has sold more than 50,000 copies.

4   Delgado's exultation was soon cut short. Graham Brough, a reporter from the London tabloid *Today* who had alerted Delgado to the latest apparition, introduced him to two landscape painters, David Chorley, 62, and Douglas Bower, 67. They had created the Sevenoaks circle while Brough looked on. Moreover, the duo revealed that for the past 13 years they have been sneaking around southern England at night, fashioning as many as 25 to 30 new circles each growing season. Their efforts apparently inspired copycats, who in the past decade have used a variety of techniques to shape hundreds of crop circles both in Britain and abroad. Said Bower to Delgado: "I'm afraid we've been having you on."

5   Delgado was crestfallen. "We have all been conned," he admitted. "If everything you say is true, I'll look the fool," Indeed.

6   The admission brought an end to one of the most popular mysteries Britain—and the world—has witnessed in years. Flying saucers, out of vogue for some time, were given new life by the whorls. Saucer enthusiasts argued that the cropland patterns marked the landing spots of UFOs bearing visitors from space. Believers in the paranormal claimed the circles radiated mysterious energy forces. The patterns

---

*"It Happens in the Best Circles" by Leon Jaroff in *Time*, September 23, 1991 and as reported by Ann Constable/ London. Copyright © 1991 Time Inc. Reprinted by permission.

spawned a kind of intellectual cottage industry: no fewer than 35 Britons claim to be experts on the phenomenon.

7   A new scientific discipline, cereology, emerged. It is practiced by members of the Circles Effect Research Unit, a privately funded group headed by Wiltshire-based physicist Terence Meaden. The group argued that a still unverified weather phenomenon is often responsible for the weird damage. It occurs, Meaden says, when whirling columns of air pick up electrically charged matter, flatten the crops below and produce the bright lights observers say they have seen above the circles.

8   Not to be outdone, a team of Japanese scientists, led by physicist Yoshi-Hiko Ohtsuki, had joined the hunt for an explanation. Ohtsuki believes a form of ball lightning generated by microwaves in the atmosphere flattened the crops; he created croplike circular patterns both in the laboratory and on a computer programmed to simulate ball lightning. Impressed by Ohtsuki's work, the authoritative British journal *Nature* published his report, leading the usually judicious *Economist* to suggest that the mystery might have been solved.

9   The hoaxers' technique required no meteorological effects and only rudimentary physics. After making a scale drawing of the intended pattern, Chorley and Bower proceeded to the wheat field with their equipment: a 4-ft.-long wooden plank, a ball of string and a baseball cap with wire threaded through the visor as a sighting device. At the center of the intended site, Bower held one end of the string. The other end was attached to the plank, held horizontally at knee level by Chorley as he circled around Bower, pushing the grain gently forward. "The heavy heads of the wheat tend to keep it down," he explained.

10   Chorley and Bower say they conceived their hoax in 1978, while sitting in a pub near Cheesefoot Head "wondering what we could do for a bit of a laugh." Inspired by reports of flying-saucer sightings, and recalling crop circles created with tractors by Australian farmers several years earlier, they decided to flatten some corn to make it appear that a UFO had landed. To their chagrin, this and other forays during the next three years went unnoticed. But one of their circles was spotted in 1981, reported in the press and promptly attributed to extraterrestrials. "We laughed so much that time," recalls Chorley, "we had to stop the car because Doug was in stitches so much he couldn't drive." It was only after circle enthusiasts began seeking government funding that the two jovial con men decided to admit to the hoax.

11   Recovering from their initial shock, Delgado and other circle specialists are hastily regrouping. "These two gents may have hoaxed some of the circles," Delgado now says, "but the phenomenon is still there, and we will carry on research." In his quest, Delgado will have the moral support of untold millions. UFOlogist Joan Creighton of

Flying Saucer Review explains why: "We all have an inner sense that there is a mystery behind the universe. We like mysteries. It's great fun."

ACTIVITY 5.7

1. What is the main idea of the article?

2. What did some people think the circles were (paragraphs 1, 3, 6, 7, and 8)?

3. What really created them?

4. Do some people still believe that there are other causes for the circles? Why do you think they feel this way?

_____

_____

_____

_____

_____

_____

ACTIVITY 5.8

1. Think about an event, situation, or condition that some people believe to have certain causes, qualities, or results, but which you feel differently about. Free write for ten minutes about the item, event, place, person, action, or whatever.
2. Decide on a main idea.
3. Write a draft in which you organize the evidence for your main idea in paragraphs. Select appropriate patterns of organization for the paragraphs and for the paper as a whole.
4. Read over your paper to see that you have held to your main idea, have supplied enough details for a reader who doesn't know about your topic, and have organized your ideas clearly and effectively.
5. Proofread, using the skills you have learned in Part II of the text.
6. Write a final draft. Edit and proofread your work one more time before handing it in.

In this chapter, your journey has taken you from using organizational patterns in paragraphs to using them in the paper as a whole. Further, you have taken another step in the process of editing for sentence level correctness and style.

Chapter 6

Getting to Know Your Reader

Different readers have different needs, and being aware of those needs helps you to decide what kind of information to include in a piece of writing. Thinking about what readers know and don't know also tells you what you can leave out and how you should organize what you want to say. To become more aware of your audience's needs, you must think about just who your audience is.

At this point you may well be asking, "But what do I know about my readers?"

Here are two passages about the same subject but designed for different readers:

> **A.** I nearly broke my axle the other day. I went down to the mall and when I got to the turnoff, you know right before, there was a giant hole. I nearly lost control of the car. What a jolt. I'm still expecting to have something go wrong with the car. A person could be killed out there.

> **B.** If the county doesn't do something about the hole at the junction of Route 54 and the interstate, about fifty feet from the turnoff to the Rheingold Mall, there may be some serious problems. At the least, there may be lawsuits from motorists. More seriously, the hole could cause motorists to lose control and serious injury and even fatalities could result.

In the first passage, the writer is addressing a friend who recently has moved away. There is no need to name specific roads and highways. The reader grew up in the area and knows immediately what the writer has in mind. Similarly, he doesn't need to be told the name of the mall where he and the writer have spent many hours.

In the second passage, the writer is communicating with the county highway department; he needs to be more specific about the exact location of the hole. His reaction to the problem is different too. Instead of just expressing his annoyance, he asks that something be done about the problem. So he doesn't dwell on his own experience, but rather calls attention to the potential dangers for all drivers. He also suggests why it is to his reader's advantage to repair the road. The style too is different. The writer, because of the difference in audience, has chosen to be more formal, less conversational, in the way he words his ideas.

ACTIVITY 6.1

Look at the following passages and working individually, in pairs, in small groups, or in the setting of the whole class, according to your instructor's directions, determine who the intended readers are. Discuss the differences in content and wording because of the needs of different readers.

> **A.**   The proposed new Stinkor, Inc., chemical facility will, we are told, provide more jobs and more taxes; however, the dangers it will present are far greater than any benefits it can bring to Gardinertown. Taxes may be lost if people are forced to leave their homes because of fumes and the very real danger of contaminated water and soil. Not only will income from property taxes decrease if there is, as there is likely to be, a mass exodus, but many business owners will find themselves in dire straits. It is the civic duty of every citizen who cares for the future of our town to let it be known that we oppose the construction of this plant.

> **B.**   Do you want your children growing up in a cloud of foul fumes? Do you want your home to reek of chemical substances? Do you want our town to be known as the stink capital of the state? If you are concerned about the quality of life here in Gardinertown, let your voice be heard. Let's keep Stinkor out of our backyards.

ACTIVITY 6.2

Form small groups. Your instructor will work out the details. In each group, choose a secretary who will write down the group's ideas and produce the final letter. Your assignment is to write a letter in which you try to sell a series of books on American history to a particular reader. The series contains twenty volumes, each priced at $19.99. Each group will tailor their style, content, and word choices to appeal to their intended reader.

Here are some intended readers. Make up others if your instructor feels you need more groups.

1. A millionaire who has an extensive personal library of expensive books and who probably would look down his or her nose at this product aimed at a mass audience.
2. A factory employee or other blue-collar worker who owns few if any books.
3. Your history professor or high school social studies teacher who, in addition to a fairly extensive personal library, has easy access to a campus or public library.
4. A member of your group or the parents or relatives of that person. He or she can fill in the details of what the intended reader is like and why he or she would or would not be likely to want the books.

After each group has finished, one member of the group will read the letter to the entire class. The class will then evaluate how successful the letter is in terms of the needs of the intended reader. If the intended reader is unknown to the class, the secretary of the group will describe him or her before the letter is presented.

Here are some issues the class might address in their evaluation of the letter:

1. Does the letter appeal to the interests of the reader?
2. Does the letter try to meet objections the reader might have to buying the books?
3. Are the style and the level of language appropriate to the reader?
4. Is the letter likely in any way to insult or offend the reader?
5. Do you think that the letter will convince the reader to buy the books? Why? Why not?

ACTIVITY 6.3

Pick one of the following situations. Free write and then develop two drafts, one to each audience described.

1. You have been appointed head of the board of education in the district that includes the high school you attended. Write two letters in which you discuss what you would do to improve the school and what you would keep the same.
   a. Write one letter to the parents of a student currently enrolled in the school.
   b. Write another to the principal of the school.

2. You have been chosen to head the anti-drug campaign in your state, or city, or county. Write two pieces in which you describe the program your office will initiate. Tell your readers why the program is needed, what it will consist of, and why you think it will be successful.
   a. Write first to your employees and volunteers.
   b. Then write to a local newspaper.

Writing to a General Audience

When you write a report, you are aware that your reader is your boss or supervisor. You know that the reader of your history final is your instructor, and the reader of a letter to the editor is both the editor and the readership of the newspaper or magazine. In tackling the writing activities in this text, you envision your classmates as well as your instructor as your audience. At other times, of course, you don't know a great deal about your readers. And that's fine. However, even in those situations, you make certain assumptions about your readers. The choices you make about what to include, what to explain fully, what to pass over quickly, are all based on who you feel is on the receiving end of your piece of writing. And the assumptions you make about your readers help you to organize your paper.

If you have a sense of your unknown readers as being interested in your topic, you will write one way. You can simply explain your ideas or argue your position. If you assume your readers don't care about your topic, you will want to use different tactics. You might, for instance, start with an anecdote or story to capture their interest. Or you might want to start by showing them that your topic is important to them. Still other strategies would apply if you believe your audience is opposed to your point of view.

It is important to maintain a consistent picture of your readers. If you write a piece that seems to be geared to readers who know a lot about your topic and agree with your position in one part of your paper and then write in another part to people who are not knowledgeable and who disagree with you, the result will be confusing.

ACTIVITY 6.4

Pick a previous paper, and write an analysis of the assumptions you made about your readers. Explain why you chose to explain various points in the particular ways that you did. Did you assume your readers were friendly or hostile? Did you assume they would be interested in your topic or not? Did you think they knew as much as you did about the topic or less? Be sure to be specific in your response. Point to the specific choices you made in terms of words and ideas that were based on your assumptions about your readers.

ACTIVITY 6.5

Using the same paper or another paper you wrote earlier, exchange papers with another student or share it with a group of readers. Ask the other person(s) to analyze the paper for the audience in the same way you did in Activity 6.4. This time they will be telling you what assumptions they thought you were making about your readers when you wrote the paper.

Writing to an Audience That Disagrees with You

If you are writing to persuade, you obviously assume your readers disagree with you. Suppose you want to convince readers who favor abortion that they are wrong. If you start out by saying abortion is wrong and those who favor abortion are bloody-handed murderers, are your readers likely to continue? Even if the readers read on, they will be less than totally receptive to your point of view.

On the other hand, if you acknowledge that you are aware of the opinions of those who disagree with you and that you understand why they feel that way, you have created a common ground on which you can have a dialogue with your readers.

Then, you can show why you feel the readers are wrong. You may or may not convince them, but you have a better chance of achieving your goal. And your readers, even if they reject your overall argument, may at least think twice about your side of the issue and may even shift a few degrees in your direction.

Acknowledging the beliefs of your readers does not mean that you must give up your own point of view or beliefs, but merely that you show you are aware of the other side. Your argument will be stronger if you can show why the opposing position is invalid. If, however, in the course of thinking about arguments for the other side you change your position, that is fine too. You can simply use your original position as the one you acknowledge and undercut. Either way, the process of thinking about your readers' attitudes and beliefs has made you think more in depth about the issue, and you have a more sophisticated view of what is involved.

Here is a poem by Andrew Marvell (1621–1678) that illustrates the strategy of acknowledging the other side, undercutting it, and then presenting one's own point of view:

To His Coy Mistress

Had we but world enough, and time,
This coyness, lady, were no crime.
We would sit down and think which way
To walk, and pass our long love's day.
Thou by the Indian Ganges' side
Shouldst rubies find; I by the tide
Of Humber would complain. I would
Love you ten years before the Flood;
And you should, if you please, refuse
Till the conversion of the Jews.
My vegetable love should grow
Vaster than empires and more slow;
An hundred years should go to praise
Thine eyes and on thy forehead gaze,
Two hundred to adore each breast,
But thirty thousand to the rest
An age at least to every part,
And the last age should show your heart.
For, lady, you deserve this state,
Nor, would I love at lower rate.
But at my back I always hear
Time's wingèd chariot hurrying near;
And yonder all before us lie
Deserts of vast eternity.
Thy beauty shall no more be found,
Nor in thy marble vault shall sound

My echoing song; then worms shall try
That long preserved virginity,
And your quaint honor turn to dust,
And into ashes all my lust.
The grave's a fine and private place,
But none, I think, do there embrace.
Now, therefore, while the youthful hue
Sits on thy skin like morning dew,
And while thy willing soul transpires
At every pore with instant fires,
Now let us sport us while we may,
And now, like am'rous birds of prey,
Rather at once our time devour
Than languish in his slow-chapped power.
Let us roll all our strength and all
Our sweetness up into one ball,
And tear our pleasures with rough strife
Through the iron gates of life.
Thus, though we cannot make our sun
Stand still, yet we will make him run.

The purpose of the speaker in the poem is to convince the woman he loves to become intimate with him as soon as possible. The woman, on the other hand, wants a long romance first, during the course of which he must spend much time flattering her, praising her, courting her.

This seduction poem does not start with a statement that the speaker is uninterested in the conventions of courtly love or that he is in a hurry to go to bed with the woman he is addressing. Rather, the speaker, in the first section, states that the beloved is worth the long courtship. She's right to want it and surely deserves it. In other words, the opposite point of view is valid. A common ground is established. The speaker would praise her for thousands of years. The lovers could sit on opposite sides of the world and sigh for each other.

Of course, the speaker is beginning to undercut this position by suggesting that it cannot be done. The time involved is obviously too great.

In the second stanza of the poem, the speaker makes explicit why the lovers shouldn't wait. If they wait too long, they won't be able to become lovers.

The final stanza presents the solution—let's make love now while we're young and eager. Let us outwit the process of aging and dying and, with the pun on "sun," he suggests having a child.

Convincing a hostile audience involves seduction, not of a sexual nature, but instead softening the readers with something they want to hear before convincing them that the writer's position is worth considering. It starts with a common, shared position.

The way to organize is no longer an intimidating worry. Seem to agree with the reader, undercut that position, and present your side.

Here is an example of the same basic technique in a draft of a paper on the use of computers in the workplace. The writer assumes that at least some of her readers do not share her point of view.

1   It's all true. Computers do make mistakes, and they have put people out of work. It also takes time to learn how to run one. But let's talk a little about the mistakes they make and about the people they have put out of work.

2   Computers can process information faster than people. That's pretty obvious. A machine doesn't take coffee breaks or gossip on the phone. It does nothing but work. It's always efficient. So why does it send you a bill for the wrong amount? Computers know only what they're told. And who tells them information? People. Every day information is fed into computers by data entry operators, people who do nothing but type information from charge slips or lists of addresses. A computer has no way to know if that information is correct (although it can be taught to refuse some information, such as a letter where only a number would be appropriate). So it makes a mistake if a human gives it misinformation. Human error is the problem, not computer error.

3   Also it's true that many people have lost their jobs to computers. But for every person who lost his job, another person was hired to take care of the computer. In fact, someone was hired to make the program for the computer. Someone was hired to enter data into that computer. Someone was hired to maintain that computer. And someone was hired to interpret or handle the information that computer produced. Many companies have found it easier to train present empoyees for these jobs rather than look on the outside for new employees. Employees trained on computers earn more money because it is a technical skill and have more chance for advancement because computers offer more opportunities to learn new skills. A secretary types, files, answers the phone, and makes appointments. A secretary trained to use a computer for her typing and filing and phone messages and appointments has time left over, time to learn other skills. Also she is now a valued employee who cannot easily be replaced because of her skills.

4   So perhaps computers aren't that bad. They increase employees' skills and, therefore, their earning power. And along with these tangible improvements come job security and satisfaction.

5   But what about learning how to run a computer? That's not easy. No, it's not. But neither is learning how to type, or sort mail, or keep books. Every job takes training. When we went to school, we had to learn how to read and write. It didn't come overnight. Some effort had

to go into it. The same is true of computers. Some basic knowledge is necessary before you can run one. The nice thing is that there are only a few basic program types used on computers: word processing, data bases, graphics, spreadsheets, desktop—and once you know one word processing program, you can use almost any word processing program and feel at home. That's true for all the other types of programs too.

6   So perhaps computers aren't that bad after all. They are efficient, have created jobs, increased the value of the employees who run them, opened up careers for people who might not have been able to advance on the job, and although they take some time to learn, once you've mastered a few basics , it's smooth sailing.

Let's look at how this writer has taken into account the fact that her readers may not share her opinions about how wonderful computers are.

ACTIVITY 6.6

1. How do this writer's first sentences show an awareness of her audience?

_____

_____

_____

2. How does she deal with the fact that some of her readers believe that to err is human, but it takes a computer to really mess up?

_____

_____

_____

3. How does she handle the argument that computers put people out of work?

_____

_____

_____

4. How does she respond to the belief that it is difficult to learn how to use a computer?

_____

_____

_____

5. Besides organizing her paper by anticipating the objections of some of her readers, the writer also used an organizing principle in deciding to talk about efficiency first, creating jobs second, and learning to use the computer third. What do you think led her to use this particular order?

_____

_____

_____

6. An awareness of the readers' needs determined the order in which the writer would present information, even within individual paragraphs. Why did she decide to discuss the jobs that would be created by a company's decision to use computers before dealing with job security?

_____

_____

_____

Writing to a Friendly Audience

Whenever you write to a large and unknown audience on a controversial topic, it is always safer to imagine that that audience is hostile. This way you will reach more readers, and perhaps even change a few minds, and the organization of your paper will be easier to determine.

But sometimes you know your readers agree with your position. You know that they don't need to be convinced. How do you organize then?

One method would be to write basically the same paper as you would write for a hostile audience. You would just change a few sentences.

For example, if the paper on computers you read earlier were revised for a friendly audience, the writer could keep the majority of the details, but simply write a different introduction and conclusion and make some minor changes in the body of the paper. She could write it this way:

1   It's hard to believe, but some people are still resisting the use of computers in the workplace. They fear computer-generated errors, loss of jobs, and the difficulty of learning how to use a PC.

2   As we know, computers can process information faster than people. Computers don't take coffee breaks or gossip on the phone. They do nothing but work. They're always efficient. But some people believe that computers are at fault when they get erroneous bills. They don't realize that computers know only what they are told by people. Those of us who use computers daily know that the problem lies with errors made by workers doing data entry and sometimes by workers designing data bases and spreadsheets, not by our faithful machines, which, barring power failures or mechanical breakdowns, do not make errors. And with the careful design of data bases on our part, like teaching the machine to refuse a letter where a number needs to be entered, we can improve, thanks to the abilities of the computers, the performance of their human operators.

3   Those who fear the age of computers talk of the loss of jobs, but they fail to realize that for every person who loses his job, another has been hired to write programs, another to enter data, another to maintain the machines, and still another to interpret and employ the computer-produced information. All of us here at this company were not let go, but were trained to learn to use PCs. We have increased our earnings and, because of our new skills, we have greater job security and more opportunities for advancement. We have more free time, because of the work our computers do for us, to learn even more and so to become still more valuable employees.

4   Sure, learning the various programs wasn't always that easy, but most of us would agree it was not harder than learning to use that horrible outmoded machine, the typewriter. My coworkers agree with me that it's like getting pickles out of a jar. Once you've gotten the first one out, the rest are easy. And the rewards are so great that the time spent learning is quickly forgotten.

5   If only those who have these unreasonable fears of PCs knew what we know, they would welcome their coming instead of fighting it.

ACTIVITY 6.7

Reread the paper on computers written to a hostile audience (on pages 115–116), and compare it with the version above written to a friendly audience.

1. How has the author of the version aimed at a friendly audience reinforced the beliefs she shares with her readers?

_____

_____

_____

2. How has the writer employed opposing opinions in writing this paper?

_____

_____

_____

3. What details has she omitted and why?

_____

_____

_____

4. What ideas has she added and why?

_____

_____

_____

Of course, in writing to a friendly audience you can omit any reference at all to the other side and include only the pros of your side. However, since the readers already agree with you, you'll have to go further and tell them some things they don't know.

ACTIVITY 6.8

1. Free write for ten minutes. Focus on a topic that you are knowledgeable about.
2. Discuss the following questions in small groups or in a whole class setting:
   a. How would you organize a paper for a friendly audience on the topic you free wrote about?

    b. Should you include the beliefs and opinions of those who disagree?

    c. If you don't make reference to the position of the other side, what organizing princi-ple would work best?

3. Write a draft of a paper to a friendly group of readers who share your beliefs about your topic.

The following piece of professional writing is an excerpt from Peter Elbow's book, *Writing Without Teachers.** As you read it, consider what audi-ence Elbow has in mind and how his writing is shaped by his audience.

1   I find free writing offends some people. They accuse it of being an invitation to write garbage.

2   Yes and No.

3   Yes, it produces garbage, but that's all right. What is feared seems to be some kind of infection: "I've struggled so hard to make my writ-ing cleaner, more organized, less chaotic, struggled so hard to be less helpless and confused in the face of a blank piece of paper. I've made some progress. If I allow myself to write garbage or randomness **even for short periods**, the chaos will regain a foothold and sneak back to overwhelm me again."

4   Bad writing doesn't infect in this way. It might if you did nothing but free writing—if you gave up all efforts at care, discrimination, and precision. But no one asks you to give up careful writing. It turns out, in fact, that these brief exercises in not caring help you care better afterward.

5   A word about being "careless." In free writing exercises you should not stop, go back, correct, or reflect. In a sense this means to "be careless." But there is a different kind of carelessness: not giving full attention, focus, or energy. Free writing helps you pour *more* attention, focus, and energy into what you write. That is why free writing exercises must be short.

6   If there is any validity to the infectious model of bad writing, it works the other way around: there is garbage in your head; if you don't let it out onto paper it will infect everything else up there. Garbage in your head poisons you. Garbage on paper can safely be put in the wastepaper basket.

7   In a sense I'm saying, "Yes, free writing invites you to write garbage, but it's good for you." But this isn't the whole story. Free writing isn't just therapeutic garbage. It's also a way to produce bits of writing that are genuinely *better* than usual: less random, more coherent, more highly organized.

---

*Peter Elbow, *Writing Without Teachers* (New York: Oxford University Press, 1973), 7–8. Copyright © 1973 by Oxford University Press, Inc. Reprinted by permission.

ACTIVITY 6.9

1. What assumptions does Elbow make about the beliefs of his readers?

_____

_____

_____

2. How do these assumptions guide his organization in the passage as a whole?

_____

_____

_____

3. In the third paragraph, how does Elbow identify with the fears of some of his readers about the so-called harmful results of free writing?

_____

_____

_____

4. In the second to last paragraph, how does Elbow turn one of the concerns of individuals who distrust free writing into proof for his side?

_____

_____

_____

5. In the last paragraph, what objection does he anticipate and how does he refute it?

_____

_____

_____

Here is a piece that Kurt Vonnegut wrote for the op-ed page of the Long Island edition of *The New York Times* in 1976, after learning that a local school board had banned one of his books, *Slaughterhouse Five**:

1   A school board has denounced some books again—out in Levittown this time. One of the books was mine. I hear about un-American nonsense like this twice a year or so. One time out in North Dakota, the books were actually burned in a furnace. I had a laugh. It was such an ignorant, dumb superstitious thing to do.

2   It was so cowardly, too—to make a great show of attacking artifacts. It was like St. George attacking bedspreads and cuckoo clocks.

3   Yes, and St. Georges like that seem to get elected or appointed to school committees all the time. They are actually proud of their illiteracy. They imagine that they are somehow celebrating the bicentennial when they boast, as some did in Levittown, that they hadn't actually read the books they banned.

4   Such lunks are often the backbone of volunteer fire departments and the United States Infantry and cake sales and so on, and they have been thanked often enough for that. But they have no business supervising the education of children in a free society. They are just too bloody stupid.

5   Here is how I propose to end book-banning in this country once and for all: Every candidate for school committee should be hooked up to a lie-detector and asked this question: "Have you read a book from start to finish since high school? Or did you even read a book from start to finish in high school?"

6   If the truthful answer is "no," then the candidate should be told politely that he cannot get on the school committee and blow off his big bazoo about how books make children crazy.

7   Whenever ideas are squashed in this country, literate lovers of the American experiment write careful and intricate explanations of why all ideas must be allowed to live. It is time for them to realize that they are attempting to explain America at its bravest and most optimistic to orangutans.

8   From now on, I intend to limit my discourse with dimwitted Savonarolas to this advice: "Have somebody read the First Amendment of the United States Constitution out loud to you, you God-damned fool!"

9   Well—the American Civil Liberties Union or somebody like that will come to the scene of trouble, as they always do. They will explain what is in the Constitution, and to whom it applies.

---

*Kurt Vonnegut, "Un-American Nonsense," *The New York Times*, March 1976. Copyright © 1976 by The New York Times Company. Reprinted by permission.

10   And they will win.

11   And there will be millions who are bewildered and heartbroken by the legal victory, who will think some things should never be said—especially about religion.

12   They are in the wrong place at the wrong time.

13   Hi ho.

ACTIVITY 6.10

1. What assumption has Vonnegut made about his audience?

_____

_____

_____

2. What has this assumption allowed him to do in writing this piece?

_____

_____

_____

3. How does he establish a common ground with his readers?

_____

_____

_____

4. How does he show, although he and his readers share a common ground, that his attitude is somewhat different?

_____

_____

_____

5. How is the piece organized?

_____

_____

_____

6. How do you think the writer decided what came first, second, and so on?

_____

_____

_____

ACTIVITY 6.11

1. Do a ten-minute free write on the subject of censorship or free writing itself or any topic you or your instructor selects.
2. Read your free writing to another student.
3. Ask for that student's opinions on the topic.
4. Write a draft on the topic. While writing, keep in mind the beliefs of the person with whom you discussed your free writing. Organize your draft to meet the needs of that person.

ACTIVITY 6.12

1. Form groups of approximately five people. Your instructor will determine the size of the groups based on the size of the whole class. Each group will pick or be assigned one of the following topics:
    a. How soap operas give people odd expectations about life.
    b. The American obsession with being thin.
    c. Should one work in a job that contributes to making nuclear weapons?
    d. Locating shelters for the homeless in residential neighborhoods.
    e. Legalizing drug use.
    f. Workaholism: Is success on the job worth the sacrifice of family and friends?
    g. Any controversial topic you and/or your instructor choose.
2. Each person in the group should free write for ten minutes. In the focused free write, explore your beliefs about a particular side of the issue your group is considering.
3. Take turns reading your free writing to the other members of the group twice.

4. After you have read, your listeners should write down:
   a. The points you made that they disagree with, since these will give you a better sense of what readers who don't agree with your position feel. Of course, they should also jot down points they agree with, for they will give you additional fuel for your side. If your listeners have no opinion or can't decide, they should copy down the best points from each side.
   b. What they think your main idea is.
   c. What they want to hear more about.
   d. What order you should present your ideas in.
5. Take notes on what your listeners have to say.
6. If everyone in the group has the same opinion, role-play being on the other side and try to come up with some arguments that might be held by individuals who disagree with the group position.

EDITING ACTIVITY

Before you take your paper any further, it's time to take another step on the writer's journey. You can do this on your own or your instructor may assign particular activities.

1. Go to Chapter 12, on editing spelling. Read over the ideas and do some of the activities on your own, or your instructor may spend some class time on the chapter or assign particular readings and activities.
2. Then, turn to Chapter 14 and complete Activity 14.5, combining the short sentences in each grouping into one sentence. Again your instructor will tell you whether to work on your own, in groups, or in the setting of the whole class. She or he will also indicate whether you will hand this in, go over it in class, or simply use it for your personal practice.
3. However you work with the materials on editing for spelling, employ those concepts and what you have already learned about sentence boundaries, verbs, pronouns, style, syntax, and diction, as well as combining sentences, to improve your paper, by correcting any errors and making the sentence level writing better.

ACTIVITY 6.13

Write a first draft of a paper in which you argue for a position on the issue. Remember, your organization will be determined by the beliefs of your potential readers, both those who agree with you and those who disagree. Remember to edit for sentence boundaries, verbs, pronouns, style, and spelling.

At the end of the paper, skip a line and write your main idea in a sentence.

ACTIVITY 6.14

1. Exchange papers with another student. Read one another's drafts and, acting as editors, check to see if the writer has a clear main idea, supported with details, and organized in the right order for the reader. *Do not write on the author's paper.*
2. Without discussing the paper with the writer, write the name of the person whose paper you read at the top of a piece of paper, and do the following:
   a. Copy the writer's main idea. If the bulk of what is written contradicts that main idea, write down what you think the main idea should be. If there is a clear main idea, but some information neither proves it nor presents the other side to be later undercut, indicate what sentences or ideas you feel don't fit.
   b. Tell the writer what specific examples you found particularly effective.
   c. Tell the writer where you need or would like more specific details to help you understand what he or she is saying or to make his or her ideas more real for you.
   d. Indicate any objections you have to the argument or points you think might be raised by someone who disagrees with the position.
   e. Point out any editing errors. Remember to be specific.
3. Sign your comments, and return them along with the piece of writing to the author.

ACTIVITY 6.15

1. When you have received your draft along with your editor's comments, on another piece of paper, state whether your editor was helpful and what you will change, if anything, as a result of the comments.
2. Rewrite your draft and make it even better.
3. Your instructor will tell you whether to submit your first version, your editor's comments, and your response along with your second version, or if you should just hand in the final version of your paper.

There is an additional or alternative writing assignment at the end of Chapter 12.

Chapter 6 has pointed out that another step on the journey to creating an effective piece of writing is thinking about your readers' attitudes and beliefs. The chapter illustrated how an awareness of your potential readers helps you organize and simplifies your choices about what to include. You have also practiced another editing skill.

Chapter 7

Creating Coherence

Listen to two students discuss the issue of where children learn violent behavior before they free write on the subject:

Student 1 "I think kids learn violence from TV shows and movies. I mean, they see *Terminator II* and then beat up another kid. I've seen it. My little cousin—he's six—he'd watch the reruns of all kinds of cop shows. *MacGyver* was his favorite. He'd walk out of the room and attack his brother. He was a couple of years younger, you know. Also I read about a kid who thought he was Superman and was killed when he tried to fly. He went right out of the window, fell four floors straight down. And kids learn to curse from watching movies, too."

Student 2 "I see what you mean about kids getting violent from watching shows and movies. My little brother tries to kick me every time he sees one of those kung fu or karate movies, but I don't see how imitating Superman fits in, or the stuff about cursing."

Student 1 "Oh. Well, what I was thinking of was that kids imitate what they see in all kinds of ways. They learn to curse. That's one way. Flying like Superman was just background or a way to show how they imitate every-thing. In the same way, they, ummm, learn to do violent things. They beat up their friends and brothers and sisters. They even attack older people, just like you said."

In this conversation, the second student didn't see how some of the first student's illustrations tied in with the point he was making. When readers have a similar experience with a piece of writing, they too become confused. But they can't ask the writer questions. So the lack of *coherence*, the absence of clear links between the various ideas, is an even more serious impediment to written than to spoken communication.

In the conversation, after the second student told the first student that she didn't understand how some of his examples supported his generalization that children learn violent behavior from TV, he reworded what he was saying. By changing the order of his points, explaining first that the boy jumping out the window and the children using obscenities were examples of how children imitate what they watch, he made these statements part of his argument. In restating his position, he could add this to his example of his "attacking" cousin and the second student's example of her martial arts fan brother to make a coherent argument. Notice also that he added a phrase—"in the same way"—to help her understand how the two ideas were connected.

In Chapter 6, you saw how concern for the needs of readers provides a guide for the organization of the paper as a whole. Now, you will apply those concerns to organizing within the paragraphs. The needs of the reader will guide you as you move from one sentence to the next. An awareness of the needs of the reader helps you create coherence. *Coherence* is the term used to describe the relationship between an idea and what came before it and what will follow it—coherent writing fits together smoothly and sensibly.

The following are several ways to make your writing coherent for your readers:

1. Using transitional words and phrases
2. Repeating key words and phrases
3. Using pronouns
4. Asking yourself how ideas are connected
5. Anticipating questions from the reader

Transitions

Transitions are words or phrases that act as signals to readers, road signs if you like, showing how one idea is related to another.

Here is part of a paper by Nislia Martinez from which I've removed the transitions she used to help her reader get from one idea to another:

1   Children of divorced parents were automatically given into the custody of their mother because people believed that women were more qualified to raise children. Women were mostly housewives whose time was mainly devoted to housework and caring for their children. Men, whose jobs kept them away from home, were felt to have little or no knowledge of how to raise children. This attitude was reflected in court decisions in divorce cases.

2   Society has changed its attitude toward women being the only ones capable of raising their children. In many cases, both parents work outside the home. Women are no longer home all day. They have less time to spend with their children. Both parents are involved in caring for their children. Many men have had opportunities to prove they are capable of raising children. It's not surprising that these changes are reflected in court decisions in divorce cases.

You can get the main drift of the passage, but as a reader you have to put more than a little time and energy into explaining to yourself how the various ideas are related to each other.

Here is the passage with Nislia's transitional words and phrases restored (and underlined) to help you see the relationships between the various ideas:

1   In the past, children of divorced parents were automatically given into the custody of their mother because people believed that women were more qualified to raise children. Women formerly were mostly housewives whose time was mainly devoted to housework and caring for their children. On the other hand, men, whose jobs kept them away from home, were felt to have little or no knowledge of how to raise children. As a result, this attitude was reflected in court decisions in divorce cases.

2   However, today, society has changed its attitude toward women being the only ones capable of raising their children. In many cases, both parents work outside the home. Consequently, women are no longer home all day, and so they have less time to spend with their children. Therefore, both parents are involved in caring for their children. Now, many men have more opportunities than before to prove they too are capable of raising children. So, it's not surprising that these changes are reflected in court decisions in divorce cases.

This second version is easier to follow because the writer is showing the reader how the various ideas are connected to each other, how they relate to each other logically.

For example, in the first paragraph Nislia has clarified that certain actions took place in an earlier period by using "in the past" and "formerly." Then she sets up a contrast between the roles of men and women by using "on the other hand," and she shows cause and effect by introducing the last sentence with "as a result." Nislia also uses transitions in her second paragraph.

ACTIVITY 7.1

How do the underlined words and phrases in the second paragraph of the excerpt from Nislia's draft connect the different ideas? You might work on this individually, in groups, or in the setting of the whole class.

1. However . . . today

_____

_____

2. Consequently

_____

_____

3. and so

_____

_____

4. Therefore

_____

_____

5. Now

_____

_____

6. more . . . than before

_____

_____

7. too

_____

_____

8. So

_____

_____

Here are some commonly used transitional words and phrases grouped by the kind of relationship they signal to the reader and followed by examples of how they can be used.

Addition or Similarity

furthermore	in the same way
also	likewise
in addition	similarly
moreover	

I find free writing has helped me overcome my fear of the blank page. Furthermore, it helps me keep my voice sounding more natural, less stuffy and artificial.

Contrast

however	conversely
on the other hand	nonetheless
although	nevertheless
even though	despite that

At first, I was unhappy when I realized that I frequently had to revise my writing. However, when I later realized that if I started with free writing, I hadn't made a major commitment to the words I put down first, and writing again wasn't such a big deal.

Time

first	soon
second	while
next	at the same time
meanwhile	before
at first	after
then	finally
later	

At first, I was unhappy when I realized that I frequently had to revise my writing. However, when I later realized that if I started with free writing, I hadn't made a major commitment to the words I put down first, and rewriting wasn't a big deal.

Cause and Effect

as a result	since
consequently	because
thus	so
therefore	in conclusion

When I wrote, I tried to get everything right the first time—the word choices, the organization, the coherence, the details, and the grammar and spelling. <u>Consequently</u>, I got stuck on the first few sentences and grew very frustrated.

Illustration

for example	in other words
thus	for instance
such as	in particular

Free writing helps you find out what you want to say. <u>For example</u>, I wasn't sure what I wanted to include in this chapter until I did some free writing on the topic of coherence in writing.

Emphasis

indeed	again
most	truly
as a matter of fact	in fact
importantly	to repeat

Trying to write a perfect piece the first time can be very frustrating. <u>Indeed</u>, it can keep you from getting to the finished paper.

ACTIVITY 7.2

Fill in the blanks with transitional words and phrases. Leave a space blank if you feel transition is not necessary. Discuss your answers with other students in pairs, groups, or in the setting of the whole class, according to your instructor's directions.

To understand some American writers in the nineteenth century,

the concept of ambiguity is important. _____, not

knowing what a certain symbol stands for or if an event really hap-

pened is a situation we find ourselves in while reading Melville and

Hawthorne. _____, in *The Scarlet Letter*, the letter *A*

that the main character has to wear stands for *adulteress*. _____,

it means other things. _____, it comes to stand for *able*

because of the skills of Hester, the main character. _____,

some of the people of Boston say the *A* stands for *angel* because of all

her good deeds.

_____, in Melville's *Moby Dick*, the white whale rep-

resents many different things to different people. _____ one

person sees it as representing a source of money if it is killed.

_____ another sees it as a symbol of nature.

_____ another character feels it is something evil to be

conquered. And so on. _____, the reader must decide

for him or herself. _____, the reader might decide that

it means all of those things at the same time.

___

Repetition

Another way writers can clarify for their readers how individual ideas and sentences in a piece of writing are related to one another is through the repetition of words or phrases.

Repeating key words or phrases or ideas, sometimes in slightly different ways, helps the reader follow the ideas smoothly, without abrupt and choppy shifts. This technique is especially helpful if the material is unfamiliar to the reader.

___

ACTIVITY 7.3

Here's part of a paper written by Joni Kindermann, a student in one of my classes. The repetitions of key words are underlined in the first two sentences. Underline other words or phrases that are repeated by Joni to help her readers follow her train of thought, and draw a line connecting the repetitions.

You might work on this exercise individually or in groups, depending on your instructor's directions.

1   In the short <u>stories</u> "The Yellow Wallpaper," by Charlotte Perkins Gilman, and "Really, Doesn't Crime Pay?" by Alice Walker, an unhappy marriage provokes, if not causes, a <u>journey</u> into insanity. In both <u>stories</u>, it is the woman who experiences this <u>journey</u>. Both women are the narrators of their stories, and they both use a journal format. Both women are also writers who have not published, and their writing is not supported by their respective husbands.

2   In both marriages, the husbands are caught up in the superficiality of what a wife should be, and they both try to control what their wives do. Both husbands not only do not support their wives' writing, but also seem afraid of it. In "The Yellow Wallpaper," John, the husband, tells his wife that with her imaginative powers her habit of writing will lead to "all manner of excited fancies" and that she should "check this tendency." It seems that John is afraid her writing will cause insanity whereas the narrator feels it will help her express her feelings in a healthy way and so control them. Ruel in "Really, Doesn't Crime Pay?" also expresses his fear of his wife's writings. He says, "No wife of mine is going to embarrass me with a lot of foolish, vulgar stuff."

Repetition for Emphasis

Writers often repeat key words to drive a point home. This technique is called *battering rams*. Look at this conclusion to a paper arguing in favor of gun control:

> <u>Gun control is necessary to protect the lives of</u> police officers. <u>Gun control is necessary to protect the lives of</u> young children. <u>Gun control is necessary to protect</u> us all from uncontrolled violence. Without <u>gun control</u> we will all be in grave danger.

ACTIVITY 7.4

Look again at the passage from *Perfume* (page 49), and underline each use of "stench" and "stank." Discuss how Suskind uses repetition to make his paragraph cohere and to drive his main point home.

Warning: This use of repetition for emphasis should be used only sparingly. Paragraph after paragraph written in this style would not be powerful and coherent, but redundant and boring.

You also want to avoid the kind of repetition that results from stating the same idea several different ways, as is the case in the following excerpt from another paper on the topic of gun control:

> I'm against gun control because it is against the Constitution. The Constitution guarantees us the right to ownership of guns. Banning guns would violate our constitutional rights. So I'm against gun control. It's unconstitutional!

(For more on unnecessary repetition see the section on wordiness in Chapter 11.)

ACTIVITY 7.5

In the space provided below rewrite the above passage to eliminate repetition that does not contribute to coherence or add emphasis.

_____

_____

_____

_____

Pronouns

Pronouns act as substitutes for other words (see Chapter 10, pages 187–202). They direct the reader's attention back to earlier words and so make sentences cohere.

Here's an illustration:

Free writing helps writers find out what <u>they</u> have to say. <u>It</u> shows <u>them</u> <u>they</u> have ideas <u>they</u> didn't know <u>they</u> had.

ACTIVITY 7.6

Read this passage from a paper by Crystal Simmons. Underline the pronouns, and draw a line from each pronoun to the word it refers to or replaces.

Sometimes a person has to support his family by doing something

that goes against his morals like working at a plant that builds nuclear

weapons. And there's no way he can support them on an unemploy-

ment check. However, in other cases, the person realizes that money

isn't everything. He realizes that it can't buy happiness and earning it

in a particular way can cost him his family. If an individual quits his job,

there are ways he can find another job. It may not pay as much as the

first job, but he and his family can cut back on some little extras. But if

he stays on a job that involves doing something immoral, he will be

eaten up inside. This emotional state will affect the family as a whole.

What happens on the job may fill him with guilt and anger at himself.

He will bring these feelings home and he might take them out on those

near and dear to him.

Asking Yourself How the Ideas Are Connected

Another way to establish coherence is this: when you are about to rewrite a draft, go through your paper and ask yourself what a given statement has to do with what goes before and what comes after it.

Here's a passage from Donald Murray's book, *Write to Learn**:

1. Sometimes we write just for ourselves, to record what we have seen or felt or thought. Sometimes we write to celebrate experience. Many times we write just to find out what it all means, for by writing we can stand back from ourselves and see significance in what is close to us.

2. Most of the time, however, writing is a private act with a public result. We write alone to discover meaning. But once meaning is discovered, once we understand what we have to say, then we want or need to share it with other people.

3. Sometimes that need precedes the impulse to write. We receive an assignment and have to write a paper, an examination, a memo for a boss, a news story. We may have to report an experiment, turn in a poem, write a skit, send out fund-raising publicity, create a job resume, complain about being badgered for a bill we've already paid. There are hundreds of writing tasks we have to perform. We may have to write speeches, books, brochures, letters of sympathy, case histories on patients. But whatever writing we do, if it is to be done well we have to go back to gather information and make sense of it.

4. We can't write writing. Some readers think professionals who turn out political speeches or company reports can use language to weave a meaning without information. I've been hired as a corporate or political ghost writer and know we can't. First we have to understand what the candidate is trying to do, or why the company has made a profit or a loss. We have to do research and attempt to build a meaning from the product of our research that a reader can understand.

The first sentence in the first paragraph above gives one reason for writing for oneself. The next two sentences are tied to that idea. They offer more reasons for writing for oneself. The second paragraph sets up a contrast with the first. It states that writing for oneself results in writing for others. And the rest of that paragraph elaborates on that idea.

---

*Donald Murray, *Write to Learn* (New York: Holt, Rinehart and Winston, 1987), 3. Copyright © 1984, 1987 by Donald M. Murray. Reprinted by permission of the author and Roberta Pryor, Inc.

ACTIVITY 7.7

Analyze paragraphs 3 and 4 of the Murray excerpt. State how the ideas in each of these paragraphs are related to each other and to the ideas in the other three paragraphs.

Your instructor will tell you whether to work alone, in pairs, in small groups, or as one large group.

ACTIVITY 7.8

1. Read the following list of information on the topic of the elderly:
   a. Older people in our society are shoved into homes.
   b. In other cultures, they are valued, honored, and are the center of the family.
   c. They have much advice and expertise to offer the younger generation.
   d. My grandfather told me about how during an epidemic at the end of the last century coffins were sold on street corners like Christmas trees.
   e. In homes, older people are often mistreated and neglected.
   f. They are lonely many times.
   g. They know folk arts that are unknown to us.
   h. Older people can make history come alive for us.
   i. My grandmother showed me how to weave shapes and designs out of the palms we got at church on the Sunday before Easter.
   j. We are busy building our careers, having fun with friends, and entertaining ourselves with movies, parties, and trips.
   k. It is unfortunate that we do this.
2. Write a main idea. In other words, decide what generalization this information can support.

MAIN IDEA

_____

_____

3. Rearrange the sentences into a coherent order. Write the letter of each sentence in order below. (There is not one right way to do this.)

   (1)_____   (5)_____   (9)_____

   (2)_____   (6)_____   (10)_____

   (3)_____   (7)_____   (11)_____

   (4)_____   (8)_____

4. Jot down for yourself an explanation of how the sentences are related to each other.
5. Copy the sentences to form an organized piece of writing. Use transitional words and phrases and add sentences that may be necessary to create a coherent whole.

ACTIVITY 7.9

Take one of the drafts you have written already. Analyze it in terms of coherence. Rewrite it adding transitions, repetitions, and any additional sentences necessary to make it more coherent.

Anticipating the Questions That Readers Have

In earlier chapters, you saw how anticipating questions from your reader could provide a guide to organizing a piece of writing. This same principle is also helpful in creating coherence within that overall organization.

Consider how this strategy may have been used by a student, Safiyah Abdur-Rahman, in this paper:

1   Although it is the parents' responsibility to teach their children about sex, many parents are not performing their duty. Some parents are ashamed to tell their children about sex. Some others are so busy, wrapped up in their own lives, they just assume their children know. Still other parents put off telling their children. They feel that their children are still too young, too sweet and innocent to know about sex.

2   In the meantime, their children have a burning desire to know about sex. They hear their friends talking about it and they want to know. Many times, their friends are giving them many misconceptions because they do not have the right or exact knowledge about sex. They learn about sex from TV, books, magazines, anything they can get their hands on, but oftentimes, they do not understand what they have heard, seen, or read. As a result, the rate of unwanted teenage pregnancies continues to rise, and sexually transmitted diseases spread at even higher rates. They need someone who is knowledgeable in the subject to teach them.

3   A teacher who is knowledgeable in the subject can give them a lot. He or she can teach them about the development of their bodies, and the different stages they go through and can teach the children about venereal diseases, the symptoms and the treatments, about contraceptives, and about AIDS. Teachers can inform them that sex involves more than just the physical act. They can talk about the emotional side too. Sure, parents could teach their children these things too, but a lot of them are not well enough informed or cannot bring themselves to discuss the matter.

4   Some people might argue that by having sex education in school, promiscuity will be promoted. But promiscuity does not come about as a result of being aware of what is involved. The knowledge does not make them run out and have sex. The knowledge will make them think twice before they act. And if they do decide to have sex, they are less likely to have unwanted pregnancies because of ignorance about contraceptives. They will be less likely to catch diseases if they know what precautions to take.

5   Sex education is no longer a private matter because sex is discussed everywhere and parents are not doing their jobs when it comes to providing correct information. Some responsible person or persons must teach the children about sex. And the greatest number of children will be reached by having sex education in the schools.

It is easy to see that Safiyah has used an awareness of her readers' needs and an anticipation that they might disagree with her to help her organize her paper. However, if you look more closely, you will see that these perceptions governed her choices when it came to getting from one sentence to the other. You can see that the paper has coherence because she envisioned her piece of writing as a dialogue, a conversation with a reader.

However, in conversations we speak in fragments and often don't name things. As a result, writing—even if envisioned as dialogue—must differ from speech. For example, here's a conversation between two people in a store:

> "John, look at this."
> "Yeah, I always wanted that."
> "I knew that. But why?"
> "Because of this thing. You remember what Ann said about how it solves lots of problems?"
> "Sure, but I was never convinced."

Obviously, this makes no sense unless you are there with the two speakers and you see they are talking about vacuum cleaners, you know what device they are looking at, what their friend said about it, and why the one person is skeptical. Many details would have to be added to put this conversation into coherent written form.

Nevertheless, you can write more successfully if you think of writing as a conversation with your reader, if you think of writing as being closer to speaking than you might realize.

Once you write a statement, think about the reader's possible response to it. That will guide you in what you ought to say in the next sentence.

Let's look at Safiyah's paper more closely. Here are her first two paragraphs again. I've interspersed her written text with the questions she was anticipating from her readers.

Reader	Parents should teach their children about sex.
Writer	Although it is the parents' responsibility to teach their children about sex, many parents are not performing their duty.
Reader	And why is that?
Writer	Some parents are ashamed to tell their children about sex.
Reader	I don't think they all are.
Writer	Some others are so busy, so wrapped up in their own lives, they just assume their children know.
Reader	You're just talking about parents who don't care.
Writer	Still others put off telling their children. They feel that their children are still too young, too sweet and innocent to know about sex.
Reader	Well, you don't want to tell them too soon.
Writer	In the meantime, children are learning about sex.
Reader	They are? How?
Writer	They hear their friends talking about it. . . .
Reader	Kids are like that.
Writer	Many times, their friends are giving them many misconceptions. . . .
Reader	Yes, so?
Writer	Unwanted teen pregnancies rise and diseases spread. . . .
Reader	So what can we do?
Writer	They need someone who is knowledgeable. . . .
Reader	Who?
Writer	A teacher. . . .

ACTIVITY 7.10

Analyze the rest of the paper on sex education. Ask yourself what questions and comments Safiyah seems to be anticipating from potential readers as she moves from sentence to sentence.

Your instructor will tell you whether to work in small groups, pairs, individually, or in the setting of the whole class.

Read the following article by Jacques Barzun, a noted cultural critic and historian.*

Multiple Choice Flunks Out

1   Many things have been urged upon the beleaguered public schools: install computers, reduce class size, pay teachers better and respect them more and give them bodyguards, reform teacher training, restore the principals' authority, purge the bureaucracy and reduce paperwork, lengthen the school year, increase homework, stick to basics, stop "social promotion," kill social studies and bring back history, and (the latest plan) pay kids not to drop out or play truant.

2   Except for the last, all these ideas have merit and some are being tried. But to the best of my knowledge the central feature of modern schooling has never been taken up: the multiple-choice test.

3   This test and its variants—filling in words, rearranging items, etc.— dominate teachers' and students' minds. Passing and failing, ratings of teachers and schools, national and state rankings, the rise and fall of literacy, admission to college all hang upon this instrument peculiar to our century.

4   It is harmful to learning and teaching. Yes. I know the arguments in favor of these "objective tests." They are easy to grade; uniformity and unmistakable answers imply fairness; one can compare performance over time and gauge the results of programs; the validity of questions is statistically tested and the performance of students is followed up through later years.

5   If the tests do test what is supposed, such advantages look overwhelming, and it must seem perverse to call them harmful. But since their adoption, the results of the huge effort and expense of public schooling have been less and less satisfactory.

6   Many studies have shown the failures of our high schools. High school graduates cannot read or write acceptably, do not know in which half of the nineteenth century Lincoln was President and can hardly identify four states on the map.

7   What has this to do with mechanical testing? Simply this: Multiple-choice questions test nothing but passive recognition knowledge, not active, usable knowledge.

8   Knowing something means the power to summon up the facts and their significance in the right relations. Mechanical testing does not foster this power. It is one thing to pick out Valley Forge, not Dobbs Ferry or Little Rock, as the place where George Washington made his

---

winter quarters; it is another, first to think of Valley Forge and then to say why he chose it rather than Philadelphia, where it was warmer.

9   In subjects that require something other than information—the development of a skill, as in reading, writing and mathematics—straining toward a possible choice is not instructional. Nobody ever learned to write better by filling in blanks with proffered verbs and adjectives. To write is to fill a totally blank sheet with words of your own.

10   Multiple-choice tests, whether of fact or skill, break up the unity of knowledge and isolate the pieces; in them, nothing follows on anything else, and a student's mind must keep jumping.

11   True testing elicits the pattern originally learned. An essay examination reinforces pattern-making. Ability shows itself not in the number of accurate "hits" but in the extent, coherence and verbal accuracy of each whole answer.

12   Science and math consist of similar clusters of thought, and, in all subjects, composing organized statements requires full-blown thinking. Objective tests ask only for sorting. So true is this that some schools have had to set up "courses in thinking"—as if thinking could or should be taught apart from curriculum subjects.

13   This is where the lost art of framing and grading essay questions comes in; such examinations imply what teaching aims at.

14   Thirty years ago, the physicist and teacher Banesh Hoffmann wrote a book, *The Tyranny of Testing*, which was attacked by the test-making industry and ignored by educationists. It showed how multiple-choice questions by their form and substance work against the aim of teaching.

15   He pointed out that these questions penalize the more imaginative and favor those who are content to collect facts. Therefore, multiple-choice test statistics, in all their uses, are misleading.

16   Instead of forcing—and coaching—young minds in form-filling exercises, telling them "choose and take a chance," schools would be well advised to return to Ralph Waldo Emerson's "Tell us what you know."

ACTIVITY 7.11

On a separate piece of paper, answer these questions about "Multiple Choice Flunks Out."

1. What is the main idea of this piece?
2. Give examples of how Barzun supports his main idea with specifics.
3. How is the piece organized? What assumptions does Barzun make about his readers? How has his recognition of their questions influenced his organization?

4. Point out some of the ways Barzun gives his piece coherence.
5. Point out some transitions, repetitions, uses of pronouns. Where does he seem to be having a conversation with his readers?

ACTIVITY 7.12

Free write for ten minutes on the topic of how high schools and/or colleges fail to properly educate their students. Suggest some possible solutions to the problem.

ACTIVITY 7.13

1. Form groups of no more than five students.
2. Take turns reading your free write once to the group. During this first reading, the others should just listen.
3. After you have finished reading, the listeners should write down what they recall most strongly.
4. Next, read your free write a second time.
5. After the second reading, the listeners should write down answers to these questions:
   a. What did they like most?
   b. What do they remember most strongly? (Here the listeners can use their notes from step 3, modifying them if necessary.)
   c. What do they feel is the main idea of the free writing? Or in what direction do they feel it is going?
   d. What do they want to hear more about?
   e. Did anything seem out of place to them? Would the writing be easier to follow if any part of it were in a different place?
   f. Did they find anything hard to follow? Did they miss any of the connections?
6. Take notes on what each of the listeners has to say. However, do not respond verbally, except to request clarification of the listeners' comments. If you explain what you intended now, you may feel the points have been dealt with, and you may fail to include them in the next draft.
7. Repeat the process for each member of the group.

EDITING ACTIVITY

Before you take your paper any further, it's time to take another step on the writer's journey. You can do this on your own, or your instructor may assign particular activities.

1. Go to Chapter 13, on editing punctuation and capitalization. Read over the ideas and do some of the activities on your own, or your instructor may spend some class time on the chapter or assign particular readings and activities.

2. Then, turn to Chapter 14 and complete Activity 14.6, combining the short sentences in each grouping into one sentence. Your instructor will tell you whether to work on your own, in groups, or in the setting of the whole class. She or he will also indicate whether you will hand this in, go over it in class, or simply use it for your personal practice.
3. However you work with the materials on editing for capitalization and punctuation, employ those concepts and what you have already learned about sentence boundaries, verbs, pronouns, style, syntax, and diction, as well as spelling and combining sentences, to improve your paper, by correcting any errors and making the sentence level writing better.

ACTIVITY 7.14

Write a draft in response to the feedback you received in Activity 7.13. Be sure to support your ideas with concrete, vivid details. Pay attention to organization and coherence, as well as editing.

At the end of the paper, skip a line and write your main idea in a sentence.

ACTIVITY 7.15

1. Exchange papers with another student. Read each other's draft and, acting as editors, check to see if the writer has a clear main idea, has supported it with details, has organized the paper with readers in mind, and has used the methods described in this chapter to build coherence.
2. Without discussing the paper with the writer, put his or her name at the top of a piece of paper, and do the following:
   a. Copy the writer's main idea. If the bulk of what is written contradicts what the writer intended to prove, write down what you think the main idea should be. If there is a clear main idea, but some of the information neither proves it, nor presents then undercuts the other side, indicate what sentences or ideas you feel don't fit.
   b. Tell the writer what you found particularly effective in the paper.
   c. Tell the writer where you need or would like more specific details to help you understand what is being said or to make the ideas more real for you.
   d. Indicate any objections you have to the writer's argument or any points you think might be raised by someone who disagrees with his or her position.
   e. Show the writer any particular spots where you believe there is a problem with coherence, any place where you don't see how one idea follows from another, where things seem to be disconnected or out of order.
   f. Give the writer specific advice on editing.
3. Return the piece of writing, along with your signed comments, to the author.

There is an additional or alternative writing assignment at the conclusion of Chapter 13.

ACTIVITY 7.16

1. When you get your draft back, along with your editor's comments, on another piece of paper state whether the editor was helpful and what you will change, if anything, as a result of his/her comments.
2. Rewrite your draft and make it even better.
3. Your instructor will tell you whether to submit your first version, your editor's comments, and your response along with your second version, or if you should just hand in the final version (for now) of your paper.

PART II
Editing and Proofreading

Chapter 8

Sentence Boundaries

After you have generated ideas, found a focus, and rewritten, you reach a point at which you feel you have the ideas and evidence you need, that you have put them in logical order, and that they are organized effectively for your readers. Now it's time for that step that you have properly postponed. Now that you know what it is that you want to say, it's time to edit and proof-read. It's time to think about how to present your ideas within sentences to your readers.

As you saw earlier, you need to be concerned with your readers' needs and attitudes. Readers certainly need to be able to grasp quickly what you have to say. They can become frustrated if your writing causes them to do double-takes, if they have to rethink and reword your ideas for themselves before they can easily understand your message. Also, educated readers make judgments about your writing based on how well you observe the conventions of Standard American English. If they react negatively to how you express your ideas, they may be less receptive to the ideas themselves.

Recognizing Sentences

One area that you may need to look at as you read over your writing to begin the editing process is sentence boundaries. If you don't observe the conventions of sentence boundaries, your reader may either become confused and frustrated or may form negative judgments about your writing. For example, fragments, groups of words punctuated as if they were sentences even though they are not, violate reader expectations. Similarly, readers expect to be given signals that indicate where one idea ends and another begins. If writers present readers with run-ons—two or more sentences incorrectly linked— readers must spend time untangling and separating the individual sentences.

Let's first look at what sentences are, what form they take, and how they function in conveying meaning.

What Is a Sentence?

From an early age we speak in units called sentences and understand the sentences that others use in communicating with us. We are surrounded by sentences, but many of us find it hard to say exactly what a sentence is. So we find it difficult to edit our own writing, to correct errors in sentence boundaries.

But as you explore the structure of sentences and how they function, you will find that you already know more than you realize.

The Form of a Sentence

A sentence starts with a capital letter and ends with a mark of punctuation—a period, a question mark, or an exclamation point. Is that all there is to it? No, for although starting and ending in these ways signals that writers think they have written a sentence, they in fact may not always have done so. Between the word beginning with a capital and the final punctuation mark there must be a subject and a verb.

The Subject-Verb Test

One way to identify sentences is based on the fact that a complete sentence must contain a subject—the *who* or *what* being discussed—and a verb—what the subject *does*, *is*, or *has*.

> John is listening to the radio.

John is the subject—the *who* being discussed.
Is listening is the verb—*what* he is doing.
If you can't divide a group of words into a subject part and a verb part, you don't have sentence.

> Waking up to a clock radio is pleasant.

This is a complete sentence, because it has a subject part—*Waking up to a clock radio*—and a verb part (also called a predicate)—*is pleasant.*

> Waking up early.

This is not a complete sentence. The reader doesn't know who is waking up early or what the writer wants to say about waking up early. A group of words like this, which looks like a sentence but is not, is called a *fragment*.

On the other hand, "Close the door!" may appear not to be a complete sentence, but it actually is. The subject, *you*, is not stated, but implied, understood.

The ing Form of the Verb and Sentences

There is one other point you need to remember. Verbs ending in *-ing* are not really verbs, but only parts of verbs. The following group of words is not a sentence:

> Young people across the country asking for Nintendo, Sega, Atari, and Genesis games.

But adding a word before the *-ing* form of the verb will make it a verb:

> Young people across the country are asking for Nintendo, Sega, Atari, and Genesis games.

ACTIVITY 8.1

In the following groups of words underline the <u>subject part</u> once and the <u>verb part</u> twice. You may find groups of words that are not complete sentences. If you find such a group of words, try adding words that contain a subject or verb to make the fragment a complete sentence. (There may be more than one way to do this.) Work individually, in pairs, or small groups, according to your instructor's directions.

For example:

> <u>Many young people</u> <u>are obsessed</u> with video games.

1. My little brother plays video games for hours.

2. I used to be addicted to these games too.

3. Spending hours at the pizzeria or the delicatessen playing on the machines.

4. I saving all my money all week to feed my favorite machine, Mortal Kombat.

5. Playing was like a drug that relaxed my whole body and transported me to another world.

6. Taking away all the tension and stress accumulated during the day.

7. These machines were my medicine.

8. At home, I also played many different games.

9. Games like Sonic Hedgehog, Streetfighter, Double Switch, and Dracula.

10. Unfortunately, these games were very expensive.

The Purpose of Sentences

A sentence, as you just saw, takes the form of a group of words containing a subject and a verb. But, in addition, a sentence also has a purpose: to convey a complete thought.

The Complete-Thought Test

Another way to recognize sentences is simply to read a sentence aloud and ask yourself if it contains a complete thought. Look at the following sentence:

I like to watch horror films.

You may wonder why the writer likes these movies, what their appeal is exactly, why the writer likes to be frightened, and so on. But you have read a complete thought. You know the writer states that she likes horror films. Now, compare your thoughts after reading "I like to watch horror films" with your response to these words:

When I watch horror films.

These words leave you hanging. You probably wonder what happens when the writer watches horror films. This feeling of incompleteness often indicates that a sentence is incomplete. Take a look at the following groups of words, and you'll see that your sense of how English works can help identify complete sentences.

She finds horror films exciting.

This sentence is complete. You may not know who *she* is, but you do know what she feels.

Now look at this group of words:

Seeing the special effects.

These words leave you hanging. You don't know who sees the special effects or what the writer wants to say about seeing them.

The trick to distinguishing between sentences and fragments is to ask yourself whether each group of words followed by a period expresses a complete thought. It doesn't matter if the next group of words, or the group before it, completes the thought. If one group of words that you've ended with a period doesn't make sense by itself, you haven't written a sentence. Look at these two groups of words:

Example 1   Some people hate horror flicks. Because they feel all the blood and gore will give them nightmares.

Together they do add up to a complete thought, but the period after *flicks* makes the second group a fragment. However, your realization that the two word groups do belong together shows you that you need to combine the word groups to correct the fragment:

Example 2   Some people hate horror flicks because they feel all the blood and
                     gore will give them nightmares.

At other times, you may simply have left out words that are necessary to
create a complete thought. Sometimes this happens because for most of us
the brain works faster than the hand. The writer of this example has a complete thought in mind but left out a key word:

Example 3   Sometimes the previews for horror movies the scariest parts.

After reading over what he wrote, he recognized what he had omitted and
inserted the missing word.

Example 4   Sometimes the previews for horror movies <u>reveal</u> the scariest parts.

Sometimes, whole ideas get lost in the rush to get them down on paper.
For example, a writer is proofreading and sees this group of words:

Example 5   However, despite what many people say about watching horror films.

She must decide what is missing, based on what the rest of the paragraph
or paper has to say. In this case, the writer decided the complete thought was,

Example 6   However, despite what many people say about watching horror films,
                     they don't give me bad dreams.

ACTIVITY 8.2

Read the following unedited excerpt from a student paper. Circle any fragments (incomplete
sentences), and explain why you feel they leave you hanging. Then correct each fragment
either by joining it to the sentence that comes before or after it, or by adding information that
turns the fragment into a complete thought. Read the whole paragraph before you start to
correct individual groups of words. Work individually, in pairs, or small groups, according to
the directions given by your instructor.

1   I love horror films. Because I like being scared. Of course, I

        wouldn't like being in a terrifying situation in real life. However,

        getting my pulse racing. At the same time knowing that I will be safe

        when the scene is over, knowing that I can close my eyes if the blood

and gore get to be too much is fun. Although I don't want to face
physical harm. There is a part of me that wants to feel the thrill of
danger. Also coming through a horrifying experience and living to tell
about it.

2   The special effects are a turn-on too. Figuring out how they are
done. Admiring the skill that is involved in creating them. On the
other hand, poorly done effects are fun too. Even though the monster
is stepping on toy cars and cardboard buildings. My friends and I have
fun screaming out loud. I remember one film in which a killer baby
attacked people. It was so funny. The rubber baby thrown through the
air.

Why Are Fragments Often a Problem for Readers?

In Activity 8.2, you practiced eliminating fragments. At this point you may be
wondering why instructors in writing classes are so concerned with fragments
when you hear them daily in conversation and even see them in print at times.

In conversation, you don't have to worry whether each group of words you
utter is a complete thought. If someone asked you why you picked "inner-city
shelters" as a writing topic, you might answer, "Because I'm interested in
housing for the homeless." There is no confusion here, nor would the person
who asked the question make any negative judgments about your answer not
being in sentence form.

It's also true that fragments can be effective in advertisements. For example, the fragment,

The best for less.

is more immediate and has a greater impact on readers than a complete sentence like,

We offer our customers the best for less.

Fragments can be effective as a strategy in a piece of writing, too. For instance, take another look at "The Safest City in the World" in Chapter 3 (pages 60–62), and you will see Lurie using fragments for dramatic effect:

> No muggers.
> No pickpockets.
> No violence.
> No thieves.

However, in general, fragments in a piece of writing don't show readers the connections between ideas and tend to create a disjointed feeling. They become annoying, and readers end up doing the writer's job—making the links between the ideas and arguments explicit. And readers, more often than not, resent doing this.

For example, look at the following excerpt from a student paper, and notice how you are frustrated as a reader. You may even find yourself making negative judgments about the writer's skill and, by extension, his arguments.

> In the essay, "Bellevue: Form Follows Function," by Gerald Weisman, there are two main parts and each has a different focus. The first discussing architecture and types of diseases. The second is concerned with the social mission of the hospital. This part being clearer and more direct.

Readers of this passage must slow down and may become frustrated because they must mentally reword the fragment, "The first discussing architecture and types of diseases," into a sentence—"The first part discusses architecture and types of diseases." In fact, readers probably have the initial expectation that this is the beginning of a sentence that might go on to say something like, "The first discussing architecture and types of diseases is interesting," or "is difficult," or "is written from a historical perspective."

Again, the fragment, "This part being clearer and more direct," leads to expectations that are frustrated. After doing a double-take, readers may decide that this idea should be joined to the preceding sentence. Obviously the reading process is slowed down considerably.

Comprehension of the passage as a whole gets lost in the course of all this work, and educated readers begin to form negative judgments about the writer's skill in following the rules of written Standard American English. And, once readers question the form of what they are reading, they may begin to have doubts about the content as well.

Therefore, editing to eliminate confusing fragments is very important for writers who are concerned with meeting the needs of their readers.

ACTIVITY 8.3

Read the following piece of writing, and correct any fragments. Turn them into sentences by adding subjects or verbs, or make the fragments complete thoughts by attaching them to the sentence that comes before or after. In many cases, there is more than one way to correct a fragment. Be sure to read the whole passage before making corrections. You need to see what comes next before you decide whether to link fragments to sentences that precede or follow them. Compare your corrections with those of others in the class. This can be done in pairs or, if your instructor prefers, as a whole group activity.

The Shakers were noted for their fine furniture and their beautiful architecture. Which were constructed with perfect proportions and balance. The Shakers felt that work was a form of prayer, so everything that they did was done the best way they knew how. With total dedication, and they left no rough edges. There were no short cuts. No unfinished corners. Their buildings reflected their beliefs in another way. Since men and women lived separately, for the Shakers did not permit sexual intercourse among members of their sect. They constructed dwellings with separate doors outside and separate staircases inside for use by members of each sex. Because they had few personal possessions. Their rooms were empty and bare. Reflecting the simplicity of their lives, their architecture, furniture, and even their utensils had simple lines. And no trim or fancy designs or carvings of any kind whatsoever. You can see Shaker villages in several states. For instance, in Massachusetts, New Hampshire, Maine, and Kentucky.

Run-ons

Fragments are one major problem involving sentences boundaries; the other is run-ons. Run-ons can be thought of as being the opposite of fragments or incomplete sentences. Run-ons contain too much instead of too little. They are produced when two sentences are incorrectly joined.

Readers expect signals that show them where one idea ends and another begins. And just as in the case of fragments, when these expectations are not met, readers become frustrated and form negative judgments about what they are reading. Look at the following unedited passage:

> Swans are beautiful, romantic creatures to many people others have very different responses to them. These people say swans destroy the environment by rooting up plants, that they chase away ducks, and even attack children. There have been quite a few cases of swans attacking humans recently in the news I read about one just yesterday.

Readers of this passage must do some extra work before they can make sense of it. The first group of words, punctuated as if it were a sentence, is really a run-on, and so can cause problems for readers. Seeing no punctuation after *people*, they continue without pausing, wondering how the word *others* can logically fit after *people*. But when readers come to the verb *have*, they come to a total halt, realizing that they are reading a new sentence. They have to go back and reread the first sentence, then mentally separate the two ideas, creating two separate sentences, one that says some people like swans and another that says others don't.

The last "sentence" creates even more problems. Not only do readers have to separate the two complete thoughts, but they must do even more of the writer's job. They must decide whether the second sentence begins with *I* or with *Recently*.

Before practicing correcting run-ons, we'll discuss types of sentences and some ways to correctly combine them.

Simple Sentences

You have already learned to recognize the simple sentence. It consists of a group of words that contains a complete thought. It has a subject—what you are discussing—and a predicate (which includes the verb part)—what you are saying about the subject. A simple sentence can also be called an *independent clause*. A clause is a group of words with a subject and verb. A sentence is an "independent" clause because it can stand alone. It is a complete thought by itself.

Subject	Predicate
The black belts	are holding a karate exhibition today.

Compound Sentences, or Coordination

The second type of sentence is the compound sentence. It is created by joining simple sentences. This can be done in three ways.

> SENTENCE, and SENTENCE.
> SENTENCE; in addition, SENTENCE.
> SENTENCE; SENTENCE.

SENTENCE, and SENTENCE Compounds

The first method of coordinating involves joining two simple sentences, two independent clauses, with a comma followed by one of the seven coordinating conjunctions. Doing this creates one type of compound sentence. Joining two or more sentences with a comma *without* using one of these seven words creates a run-on. I always found it hard to remember the seven coordinating conjunctions until someone told me about FANBOYS. It is a mnemonic device, an aid that helps us recall information. Each letter of FANBOYS is the first letter of one of the seven coordinating conjunctions.

> **F**or
> **A**nd
> **N**or
> **B**ut
> **O**r
> **Y**et
> **S**o

For example, here are two simple sentences:

George is going to the registrar's office.

He is going to get a credit/no credit form.

They can be combined by using a comma and the coordinating conjunction *and*, as follows:

George is going to the registrar's office, and he is going to get a credit/no credit form.

Here are examples of the other six words used to form compound sentences:

I am going to the office, but I won't complain.

He went shopping for days, yet he didn't find what he wanted.

She is taking biology, for she is a pre-med major.

Harry is from Boonville, so he knows the central part of Missouri very well.

You must hand in your paper on time, or you will have your grade lowered.

He didn't know the language, nor did he understand the customs of that country.

The two halves of each of these compound sentences can be separated into two sentences, and clearly each can stand alone. For example,

It snowed heavily that day, so the opening of the baseball season was postponed.

can be changed to

It snowed heavily that day.

So the opening of the baseball season was postponed.

As you can see, despite what you may have heard in school, the seven coordinating conjunctions (FANBOYS) may sometimes begin a sentence. Any sentence they start, of course, must be logically connected to the previous sentence. Using conjunctions to begin sentences is especially effective if you have a short sentence following a long one. For example,

At a meeting last week, representatives from fifty nations discussed solutions to world hunger, unemployment, problems of the homeless, and oppression of minorities. But they failed to find any solutions.

Joining Short Sentences with a Comma. One exception to the rule that states that you can't join two simple sentences with a comma unless you use one of the coordinating conjunctions (FANBOYS) involves joining short, linked sentences like

Roses are red, violets are blue.

Using only a comma here is acceptable.

Run-ons with Commas. In general, joining two sentences with a comma, without using one of the seven coordinating conjunctions (FANBOYS) produces a run-on.

I am going to register on Thursday, I hope I get the classes I want.

This is as much of a run-on, and as incorrect, as is joining two sentences without any punctuation.

I am going to register on Thursday I hope I get the classes I want.

This can be corrected in several ways.

1. You can make two separate sentences.

   I am going to register on Thursday. I hope I get the classes I want.

2. You can add a coordinating conjunction (FANBOYS) and create a compound sentence.

   I am going to register on Thursday, <u>and</u> I hope I get the classes I want.

Here's another kind of run-on:

I'm going to register early on Thursday, then I'm going to work.

This run-on too can be corrected in several ways.

1. You can transform it into two separate sentences.

   I'm going to register early on Thursday. Then I'm going to work.

2. You can use a coordinating conjunction (FANBOYS) and make a compound sentence.

   I'm going to register early on Thursday, <u>but</u> then I'm going to work.

3. You can turn the run-on into a simple sentence.

   I'm registering early on Thursday and then going to work.

SENTENCE; in addition, SENTENCE Compounds

A second way to join sentences into a compound sentence is with conjunctive adverbs, which are words or phrases that function like FANBOYS. However, only FANBOYS can join sentences with a comma. When you use conjunctive adverbs, you need a semicolon.

He is taking 18 credits; in addition, he is working at a full-time job.

Once again each clause is a complete sentence and could stand alone, but the second sentence makes little sense unless it is linked to the first.

He is taking 18 credits. In addition, he is working at a full-time job.

Here is a list of conjunctive adverbs, grouped by the logical relationships they establish between two simple sentences:

ADDITION

also	in addition
besides	moreover
furthermore	similarly

CONTRAST

however	on the contrary
in spite of that	on one hand . . . on the other hand
instead	still
nevertheless	

RESULT

accordingly	consequently
as a result	therefore

CONDITION

otherwise

TIME

later	then
meanwhile	

EXAMPLE

for example	in other words

SENTENCE; SENTENCE Compounds

The third way you can form a compound sentence is to join simple sentences using just a semicolon, rather than adding a comma and a conjunction.

Ms. Smith is his advisor; she gave him help whenever he needed it.

This method is used less frequently than the other two because it does not make explicit the relationship between the two simple sentences, but rather leaves the connection up to the reader to some degree.

Here are some ways for editing run-ons using compound sentences without FANBOYS.

> Learning to use the computer took a long time however, now I find it easier to write my papers.

is a run-on, as is

> Learning to use the computer took a long time, however, now I find it easier to write my papers.

These run-ons can be corrected by writing two separate sentences:

> Learning to use the computer took a long time. However, now I find it easier to write my papers.

Or you can correct them by using a semicolon:

> Learning to use the computer took a long time; however, now I find it easier to write my papers.

Complex Sentences, or Subordination

We have seen that there are three ways to form a compound sentence.

> SENTENCE, and SENTENCE.
> SENTENCE; in addition, SENTENCE.
> SENTENCE; SENTENCE.

In each of these kinds of compound sentences, each of the two simple sentences is an independent clause and could stand alone. Another category of sentence, called *complex*, is created when one of the sentences being combined is a "dependent" clause and so is unable to stand alone.

Look at this simple sentence:

> 1. It is cold today.

This group of words is clearly a sentence because it contains a subject *it* and a verb *is* and presents a complete thought. But if we add *because* in front of it, we no longer have a complete thought.

> 2. Because it is cold today.

We can say that number 2 consists of *because* and a sentence. By adding a word like *because* we turn a sentence into a fragment. The pattern is:

Because SENTENCE. If we attach this fragment, this dependent clause, to another simple sentence, we will end up with a complete sentence.

Dependent Clause	Independent Clause
Because SENTENCE,	SENTENCE.

Because it is cold today, I wore my heavy coat.

A clause is a group of words containing a subject and predicate. A simple sentence is an independent clause. A simple sentence that is introduced by a word like *because* is still a clause. It has its own subject and predicate. But it is a *subordinate or dependent clause* because it depends on another sentence to complete its meaning. A word like *because* is called a *subordinator*.

Here are some subordinators grouped by the relationships they create between independent and subordinate clauses (also called a dependent clause).

TIME

as	since
as soon as	until
before	when
by the time that	while
once	

PLACE

everywhere	wherever
where	

CAUSE

as	now that
as long as	since
because	

CONDITION

even if	unless
if	whether (or not)

CONTRAST

although	though
even though	whereas

Front Shifters

Sometimes a word or a group of words that tells you something about the verb (usually they answer the question How or When) appears at the beginning of a sentence, before the subject.

Next Wednesday, the first draft of your research paper will be due.

The words *Next Wednesday* (which answer the question When) can be removed and the rest—*The first draft of your research paper will be due*—can stand alone. They still make up a complete sentence, even if it does have a different meaning. Words or groups of words that are separate from the independent clause, the part of the sentence that has a subject and verb and makes sense by itself, are called front shifters. They are separated from the subject with a comma when they come at the beginning of a sentence, before the subject. And they can also shift to the end of the sentence.

The first draft of your research paper will be due next Wednesday.

When shifters come at the end of the sentence, however, they are not usually preceded by a comma.

Let's look again at the sentence that was used to illustrate the first type of complex sentence (page 163), a dependent subordinate clause followed by an independent clause:

Because it is cold today, I wore my heavy coat.

Since the subordinate clause functions as a front shifter, you can see how we get a second kind of complex sentence. The front shifter moves to the end of the sentence, and the pattern is an independent clause followed by the subordinate clause.

<pre>
Independent
  Clause   Dependent Clause
┌───────┐┌──────────────────────┐
SENTENCE because SENTENCE.
</pre>

I wore my heavy coat because it is cold today.

Subordinate clauses can also be imbedded in the middle of a sentence, as in these two examples.

<pre>
            Independent Clause
┌───────────────────────────────────┐
Subject that SENTENCE Predicate
           └─────────────┘
            Dependent Clause
</pre>

The tape that I wanted was hard to find.

Independent Clause (Sentence)
<pre>
┌──────────────────────────────────┐
Subject that predicate Predicate
       └─────────────┘
       Dependent Clause
</pre>

The tape that was unavailable will be ordered soon.

Correcting Run-ons

Now that you have seen all the sentence patterns—simple, compound, and complex—let's take another look at the various ways you can correct run-ons.

I am writing a research paper about a movie I have never written one before.

Clearly there should be two sentences here since there are two complete thoughts, each containing subjects and verbs, two independent clauses.

I am writing a research paper about a movie.

and

I have never written one before.

You could correct this run-on in several ways. You could make it into a compound sentence using a comma and coordinating conjunction (1), using a semicolon and a conjunctive adverb (2), using a semicolon only (3), or you could transform it into a complex sentence (4).

1. SENTENCE, but SENTENCE.

   I am writing a research paper about a movie, but I have never written one before.

2. SENTENCE; however, SENTENCE.

   I am writing a research paper about a movie; however, I have never written one before.

3. SENTENCE; SENTENCE.

   I am writing a research paper about a movie; I have never written one before.

4. SENTENCE even though SENTENCE.

I am writing a research paper about a movie even though I have never written one before.

ACTIVITY 8.4

Read the following excerpt from an essay on getting a personal computer, and correct any run-ons. Refer to the various sentence types. Use coordination or subordination to join clauses. There is more than one way, in many cases, to correct a particular error. Be sure to read each paragraph in its entirety before making any corrections. Discuss your answers in small groups or in a whole class setting.

1   I have always been interested in gadgets. Every household gadget that comes on the market is fair game for me, I have had food processors, toaster ovens, electric can openers, and electric toothbrushes by the dozens. Whenever I hear about a new toy, I have an urge to get it, however, something about the personal computer scared me.

2   My initial reaction was that I didn't need one, then some close friends bought one. At their house, I played a game on the computer called Dungeons and Dragons. I was fascinated I felt that a computer was one toy that was just too expensive. I pondered this for about two months meanwhile I recalled what another friend told me when I bought an electronic typewriter. At the time, I was overjoyed with its ability to correct typewritten material without my needing to use whiteout. She said to me, "That's great, but it's nothing compared to a word processing program on a computer." With this in mind, after

reading up on computers and going to many stores to do comparison

shopping, I took the plunge.

3   I got the boxes home, unpacked them, then I panicked and started

making phone calls. Some friends helped me set up the computer they

put some word processing programs on it as well as my beloved

Dungeons and Dragons. They then told me to read the books on DOS

and BASIC, they left I was left with two tomes. Perhaps I should call

them tombs. Anyone who has read, or rather attempted to read, a

computer manual knows how I felt I couldn't understand a word I was

reading.

ACTIVITY 8.5

Here's some more of the same paper. This time be on the lookout for both fragments and run-ons. Identify and correct any that you find. In many cases, there is more than one way to improve the sentence boundaries. Remember, read each paragraph in its entirety before making any corrections. And again, discuss your changes with others, either in small groups or as part of a whole class discussion.

1   Terror set in fear came with every breath. What if I break the

computer? "You idiot." I said to myself. Then making more phone

calls. Daily, I called friends for help and instructions. Sometimes, they

were quite patient other times they told me. "Read the book it's there,

look it up in the index."

2   I found a book on DOS. While visiting a bookstore. I bought it it

made sense. Some computer person knew how to write English. After

I made it halfway through this book. Suddenly, all the instructions made sense. I saw the light! I played Dungeons and Dragons until the wee hours of the morning. Played with the word processor. I even bought some new games. Becoming hooked on that little television-like screen.

ACTIVITY 8.6

1. Free write on one of these topics: computers, video games, a type of movie, such as horror, comedy, adventure, for example. Or write on a topic suggested by one of your journal entries.
2. Find a focus, expand the details, and organize the material.
3. After you have a workable draft, but before you edit for sentence boundaries, exchange papers with another student.
4. Read the other person's paper, but don't write on it. On a separate piece of paper, in addition to commenting on how clear the main idea is and how well it is supported by details, indicate any problems with sentence boundaries. It is important to be specific and to point to particular fragments and run-ons in given paragraphs.
5. After you get your draft back along with the reviewer's comments, rewrite and then check once more for any sentence boundary problems before handing in the paper to your instructor.

Chapter 9

Editing Verb Usage

Before we look at what's involved in editing for grammar and usage problems within the boundaries of the sentence, here's a reminder of the parts of speech. The top row of the chart tells how words can function in a sentence; the bottom row names the corresponding part(s) of speech.

Name Someone or Something	Show Action or State of Being	Join Elements in a Sentence	Describe Things, Qualities, or Actions	Express a Speaker's Emotion
nouns pronouns	verbs	conjunctions prepositions	adverbs adjectives	interjections

Verbs are, as the chart illustrates, words that show action or state of being.

Identifying Verbs

When you read about sentence boundaries in Chapter 8, you learned that sentences contained subject parts (what you are writing about) and predicates or verb parts (what you have to say about the subject). Within the predicate, the verb is the word that shows the action or state of being. The subject names someone or something. The verb shows what that someone or something is or does.

Look at this sentence:

<u>Karen</u> **reads** the novels of John Irving.

The subject is <u>Karen</u>, the person the writer is talking about. The verb is **reads**; it is what the subject does. (In this chapter, you will find that <u>subjects</u> are underlined and **verbs** are in bold print whenever your attention is being directed to how these items function in a sentence.)

This relationship can also be seen with state-of-being verbs. Look at this sentence:

<u>Linda</u> **is** a fine student.

Linda is the subject, the person who is, the who or what, and **is** is the verb. It shows Linda's state. She is. In this case, the verb sets up an equation or definition.

Other state-of-being verbs include *are, was, were, seems, appear,* and *exist.*

ACTIVITY 9.1

Circle the verbs in the following sentences. Work individually, in pairs, or in small groups, depending on the directions given by your instructor.

1   I have mixed feelings about TV talk shows. In some ways they are good. After all, they enlighten the public about injustices, unfair laws, corrupt practices in government and business, and environmental issues. They may change peoples' attitudes about sex roles, members of various ethnic groups, and people who think or act differently than the majority of viewers.

2   However, these shows are often silly and deal with unimportant issues like the lives of celebrities or offer empty, unrealistic solutions to serious problems. For example, a talk show host asks a guest or a member of the audience how a situation like drug use can be corrected. The answer nine times out of ten will be "We all have to work together." That really tells the viewer a lot. Many people watch these shows just to see what kind of outrageous thing will happen. Will Donahue wear a skirt again? Will someone punch Geraldo in the nose, or will he go to a nudist colony? For these reasons, I often think that it is a waste of time to watch these shows.

Subject-Verb Agreement

In earlier chapters, you learned that writing, like speaking, should not be unnaturally formal or convoluted. When it comes to the editing process, to grammar and style, writers must be more careful than speakers to observe the rules of Standard American English. In conversation, a speaker of black American English would be correct to say, "He be here," or "She eat now." A speaker of Cajun dialect would correctly say, "Pie are round." These expressions are not wrong. They are appropriate in conversation with other speakers of the same dialect. In academic or business writing, however, readers expect Standard American English and are frustrated or annoyed with any other kind of usage.

So when you edit your writing, you need to be sure you are observing the rules of Standard American English that govern subject-verb agreement.

Verbs agree with subjects in two ways: in number and in person. *Number* refers to whether a word is singular or plural. *Person* refers to who or what is doing the action or existing.

The following chart shows the person and number of two verbs. The first, **be**, is a state-of-being verb, in fact the most common one. And the second, **cook**, is an action verb.

Be

| | Number | |
Person	Singular	Plural
First person: the speaker or writer	I am	We are
Second person: the person being addressed	You are	You are
Third person: the person or thing being spoken about	He, She, It is	They are

Cook

First person: the speaker or writer	I cook	We cook
Second person: the person being addressed	You cook	You cook
Third person: the person or thing being spoken about	He, She, It cooks	They cook

Look at this sentence:

He **finds** novels easier to read than poetry.

In the sentence above, the subject <u>He</u>—the person who does the finding—is singular in number and is third person, so <u>He</u> requires a singular verb, **finds**, not **find** as would be the case in the following sentence:

<u>They</u> **find** poetry to be more interesting than fiction.

The third person plural subject <u>They</u> takes the plural verb form **find**.
Remember that dependent clauses also contain subjects and verbs that have to agree.

<u>He</u> **helps** me proofread because <u>I</u> **find** it hard to see my own misspellings.

ACTIVITY 9.2

Fill in the blanks in the following draft with the appropriate form—number and person—of any verb that fits. Work individually, in pairs, or in groups, according to your instructor's directions.

What does an employee do when the company she works for

_____ to move to another location? I guess, it

_____ on whether the worker _____

to move to another town. Making this decision _____

thinking about the wishes of members of the family. What the new

location has to offer also _____ a factor. A person who

_____ to go to the theater, for example, would be

miserable if she _____ to a location far from a major

city. If the worker _____ a home, how much she can

get for her house and what homes cost in the new community

_____ major concerns. If she rents, then she is

concerned with rents in the new location. Sometimes, companies

_____ bonuses to workers who go with them to the

new location. This _____ some people to make the

move while the offer of extra money only _____ things

harder for others. Still other employees _____ to

decide whether the disadvantages of a long commute _____

outweighed by the advantages of staying with a company where they

_____ accumulated retirement and where their

chances for advancement _____ good. All of these

concerns _____ the decision to stay with the company

or to look for work elsewhere very difficult.

Several situations that can complicate subject-verb agreement are discussed in the following sections.

1. Words between Subjects and Verbs

Sometimes words that are not part of the subject come between the subject and verb. These are usually surrounded by commas. The words between the commas do not affect the agreement of the subject and verb. You can think of the words between the commas as being an aside, words that contain additional information. They are like words in parentheses, and in terms of the relationship between the subject and verb, can be skipped over.

Maria, together with her friends, **is** (not **are**) going to that concert.

Alexander Borodin, along with other composers who were part of nationalist movements, who insisted on the freedom of art in their countries from outside influences, **uses** (not **use**) folk tunes in his works.

2. Words That Rename Subjects Later in the Sentence

The verb agrees with the subject, not words that rename it later in the sentence.

My main concern **is** (not **are**) my readers' reactions to what I write.

The subject is <u>concern</u>, not *reactions*, which is a renaming of the subject.

3. False Subjects

Words like *here* or *there* do not affect the person or number of the verb. You have to look ahead in the sentence to find the actual subject.

Here **is** the <u>book</u> I've been looking for.

Ask yourself what is here? The answer, the <u>book</u>, is the subject. Since <u>book</u> is singular, it takes a singular verb, **is** (not **are**).

There **are** (not **is**) many <u>students</u> in the class.

In this case, it is many <u>students</u> who are there, so the verb must be plural to agree.

4. Subject and Verb Reversed

The same holds true for sentences in which the usual subject-verb order is reversed.

Under the leaves **is** (not **are**) the <u>snake</u>.

What is under the leaves? The <u>snake</u>. And since <u>snake</u> is singular, a singular verb form is needed. Of course, you could avoid this situation by rewriting the sentence in a much more straightforward way. You could write:

The snake is under the leaves.

This makes it easier not only for the writer to see the relationship between the subject and verb but also for the reader to understand.

ACTIVITY 9.3

Correct any errors in subject-verb agreement in this unedited excerpt from a student paper. Work individually, in pairs, or in small groups, according to your instructor's directions.

1   There is different ways of studying. Some students, like my friend

Janet, prefers to study while watching television or listening to the

stereo. However, other students, including another friend, Joan, feels that studying in a quiet place with no distractions is best. And I

agree with Joan.

2   Janet says that distracting noises is not a problem for her. She

claims that music and TV shows relaxes her so she can do a better job

on her assignments and papers. Behind her claims are just an excuse

for not wanting to concentrate on her work. At least that's what I

think. Janet is getting low grades. Here are the cause—she can't give

her full attention to what she is doing. She, as well as many other stu-

dents, don't realize how distracted she is by what's going on around her.

---

5. Plural Subjects Joined by *And*

Two or more subjects connected by *and* take a plural verb.

His complicated <u>ideas</u> and long <u>sentences</u> **make** reading difficult.

However, two closely related nouns joined by *and* or two nouns joined by *and* that describe the same person are usually followed by a singular verb.

<u>Ham</u> and <u>eggs</u> **is** my favorite breakfast.

The ham and the eggs together are considered one item, which takes a singular verb.

The best <u>student</u> and <u>teacher</u> **is** the person who keeps an open mind.

The student and the teacher are one and the same individual, so a singular verb is correct.

6. Subjects Joined by *Or* or *Nor*

When two or more subjects are joined by *or* or *nor*, the verb form is determined by the subject that is closer to the verb.

Neither the <u>instructor</u> nor the <u>students</u> **like** the long evaluation form.

Neither the <u>students</u> nor the <u>instructor</u> **likes** the long evaluation form.

7. Subjects Containing Prepositions

When you have a complete subject that contains several nouns joined by prepositions (words like *on*, *in*, *around*, *beside*, an so on), the subject always comes before the preposition. Or, to put it another way, the subject is the noun farther from the verb.

Acres of land **are** being planted with corn.

Even the first of his many paintings **shows** his skill with colors and shapes.

8. Singular Pronouns as Subjects

The following pronouns are singular and require singular verbs: *either, neither, each, another,* and any of the pronouns that end in *-one*, *-body*, or *-thing*, such as *anyone, anybody, anything, no one, nobody,* and *nothing*.

Each **is** made by hand.

Everyone **wants** to succeed.

When words come between a singular pronoun and its verb, the situation is the same as in the case of nouns, except there are no commas. The verb must agree with the pronoun subject.

Each of her computer disks **is** easy to find.

9. Nouns with Plural Form but Singular Meaning

Subjects that indicate distance, money, or time, take singular verbs.

Nine miles **is** a long way to walk every day.

Nine miles is thought of as one distance.

One hundred thousand dollars **is** a great deal of money.

Six hours **is** a long time to study without a break.

Subjects that name a field of academic study—*mathematics, economics, physics*—also take a singular verb. *News* and *headquarters* are singular, too.

Physics **is** a difficult subject for some people.

Titles of novels, movies, and other works of art that have plural words in them take singular verbs if they refer to only one work.

The Birds **is** one of Hitchcock's scariest movies.

10. Gerunds as Subjects

A verb form that ends in *-ing* and functions as a noun is called a *gerund*. A gerund subject is always singular and, of course, so is its verb.

Cooking **is** fun, sometimes.

Cooking is a singular action, so the verb is singular, **is**, not **are**.

ACTIVITY 9.4

Correct any errors in subject-verb agreement in these unedited passages. Work individually, in pairs, or in small groups, according to the directions given by your instructor.

A. Joan and I agrees about the best kind of environment in which to study.

Each of us find that distractions cause problems. For example, Joan says

that if she hears a song on the radio while she is writing a paper, she finds

that words from the song ends up on her page. I, too, have discovered that

either words or an idea from a TV show find its way into my thoughts if I

try to study with the TV on in the same room. As a result, I misunderstand

what I am reading, or many hours of my limited time after work in the

evening is wasted because I have to read the chapter or section all over

again. Everyone have the right to his or her own opinion, but, as a result of

our experiences, Joan and I always studies in a quiet place.

B. Attending college classes regularly are very important. Economics are

one class many students feel they can cut if they follow the syllabus and

read the chapters. They feel that the three hours a week spent in class are

a waste of time. Students who cut regularly don't realize what they are missing. In class, there are discussions about points that are not covered in

the text. In many of these classes that students feel they can cut, the

instructor give examples that help students understand ideas that aren't

clear in the text. For example, *Microeconomic Practices* are a difficult text-

book. Grasping its ideas are difficult, without having them illustrated by an

instructor.

---

11. *A Number* and *The Number*

A number, which means more than one person, object, or idea, used as a subject, requires a plural verb. The number, on the other hand, which means a single amount, is always singular.

A number of dishes at that restaurant **are** really wonderful.

The number of people who dine there **is** really amazing.

12. Subjects That Can Be Singular or Plural

Some words such as *some*, *none*, *any*, *all*, and *most* can be singular or plural, depending on whether the noun they refer to is singular or plural.

All of the butter **is** rancid.
(All of one thing, the butter, is rancid.)

All of the plants **are** in need of water.
(All of more than one thing, the plants, need watering.)

13. Collective Nouns

A collective noun names a group that is regarded as a single unit. Some examples are *committee*, *family*, *jury*, *team*, and *faculty*. If you are talking about the group as a singular unit, use a singular verb. If you are talking about the individual members of the group, then you need a plural verb.

The faculty **is** meeting today.

In other words, this sentence says that the group as a whole is meeting together.

The <u>faculty</u> **are** in different cities right now and so can't meet today.

This sentence means the individual members of the faculty are in different places.

ACTIVITY 9.5

Correct any errors in subject-verb agreement in this unedited excerpt from a student paper. Work individually, in pairs, or in small groups, according to your instructor's directions.

> A number of people feels they write best early in the morning. Others
>
> like to work later in the evening. Some people write best after drinking
>
> coffee; others need to meditate and calm themselves down first. Some of
>
> these approaches works for some people, some work for others. There is
>
> no one right way for all writers. My class have widely differing opinions
>
> about the best way to write and the best time to write.

ACTIVITY 9.6

Exchange a draft of a paper you are currently working on with another student. Read each other's paper and check for any problems with subject-verb agreement.

Tenses

When you edit your writing, you need to give special attention to verb tenses—the different forms verbs take to show the time frame of an action or a condition.

Present Tense

In the section you just read, Subject-Verb Agreement, you concentrated mainly on the *present tense*, which indicates an action or condition taking place or existing right now. The present tense is also used for an action that usually happens or exists.

<u>Jim</u> **looks** like a different person in that suit, doesn't he? (right now)

Looks is the present tense (third person singular) form of the verb *look*, and it describes Jim's condition right now.

Your <u>friends</u> always **influence** your beliefs and attitudes. (usually)

Influence is the present tense (third person plural) form of the verb *influence*.

Future Tense

The *future tense*, which, of course, shows action in the future, is formed by adding a helping verb like *will* or *shall* to the predicate.

<u>Trying</u> to write a perfect paper on the first draft **creates** problems. (now or usually)

<u>Trying</u> to write a perfect paper on the first draft **will create** problems. (in the future)

ACTIVITY 9.7

Write a paragraph about an activity you do almost every day. You could write about what you do at work if you have a job, how you study, how you write a paper, or whatever you wish. Write it in the present tense. After you edit the paragraph, underline every verb. Then cross out the verb in the present tense, and above it write the future tense of that verb. Finally, change the opening of the paragraph from "Usually" or "Every day" to "Tomorrow" or "Next week."

Past Tense

In the *past tense*, the verb shows that the action or condition named in the sentence is finished, that it has already occurred. The past tense is usually formed by adding *-ed* to the present tense form.

The <u>use</u> of empty space in Japanese painting greatly **impressed** French artists in the last century. (in the past)

There are, however, irregular verbs that have different forms—for example, *sit*.

<u>She</u> always **sat** in the front of the class. (in the past)

A list of some of the most common irregular verbs is included in the following discussion of past participles.

Past Participle

The *past participle* used with *has* or *have* shows an action or condition that began in the past and is still going on.

> <u>My family</u> **has attended** opening day at the baseball park since I was a first grader. (begun in the past and still going on)

The past participle is also used with *had* to show an action completed in the past before another action that was completed in the past too, but at a later time.

> <u>I</u> **had wanted** (past participle) to be an art history major before <u>I</u> **realized** (past) there were few job opportunities in the field.

Wanting to be an art history major, in other words, occurred before the realization that there were few job openings; it is no longer continuing.

The participle form is used with *was* or *were* in passive sentences to show the simple past:

> **Active:** <u>The members</u> **chose** her as president.
>
> **Passive:** <u>She</u> **was chosen** to be president by the members.

(See Chapter 11, pages 205–206, for more on active and passive voice.)

The participle form is also used for adjectives.

> The *broken* <u>chair</u> **is** in the barn.
>
> The <u>chair</u> **is** *broken*.

The past participle is formed by adding *-ed* to the present form. Often it follows a helping verb such as *have, has, had, am, is, are, was,* or *were*. Again, as was the case with the past tense, there are some irregular verbs.

> <u>I</u> **had forgotten** to defrost, so there was a great deal of ice in the freezer. (past participle of *forget*)

The irregular verbs are usually short, simple words that come from Anglo-Saxon, an ancient Germanic language from which modern-day English has, in many ways, evolved. They are among the oldest words in modern English. On the other hand, verbs that come from Latin, French, or Greek roots tend to add *-ed* to form the past and past participle forms; they are called regular verbs.

Following is a list of the principle parts of some commonly used irregular verbs:

Verb	Past	Past Participle
to be	was, were	been
to become	became	become
to begin	began	begun
to bite	bit	bitten
to blow	blew	blown
to break	broke	broken
to bring	brought	brought
to build	built	built
to burst	burst	burst
to buy	bought	bought
to catch	caught	caught
to choose	chose	chosen
to come	came	come
to deal	dealt	dealt
to dive	dove (dived)	dived
to do	did	done
to draw	drew	drawn
to drink	drank	drunk
to drive	drove	driven
to fall	fell	fallen
to feel	felt	felt
to fly	flew	flown
to forget	forgot	forgotten
to freeze	froze	frozen
to go	went	gone
to grow	grew	grown
to have	had	had
to hit	hit	hit
to hold	held	held
to know	knew	known
to lay (place)	laid	laid
to lead	led	led
to lie (recline)	lay	lain
to make	made	made
to read	read	read
to ride	rode	ridden
to ring	rang	rung
to rise	rose	risen
to run	ran	run
to see	saw	seen
to shake	shook	shaken

Verb	Past	Past Participle
to shrink	shrank (shrunk)	shrunk (shrunken)
to sing	sang	sung
to sink	sank	sunk
to sit	sat	sat
to speak	spoke	spoken
to spring	sprang	sprung
to sting	stung	stung
to stride	strode	strode
to strike	struck	struck
to swim	swam	swum
to take	took	taken
to teach	taught	taught
to tear	tore	torn
to tell	told	told
to throw	threw	thrown
to wake	woke	waken (woken)
to wear	wore	worn
to weave	wove	woven
to write	wrote	written

If you are in doubt about a particular verb that is not on this list, consult a dictionary.

ACTIVITY 9.8

Free write about a situation on campus or an activity in your life. Find a focus, and then write a descriptive draft. Assume that this situation is happening right now or always happens the same way. In other words, keep the whole piece in the present tense. You might begin this way:

> Registration is always a pain in the neck. There are long lines to see advisors, to sign up for courses, and to pay for them.

ACTIVITY 9.9

Rewrite the draft you wrote in Activity 9.8 in the past tense.

> Registration was a pain in the neck. There were long lines to see advisors, to sign up for courses, and to pay for them.

ACTIVITY 9.10

Rewrite the draft you wrote in Activity 9.9 using the past participle throughout the piece.

> Registration has always been a pain in the neck. There have always been long lines to see advisors, to sign up for courses, and to pay for courses.

Editing for Tense Consistency

One problem that sometimes occurs is that writers are not consistent in their use of tense. The tense that a writer uses tells readers the time in which the events being described take place. If the writer switches tenses for no apparent reason, the reader will become confused. One cause for this shifting in tense is that writers want to make their illustrations present and immediate. But if the events being used as illustrations occurred in the past, readers will be confused about the time frame of these events if writers narrate them in present tense. Take a look at this passage from a piece of unedited student writing:

> After my daughter was born three years ago, I stopped working. It was fun being home with her all day, but there is one problem for me. When I was home, I got bored. My solution is to go to the refrigerator. I open that door every hour. So I guess I shouldn't have been surprised that I gained so much weight. Now that I'm working again and going to school, I'm busy and don't feel the need to fill my mouth to make the time go by, and I'm not as heavy as I was.

When you read this, you are confused. You think the writer is telling about what happened at some point in the past, three years ago. Then she tells you about her eating habits in the present. In the next sentence, she's back in the past. The last sentence is taking place in the present, but that's fine since she is contrasting the present with the past. You are distracted from the content of the passage as you try to figure out the reason for all these shifts in time.

Here is the writer's revision, which is much easier to follow:

> After my daughter was born three years ago, I stopped working for a couple of years. It was fun being home with her and watching her grow, but I ran into an unexpected problem. When I wasn't caring for her or playing with her, I was bored. My solution was to make frequent trips to the refrigerator. I opened that door every hour. I gained a great deal of weight. Now that I'm working again and going to school, I don't feel the need to stuff my face with food because there's nothing else to do. Now, I'm almost back to what I weighed before I stayed at home.

The passage is now less confusing, isn't it? It's easy to place the events the writer is describing in a time frame. Also notice that the writer changed a few words in the revision. As you are learning, writing is always in flux, always changing.

ACTIVITY 9.11

Correct any inappropriate tense shifts in the following unedited piece of student writing. Work individually, in pairs, or in small groups. Use the past tense for events that are over and done with, but use the present tense for generalizations that are always true.

1   In Maxine Hong Kingston's book, *The Woman Warrior*, I read a

horrifying description of what happened to the author's aunt back in

China. Her aunt was married to a man who migrated to America to

earn more money than he could in China. He leaves his wife alone for

many years, and she forgets what he even looks like. The aunt lives

with her parents. After several years, she became pregnant. When the

villagers find out, they break into the family home and destroy

everything. They killed farm animals and destroy the furniture. They

stole food and various items from the kitchen. They do this to show

their disapproval of what she has done, committing adultery and

having an illegitimate child.

2   The aunt was forced to leave her family's house because of the

disgrace and to give birth to her child in a pigsty. It is horribly filthy.

She kills herself and her baby by drowning in a well. The worst thing

was that her family denied her existence. They would never speak her

name. And the belief in Chinese society was that offerings of food must be made to the dead. So the aunt is forever doomed to be a

nameless and hungry ghost.

ACTIVITY 9.12

Using an entry from your journals, or beginning from scratch, choose a topic that allows you to compare and contrast a situation in the past with one in the present. Free write or cluster, and then find a focus and write a draft. You might compare a neighborhood or area in which you once lived with the one in which you live now. You might compare a job you once had with the one you have now. Or you might compare a former friend with a current friend. Whatever you pick should require you to write about one area, object, or person in the past, and the other in the present.

If you haven't worked with comparison/contrast yet, you need to know that any quality or trait you discuss in writing about one area, job, or person in the first, you must mention when you discuss the other. (See Chapters 4 and 5 for more on comparison/contrast.) Your instructor will indicate whether you should exchange papers with another student. Either the other person or you yourself should proofread what you've written for verb tense consistency and subject-verb agreement as well as for unity, coherence, and development.

Chapter 10

Editing Pronoun Usage

In the last chapter, you saw how careful editing of verbs makes the reader's job easier. Accurate use of pronouns is also necessary if readers are to understand what you as a writer wish to communicate.

If you look back at the chart on page 169, you'll see that pronouns are one of the two parts of speech that name persons or things. *Pronouns* are words that refer to persons, objects, concepts, and situations that usually have already been named by nouns. One writer has referred to pronouns as a tap on the shoulder, directing your attention back to an earlier word. The word the pronoun refers to is called its *antecedent*. Antecedent means something that goes before, something that precedes something else.

For example, take a look at this sentence:

Regina said that she wanted to get her degree in three years.

The pronouns *she* and *her* direct the reader back to their antecedent, *Regina*.

In spoken English, we can use pronouns without antecedents. Imagine that a friend is working on his car. He is lying underneath the car, and a wrench is lying on the ground out of his reach. If he calls out, "Hand it to me, will you?" you will look around, see the tool, and have no problem deciding what the pronoun *it* refers to. In writing, readers also need to know precisely what a pronoun refers to. They must locate a word that clearly functions as the antecedent of the pronoun. And there is no place readers can look but to the preceding words and sentences. If readers can't find a clear antecedent, or if there are several possible antecedents, they will become confused and frustrated. Their time is wasted, and they may lose interest in what the writer is saying.

Before looking more closely at some of the problems that result from the misuse of pronouns, here's a chart to remind you of the different forms of the personal pronouns:

Pronoun Forms

	Subjective case	*Objective case*	*Possessive case*
	Functions as a subject of a verb	Functions as the object of a verb or preposition (words like *by, with, in, on, between,* or *from*)	Functions to show possession or ownership
Number—Singular			
First person	I	me	my, mine
Second person	you	you	your, yours
Third person	he, she, it	him, her, it	his, her, hers, its
Number—Plural			
First person	we	us	our, ours
Second person	you	you	your, yours
Third person	they	them	their, theirs

In this chart, *person* refers to the person or thing being described by the pronoun. *Case* points to function, whether the pronoun exists or is doing an action (subjective), whether it is on the receiving end of an action (objective), or whether it signifies belonging to someone or something (possessive). *Number* describes whether a pronoun is singular, referring to one person or thing or concept, or whether it is plural, referring to more than one.

Pronouns Agree with Their Antecedents in Number and Gender

As a person who speaks English daily, you know almost instinctively that pronouns agree with their antecedents in number and gender. You would write,

> Albert had to produce several drafts of *his* research paper before *he* was satisfied with *it*.

and not,

> Albert had to produce several drafts of *her* research paper before *it* was satisfied with *them*.

Since you know that *Albert* refers to a male, you'd use *his*, not *her* (unless he is writing a female's research paper for her, and that's too unethical even to talk about!) and *he*, not *it*. Also, *it* in the first example above is correct since the pronoun refers to one research paper. *Them* would be appropriate only if there were more than one final version or more than one research paper.

However, in creating long sentences or sentences that begin on one page and end on the next, writers sometimes lose sight of a pronoun's antecedent and so make errors in number and gender agreement.

ACTIVITY 10.1

Correct any errors in pronoun agreement in the following passage from an unedited student paper. Work individually, in pairs, or in small groups, according to your instructor's directions.

1   Teachers should not be blamed if his students fail because high school students have a mind of his own. They are the ones who decide if they want to be educated or not. He makes the decisions for himself when they don't pay attention in class or decide to cut. Teachers can only do so much with unwilling students. She can't teach a student if they are always acting up and disturbing the class. Giving extra work and shouting at troublemakers will not make a student learn; it will not change her mind if they don't want to learn.

2   The school boards are also to blame. It has rules and regulations that prevent the teachers from doing the best job possible. For instance, the board may say that the teacher must spend six weeks teaching his or her class about probability theory, but the students know all about that part of the curriculum. She needs help in percentages or some other area. So valuable time is wasted. They

could have been used more profitably, giving the student what they

really need.

Special Situations in Pronoun Agreement

1. Indefinite Pronouns as Antecedents

Sometimes a pronoun may refer to another pronoun—called an indefinite pronoun—instead of a noun. These indefinite pronouns are often used when writers don't know the exact name of the person or thing they are discussing or when they want to talk about people or things in general.

Here is a list of some indefinite pronouns:

anyone	neither
anybody	either
anything	each
someone	everything
somebody	everybody
something	everyone
no one	nothing
nobody	

Each of these words is singular and takes a singular pronoun. For example:

Someone left *his* or *her* book here.

Both, *many*, and *two* (or any number greater than *one*) are always plural and take plural pronouns.

Many turned in *their* papers early.

2. Collective Nouns

Words like *family*, *class*, and *committee* can be either singular or plural. In Chapter 9, you learned that these words took singular verbs if the collective noun was thought of as one unit, and plural verbs if the writer was talking about the individual members of the group acting independently. The same principle applies to pronouns when they refer back to these words.

The family all have *their* own ways of dealing with unpleasant tasks.

The family is united in *its* approach to that problem.

3. Antecedents Joined by *Or* or *Nor*

When two nouns are joined by *or* or *nor*, a pronoun that refers back to them agrees in number with the noun that is closest to it.

Either Sarah or her friends will bring *their* favorite tapes.

Neither the workers nor the boss will get *her* raise this week.

ACTIVITY 10.2

Correct any errors in pronoun agreement in the following excerpt from an unedited student paper. Work individually, in pairs, or in small groups, according to your instructor's directions. Correct any other errors that appear here as well.

Doing research for my African history class made me realize how true the saying is that there is no history, only the opinions of historians. Many of the books I read about Ethiopia contained the same facts, but it offered different opinions about what these facts meant. The one group of writers interprets the facts from its socialist, leftist perspective. The writers who were members of another group interpreted the facts to fit its conservative beliefs. Either the virtues of nationalism or an attempt to find value in colonialism was secretly being fed to the reader. Somebody who wasn't aware of the particular beliefs held by the writer might believe they were reading objective information. For example, each of the books I read about Menelik II presented their own point of view about this ruler. Anybody could be confused in their reading. Was Menelik II a great figure who freed his country from foreign domination, or was he a cruel ruler who tortured prisoners and created the system of land ownership that has caused famine and the deaths of so many in the past few years? I guess everybody who reads more than one book on a historical topic has to decide what is true for themselves.

Editing for Errors in Case

As you saw in the table on page 188, pronouns have different forms, depending on whether they are used as subjects (doers), or objects (receivers), or to show ownership.

Pronouns Used as Subjects

Most writers have little trouble with case when there is just one pronoun being used as a subject in a sentence. Few writers, unless they were intentionally reproducing a dialect, would write:

Her is looking for a new car.

Without even having to think about it, we use the subjective form *she*, not the objective *her* (see table, page 188).

She is looking for a new car.

Problems sometimes arise, however, when pronouns are part of a compound subject. Often speakers, and therefore writers, use the objective form instead of the subjective form. For instance, they say:

Richard and *me* are going to the show.

The trick is to cover up the other word in the compound and see if the pronoun could work alone as the subject. In this case it can't. Clearly, it is not,

Me is going to the show. (objective case)

but rather,

I am going to the show. (subjective case)

Therefore, the correct sentence is,

Richard and *I* are going to the show.

Pronouns Used as Objects

It is unlikely that native speakers of English would write the following:

> I gave it to *she*. (subjective)

They would realize that an objective case pronoun is needed here.

> I gave it to *her*.

Yet writers often make the same kind of mistake in pronoun case for compound objects that they make with compound subjects. They often use the subjective case, especially *I*, when the objective case is needed, and they produce errors like this:

> Let's keep Bill's gift a secret between you and *I*.

Since *between* is a preposition, you need the objective form *me*.

> Let's keep Bill's gift a secret between you and *me*.

A way to check for correct case use in compound objects is to reverse the order in the compound.

> Let's keep Bill's gift a secret between (*I* or *me*) and you.

Clearly, *between me and you* makes sense and *between I and you* does not.

One more point: After *than* and *as*, a pronoun may be the subject of an "implied sentence," and so you may need to use the subjective form.

> She is learning to use the computer faster than *I* (not *me*).

You can check to see whether the subjective form is correct by completing the implied sentence mentally. Of course, there's no need to actually write it out.

> She is learning to use the computer faster than *I* (am learning to use it).

ACTIVITY 10.3

Correct any errors in pronoun use in this unedited excerpt from a student paper. Work alone, in pairs, or in small groups, according to your instructor's directions.

Have you ever been disoriented when you visited a place you haven't seen for a long time? My friend Kim and me paid a visit to our favorite teacher back at our junior high school. Everything in the building had changed size and shape. I was surprised how small and narrow the hall seemed. Kim felt this even more strongly than me. The classrooms were so tiny; it was much larger in our memories. The desks were so close together that we couldn't believe there had once been room for we to walk between they. They were tiny, too. Had we really sat in it? And the blackboard was so low that us couldn't imagine that we had had to stretch to write on them. Of course, Ms. Coles looked much older. Kim and me remember she as being a young woman. We hoped she didn't notice the looks that passed between we two.

Editing for Possessive Case Usage

In the possessive case, a pronoun shows that an object, idea, or person belongs to someone or something already named. (See the chart on page 188.)

Here are just a few points you need to be aware of about possessives:

1. Remember, the apostrophe is *not* used with the pronoun *its*. You write, "That solution has *its* problems." (The word *it's*, on the other hand, is a contraction, a combination of the words *it* and *is*, as in "*It's* really busy at the shop now.")

2.   Also, the possessive forms *mine, yours, hers, ours,* and *theirs* never come before the word that names what is possessed. You can say,

That book is *mine.*

But you can't say,

Give me *mine* book.

3.   In Standard American English there is never an *s* on the end of *mine,* as is the case in some dialects. For example:

That is *mine* (not *mines*).

Pronouns with *-Self*

Sometimes *-self* or *-selves* is added to a pronoun for emphasis or clarification or for an action reflected or directed back to the subject: *myself, ourselves, yourself, yourselves, himself, herself, itself,* and *themselves.*

I did it *myself.* (Emphasis: I didn't have help.)

They *themselves* have the solution. (Clarification: They, rather than someone else, have the solution.)

He hurt *himself.* (Reflexive: He hurt no one else, just himself.)

These reflexive forms seldom cause problems. However, remember that *hisself, theirselves,* and *themself* are not used in Standard American English. Also, *myself* cannot be used as a substitute for *I.*

My friends and *I* (not *myself*) are taking Accounting 101.

Ambiguous Pronoun Agreement

Your reader can easily become confused if there is more than one antecedent to which a pronoun can refer. Look at these sentences:

The coach and the quarterback were discussing the game. *He* told *him* that the final play had been a mistake.

We might assume that the coach made the statement, but that is not necessarily the case. The coach may have decided on the play, and the quarterback felt it was wrong. So just who *he* and *him* are in the second sentence is unclear. The solution is to repeat one of the antecedents from the first sentence in the second one.

The coach and the quarterback were discussing the game. The coach told *him* that the final play had been a mistake.

When the pronoun *he* is replaced with its antecedent, the coach, it becomes clear that *him* refers to the quarterback.

Here's another situation in which the antecedent of one of the pronouns is unclear:

> The president told his public relations advisor that *he* had a meeting the next day.

Now if the public relations advisor is a male, you can't tell whether it is he or the president (who we know is male because of the pronoun *his*) who has to attend the meeting. One solution is to repeat the antecedent, but that would create a clumsy and wordy sentence in this case. A better solution is to use direct quotes.

> The president told his public relations advisor, "You have a meeting tomorrow."

ACTIVITY 10.4

Correct any ambiguous pronoun references and any other problems in pronoun usage in the following excerpt from an unedited student paper. Work individually, in pairs, or in small groups, depending on your instructor's directions.

Virgil remembers his grandfather well even though he died ten

years ago. He would always watch baseball games with him. Grandpa

would say, "It's hard to tell the difference between a ball and a strike

on the TV screen." He said he didn't understand how this could be.

The cameras, which were positioned in different places around the

park, always showed it clearly. But he disagreed. He said the cameras

distorted everything. For example, Grandpa said the distance between

the bases looked different on the screen. But he said everything looked

different in the ballpark, too, depending on where he sat. Anyhow, he

would disagree with what the umpire said. He was sure he couldn't see either. At the time, it seemed silly and annoying. Now he misses those

arguments with him. He recalls those arguments now and realizes how

lonely he feels not being able to argue with him anymore. It brought

his grandfather and himself together in many ways.

Editing for Misuse of the Pronoun It

One exception to the rule that pronouns must have their antecedents, the words they refer to, clearly stated in your writing occurs in sentences like, "*It's* a nice day." The *it* refers to the weather and is easily understood by all English speakers. However, *it* can be misused. For example:

In the newspaper today, *it* said that there is a water shortage.

Using *it* in this way has become fairly common. But readers who are sensitive to how words are used wonder what the *it* in the newspaper is—an article, a sentence, a column, or is *it* referring to the newspaper? In that case, there is a newspaper inside the newspaper. *It* may refer to a writer, in which case *he* or *she* should have been used.

The sentence could be rewritten in either of the following ways:

In the newspaper today, I read that there is a water shortage.

According to today's newspaper, there is a water shortage.

Either of these revisions eliminates the use of the pronoun *it* that had no clear antecedent.

Editing for Misuse of They

Often, the pronoun *they* is misused in a way that is similar to the misuse of *it*. *They* is used without a clear antecedent. Look at this sentence:

In New Orleans, *they* have lots of good food.

Assuming that there is no clear antecedent for *they* in a preceding sentence, careful readers will have a problem with this sentence. Certainly, readers understand that the writer is saying that good food can be found in New Orleans, but once again, they are distracted by having to figure out just who *they* are. The city itself? No, New Orleans would be referred to as *it*. The citizens? Maybe . . . but then again, the writer could be talking about restaurants. Confusing, isn't it?

In the above sentence, the writer could have been referring to many different nouns by using the pronoun *they*. The reader cannot tell. Here are two possible solutions. But notice that each has a different meaning.

In New Orleans, a visitor can find lots of good food in stores and restaurants.

People who live in New Orleans are lucky because *they* can get good food on almost any block.

Clearly, careful use of pronouns helps get your meaning across to readers accurately, with less ambiguity.

Pronouns and Gender

As people have become more aware of the sexist nature of certain aspects of the language, the use of the masculine *he* or *him* to refer to an individual who might be either male or female has fallen out of favor. Formerly, writers would produce a sentence like this:

A manager must check the quality of work generated by workers in *his* department.

Certainly, in a particular case the manager could be male, but if you are writing about managers in general, the manager could be either male or female. And to assume the manager is male is to reinforce sexist stereotypes that hold that a woman could not have a position of authority. However, the desire to avoid assumptions about gender has led to common pronoun disagreement errors, as seen in this sentence:

A manager must check the quality of work generated by workers in *their* department.

This creates all kinds of problems. The writer means that work in a manager's department must be checked. A *manager* is singular, but *their* is plural, and so it shouldn't refer to the manager. As a result, the reader is left wondering whose department this plural form *their* points to.

There are two solutions to this problem. One is to use *his or her*.

A manager must check the quality of work produced in *his or her* department.

This eliminates the problem of excluding women and is grammatically correct in terms of pronoun agreement. However, a page of *his or her*s can become tiring to read, so another solution is to use the plural pronoun and make the antecedent plural as well. There is, after all, no indication of gender in the plural. So the sentence could be written this way:

> Managers must check the quality of work produced in *their* departments.

ACTIVITY 10.5

Correct any errors in pronoun agreement, any use of sexist language, or any ambiguous pronoun references in the following passage from an unedited student paper. Work individually, in pairs, or in small groups, according to your instructor's directions.

1   A friend told me that when she was in high school that they would make fun of her because she wore a certain brand of jeans. At first thought, it seems foolish for a person to be so concerned about their clothes. A student, especially one who doesn't have a lot of money, shouldn't have to spend more of his money, or his parents', to buy a particular brand. And they are being insensitive and tyrannical in forcing them to conform to the group's standards.

2   But there's another way to look at this situation. A person in their teenage years is learning behavior they will need as adults. When someone graduates and finds a job, he often must dress in a particular way. A businessman must wear a suit and tie. A businesswoman wears suits, too. And not only does he have to wear certain types of clothes, but they can't wear certain colors and materials if they don't want the people they deal with to form negative judgments about him and his company.

3   I've noticed that teachers, too, conform to peer pressure when it comes to what she wears. If the head of the department and other powerful members of the staff dress casually, the newer employees will follow the same pattern after a few weeks. Also, many other workers, like salespersons in stores, have to follow dress codes. My cousin works in a clothing store, and her boss said that she always had to wear dark, conservative colors. Thus we can say that the pressure teenagers put on her friends to dress in a particular way is not harmful to him, but trains them to adapt to rules they will have to follow as adults.

Editing for Voice

The pronouns writers choose to use affect the tone of a piece of writing, the way the writing sounds. For example, writers who use *one* a great deal in their writing create a formal and distant tone.

If *one* rewrites a great deal, *one's* writing will improve.

On the other hand, using the second person, *you*, will make the tone less formal and more conversational.

If *you* rewrite a great deal, *your* writing will improve.

Using the first person, *I* and *me*, also creates a personal tone.

When *I* rewrite a great deal, *my* writing improves.

No one choice is correct for all writing situations. If I were a scientist writing an article or a report, and I wanted my readers to be aware of my authority and objectivity, I would most likely choose to create a sense of distance and formality. And my choice of pronouns would be one way I could do this. I might use *we* a great deal to show that others agree with me. In this book, I want to talk to my readers as one writer to other writers, so I've used different pronouns than the scientist might have employed. I chose to use *you* frequently.

What you want to write and the audience for whom you write will determine your choices.

Editing Pronoun or Voice Shifts

Readers can become confused if you shift your point of view (your pronouns, your voice) frequently in writing. For example:

A student should do *your* work in a quiet setting.

Literally, this sentence says that a student should *do the work of the reader* in a quiet setting. And I don't think that's exactly what the writer had in mind. What the writer meant was:

A student should do *his* or *her* work in a quiet setting.

or

Students should do *their* work in a quiet setting.

Sometimes the results of voice shifts or the inappropriate choice of pronouns can be unintentionally humorous or absurd. Look at this:

When a woman becomes pregnant, she has to be careful about what she eats. *Your* unborn baby will suffer if *you* live on junk food.

This second sentence is a very strange one for a male reader.

Similarly, an instructor or older student may do a double take when a writer states,

Teenagers have to deal with many restrictions. For instance, *your* parents may insist that *you* come home by a certain time.

"Me?" the reader says. It may be that writers are seduced into using these shifts because they want to involve their readers by addressing them directly. Also, writers are bombarded by commercials that use the tactic successfully with declarations like, "Everyone needs Kindfoot shoes. You do too!" In the ad, the voice shift works to involve the reader or viewer. In the examples above, it doesn't.

ACTIVITY 10.6

Correct any errors in pronoun (voice) shifts in the following unedited excerpt from a student paper on peer pressure. Work individually, in pairs, or in small groups, according to your instructor's directions.

1   Whether peer pressure is harmful or beneficial depends on your peers. After high school, I had no plans to attend college, but several of my friends from high school went immediately. When we got together, they would talk about ideas and books you'd never heard of. You felt left out of the conversation, and even worse I felt inferior. So, following their example, I enrolled. And I'm glad I did. Now you're a part of their conversations and I already have gotten the chance to have a better-paying job.

2   At other times, peers can have a negative influence. If they feel that a course is a waste of time, you may begin to feel that way too. As a result, a student misses classes, his or her grades drop, and the grade point average goes down. When you have friends like this, you will stop striving to reach his or her goals, and you will regret it later.

ACTIVITY 10.7

Free write or cluster about your experiences with peer pressure, or a topic suggested by one of your journal entries, or a topic selected by your instructor. Then find a focus, and write a draft of a paper in which you move from your experience to a broader discussion of how peer pressure can be helpful or harmful. Exchange papers with another student. Proofread, but do not write on, the other person's paper. After you have checked for subject-verb agreement, use of verb tenses, pronoun agreement, and sexist language, on a separate piece of paper write notes to the author pointing to specific problems you found. Of course, you should also give advice on unity, coherence, use of details, and make the writer aware of how his or her readers' needs are or are not being met in the paper.

Chapter 11

Editing Style, Syntax, and Diction

Wordiness

> Clutter is the disease of American writing. We are a society strangling in unnecessary words, circular constructions, pompous frills and meaningless jargon. . . . (William Zinsser, *On Writing Well*)

Wordiness is a problem that frustrates readers, and so writers should seek to correct it when they edit their work.

Sometimes wordiness grows out of a writer's desire to impress readers. Of course, what really impresses people are your ideas and your examples, not fancy words.

I recently had to take my son to the doctor. The doctor spoke plainly until he asked me what I did for a living. After I told him that I taught college-level writing, he started saying things like this:

> On certain days, multiple stimuli impose themselves on one, and one is thus at a considerable loss to maintain a state of equanimity in the face of those forces.

I thought about that for a while and decided that he meant he was cranky that day because a lot of stressful things were happening to him at once.

Writers in academic and business situations get carried away in a similar fashion. I used to be embarrassed to walk into a particular building on the campus of a major university where I once worked. The building had a wheelchair ramp with a railing. And on it was a sign that read, "Bicycles are not permitted to be chained to the rail." I guess someone thought that sounded impressive. I thought it was foolish. "Don't chain bikes to the rail" would have served the same purpose and certainly would have been clearer and more direct.

At another school, I cringed when I had to hand out this letter to my class from the head of the department:

> This letter is to inform you that students are not permitted to accumulate more than six hours of absences in the course of the semester. If this limitation is surpassed, continuance in this course will be terminated and participation in the final examination process will be denied.

What the writer of that letter wanted to say was that if you miss six hours of class, you'll be dropped from the course and you won't be allowed to take the final. If he had said that, students would have gotten the message more quickly, and they would not have gotten the mistaken idea that professionals admire inflated writing.

The wordy writing in this letter not only wastes your time and presents a false model of style, it also illustrates another problem caused by using unnecessary words: wordiness can distort the message. This letter doesn't say what the writer really wants to say. Look at it again.

What it says is that I'm writing to you for a particular purpose. But you don't have to tell readers this. Just do it. It also says that "continuance will be terminated." Readers have to figure out whose "continuance" is being terminated. The last clause is even stranger. If the writer had said, "You can't take the final," I'd know what he meant. But that long-winded phrase "participation in the final examination process" has me wondering. Is the writer talking about taking the test, marking it, collecting test papers, or what? The extra words introduce extra ideas.

Some wordy constructions are the result of imitation. During the Watergate hearings, every day on TV millions of Americans heard government officials saying "at that point in time" instead of "then" and "at this point in time" instead of "now." The infection spread, and now you regularly hear and read five words where one would suffice.

ACTIVITY 11.1

On another piece of paper, rewrite the following excerpt from an unedited draft of a student's paper. Eliminate wordiness. Discuss the changes you've made either in pairs, in small groups, or with the whole class, according to your instructor's directions.

1   In our country the process of education is extended in time to a degree that is extreme. We have come to accept that pre-college schooling must take far more years than is necessary to provide students with the information required for the positions that are the goals of their involvement in academic activities. As a result of this situation, large amounts of time are wasted and colossal amounts of money are spent.

2   The final years of my stay at my high school were, I feel in my opinion, an example of the wasteful nature of this process of overly extended education. These years mainly consisted of a review of the materials presented by the instructional staff of that institution of learning in previous years. At that point in time I could have easily slept through the hours of classroom instruction and still have

obtained an adequately decent grade point average. Resulting from this situation was the fact that I did not learn any material that was new, and these years, as a consequence, were timewise a total waste.

Active and Passive Voice

Most readers find that sentences written in the *active* voice are easier to read and less wordy than sentences written in the *passive* voice. In the active voice, the doer comes before the verb. In the passive voice, the doer follows the verb or does not appear in the sentence at all. Readers can grasp the writer's ideas more quickly if they are presented in normal English word order—that is, if the doer of the action comes first. Look at these two sentences, A and B. Both express the same idea, but the first is written in the active voice.

A. The government reduced the number of student loans.

B. The number of student loans was reduced by the government.

Sentence A is easy to read. The doer, *the government*, comes first, followed by what it did, *reduced*, and concluding with what was reduced, *the number of student loans*.

Passive sentence B not only adds unnecessary words, which slow readers down, but it also requires more time to comprehend. You start out thinking that *the number of student loans* is the doer. Then you reach *was reduced* and have to reorient yourself to think not that the number of student loans did something, but rather that something was done to them. Finally, you reach the doer, the who or what that did something to the number of student loans.

Compare the length of the paragraph above that describes the thought process required to understand the active sentence (A) with the paragraph that explains what goes on while reading the passive sentence (B). The reasons why writers and readers prefer the active voice are apparent.

So why do writers sometimes overuse the passive? They do so for the same reasons they become wordy. They feel that passive is fancier. They feel it sounds "educated," and so their readers will be impressed. But as is the case with wordiness, their readers only get tired, suffer needlessly, and probably lose interest in what the writers have to say. The passive is the curse of much bad academic, business, and government writing.

The passive voice is also used for deceptive purposes. The English writer George Orwell once said that the passive is used to defend the indefensible. In other words, writers hide their guilt or responsibility by using the passive. If the governor decides to raise your taxes, he or she doesn't usually say, "I'm raising taxes." Instead, he or she usually says something like this, "A decision was made to raise taxes." In this kind of passive construction, the doer of the action isn't even mentioned.

Of course, there are occasions when the passive is appropriate. For example, sometimes the writer doesn't know who or what caused a certain result, or maybe doesn't care.

My car was stolen.

More compact discs are being purchased today than cassettes.

Also, the passive provides a way for writers to avoid using the pronoun *they* without an antecedent. You remember in Chapter 10 you learned to avoid using this pronoun in sentences like,

They talked about two-career families on the talk show yesterday.

This sentence could be rewritten using the passive this way:

Two-career families were discussed on the talk show yesterday.

Also the passive is often used in technical writing, where the agent of an action (the doer) is not important. That "the enzyme was isolated" might be of more importance than the fact that "Dr. Johnson isolated the enzyme." The use of the passive in these situations puts the key word or idea at the front of the sentence for emphasis.

In general, however, the active will make life easier for your readers and will keep you honest.

ACTIVITY 11.2

On another piece of paper, rewrite the following excerpt from a piece of unedited writing to correct unnecessary use of the passive voice. Work individually, in pairs, or in small groups, according to your instructor's directions.

1   Many problems are encountered by left-handed people. For example, in a typical college classroom few desks designed for the left-handed can be found by those who need them. This means that left-handed people have to sit in desks made for the right-handed. Twisting of the body and reaching across their chests must be done by lefties so they can write. This is found by many of them to be extremely uncomfortable.

2   Another problem is also encountered by the left-handed. When right-handed people write with a pen or pencil, their hand is moved across the page in front of what is written by them. However, the writing hand of lefties is moved across what has already been written. So, often, they smear and smudge what has been written. When I was

in grammar school it was insisted upon that I use a fountain pen. You can imagine what a horrible mess was made by a lefty like me. Ballpoint pens were found to make life much more pleasant for people like me. And typewriters and computers really improved my life.

Overly Simplistic Writing

Of course, the extreme opposite of wordiness is not much fun for the reader either. As the ancient Greeks knew, balance is needed in every aspect of life. In writing, you need to strike a balance between wordiness and simplistic writing like this:

> I went to the store. I bought bread. I bought some meat. I did this yesterday.

This represents an extreme illustration of what many people call writing "baby sentences." These four sentences could be more effective if they were combined into one sentence.

> Yesterday, I went to the store and bought bread and some meat.

This saves time for readers and keeps them from forming negative judgments about the skills and intelligence of the writer.

ACTIVITY 11.3

If you've been working on sentence combining in Chapter 14, you won't have any problems with this activity. Rewrite the following passage from a student paper. Combine short sentences into longer sentences. Add subordinators and coordinators. Also, look at the sentence patterns and delete repeated words. (See Chapter 8, pp. 123–165.)

There is more than one way to combine the sentences. Read whole paragraphs before deciding how to combine the short sentences. Work individually, in pairs, in small groups, or in the setting of the whole class, according to your instructor's directions. This first paragraph has been done for you as an illustration.

> Last night I watched my local public television station. I saw an interesting show. It was about Richard Feynman. He won a Nobel Prize. He was a physicist. The show wasn't really about physics.

Here's one possible revision to make the paragraph less simplistic:

> Last night, I saw a show on my local public television station about Richard Feynman, a physicist who won a Nobel Prize, but the show wasn't really about physics.

Now you try. Here's the rest of the first paragraph:

> It was really about the way a scientist thought. The scientist was Feynman. It was about the way a scientist dealt with a problem. The problem was not a scientific one.

And here's more of the draft:

1   There is an example. Feynman was a young boy. He collected stamps. He got stamps from a place called Tuva. It used to be an independent country. At the time, it was in Central Asia. It was a part of the Soviet Union.

2   He was fascinated by this place. Almost no one ever heard of this place. He became an adult. He was determined to visit this place. He wrote a letter. The letter was to the Soviet Travel bureau. It was in Moscow. It was not in Tuva. He made a request in the letter. He requested permission to visit Tuva. He received an answer. It stated there were no tours there. In the U.S.S.R., travelers could only visit places with a tour. He didn't get permission to go there.

3   He didn't give up. He read all he could about Tuva. He learned some of the language. He learned this from a book. It contained phrases and sentences. The phrases and sentences were in two languages. They were in Tuvan and Russian. Feynman had to translate the Russian. He translated it into English. He did this to learn to say some things in Tuvan. He wanted to write another letter. The letter was to someone in Tuva.

4   A long time passed. He got an answer. It was written in Tuvan. He didn't understand Tuvan. He translated it into Russian. He, then, had to translate the Russian into English. The answer told him about Tuva. The answer told him about a special kind of singing people there do. The song sounds like a voice and a flute. Both sounds are really made by one person.

5   More time passed. Feynman learned there was going to be a contest. The contest was for people who sing this way. It was to be held in Tuva. He tried to get invited. The contest was cancelled.

6   Then there was an art exhibit in Sweden. The exhibit contained art from Tuva. Feynman and a friend contacted the people in charge of the exhibit. Feynman and his friend said, "We want to bring this show to America." Feynman and his friend succeeded. They brought the

exhibit. A Russian expert on art from Tuva came to America. He came with the exhibit. Feynman talked to the Russian expert. Feynman said to the expert, "I need to go to Tuva." Feynman said, "I need to see the places the art came from." Feynman finally got permission to go to Tuva.

7   This TV show didn't tell me about a problem in physics. This show told me how one scientist worked on a problem. He became interested in something. He tried different ways to find out about it. He studied different fields. He used different tactics. He didn't give up.

Modification

Words that describe other words are called *modifiers*, because they change the meaning or importance of that word in some way. If you look at the chart in Chapter 9, page 169, you will see that adjectives describe or modify nouns and adverbs describe or modify actions. They also modify adjectives as well.

Feynman, a *famous* physicist, *continuously* tried *different* approaches to reach his goal.

Famous is an adjective that describes the noun *physicist*, and *different* is an adjective that describes *approaches*. The adverb *continuously* modifies the verb *tried*.

She is a *good* student, and she writes *well*.

The adjective *good* modifies *student*—it describes what kind of student the writer is talking about—and the adverb *well* modifies *writes*—it describes how she writes.

Phrases (groups of words without subjects and verbs) and clauses (groups of words with subjects and verbs) can also act as modifiers.

Misplaced Modifiers

Modifiers should be placed as close as possible to the words they describe. When other words come between modifiers and the words they describe, the results can be unintentionally funny. For example:

Amy served Turkish coffee to her friends in small cups.

In this sentence the phrase *in small cups* follows the words *her friends*, and so seems to suggest that somehow her friends are in small cups. The sentence could be rewritten this way:

Amy served Turkish coffee in small cups to her friends.

Now it is clear that the coffee, not the friends, is in the small cups.

Here is a sentence in which a misplaced clause can cause confusion:

Bill is going to buy a new word processing program that he can use in writing his term paper while he is shopping in that store.

Taken literally, this sentence says that Bill is going to write his paper while he is shopping in that store. That's not very likely unless the store employees allow him to use a floor model computer and the program for a considerable length of time. The clause, *while he is shopping in that store*, is misplaced and should not follow the words, *is writing his term paper*. The sentence can be rewritten this way:

While he is shopping in that store, Bill is going to buy a new word processing program that he can use in writing his term paper.

Here's another example:

I found my keys walking down the street.

Do you see what's wrong here?

Dangling Modifiers

Dangling modifiers occur when a phrase describes an action or state of being but the person or thing the phrase refers to is not in the sentence.

Being very tired, mistakes are often made.

The phrase *Being very tired* seems to modify *mistakes*, but that doesn't make sense. How can a mistake be tired, or wide awake for that matter? Clearly something is missing in this sentence. This sentence also shows another good reason to be wary of the passive voice. Here are two corrections, both of which are written in the active voice:

Being very tired, students often make mistakes.

Students who are very tired often make mistakes.

ACTIVITY 11.4

On a separate sheet of paper, correct any misplaced or dangling modifiers in this unedited draft adapted from a student writer's paper. Work individually, in pairs, or in small groups, according to your instructor's directions.

1   In the past, to have a baby of their own, adoption was the only option for infertile couples. Today, these couples have another choice, surrogate motherhood.

2   Being paid $10,000 or more, a child is carried by a surrogate mother for a woman who cannot have a child. Artificially inseminated with the husband's or another man's sperm, the child is carried for nine months until it is born.

3   I feel it is better to adopt for both parents and for the child. Being unwanted, I would rather provide a home for some poor child than bring another child into the world. Also, after having carried the baby for nine months, some of these children end up in the middle of a custody fight between the surrogate mother and the woman who hired the surrogate. I know of one surrogate mother who sued to keep the baby from reading the newspapers. Then too, the surrogate may smoke, drink, and do other things that may harm the baby who is picked.

4   By using an adoption agency, a child can be picked according to the sex and appearance the would-be parents want. Health records are available, so parents can know about the health of the child in the case of adoption which is a major concern to many of them.

Parallel Structure

Another aspect of drafts that sometimes needs editing is parallelism. This term refers to the idea that similar ideas should be expressed in similar grammatical forms. You can write about your favorite sports these two ways:

I like *swimming* and *skiing*.

I like *to swim* and *to ski*.

But in Standard American English you shouldn't write this way:

I like *swimming* and *to ski*.

This type of sentence is inelegant and slows the reader down. So if you have two verbs that refer to the same subject, they should have the same form—they should both end in *-ing*, or *-ed* (or both be in the past tense if they are irregular verbs (see Chapter 9), or be preceded by *to*. Similarly, if you have a series of adjectives, you shouldn't shift to a clause—a group of words with a subject and verb—to describe what you could show by another adjective. For instance:

> The books in that corner of the library were old, dusty, and they were not used.

If, instead, you make all the modifiers into adjectives, the sentence is more direct.

> The books in that corner of the library were *old*, *dusty*, and *unused*.

ACTIVITY 11.5

Correct any errors in parallelism in the following sentences. Work individually, in pairs, or in small groups, according to your instructor's directions.

1. When I have to do a research paper, I like to find the call numbers, go to the shelves, seeing what is available on my topic.

   _____

   _____

2. My art history course gave me a better sense of beauty, the texture of life in other times, and to see how other cultures see the world.

   _____

   _____

3. To deny a woman the right to an abortion is held by some to deny her freedom of choice, to take away her control of her own body, and it could be seen as tyrannical.

   _____

   _____

4. Others feel abortion is a selfish, cruel act that is murderous.

   _____

   _____

5. Working in groups has helped me to learn from others and not feeling alone when I write.

_____

_____

6. Video games encourage hand to eye coordination, alertness, and they can improve reflexes.

_____

_____

7. He expected to drive there, find the house, and to be able to buy it.

_____

_____

8. When he moved, he found his new neighborhood had convenient shopping, friendly neighbors, and there were many trees.

_____

_____

9. She wanted to free write, write a draft, and to have edited her paper by Monday.

_____

_____

10. We will go swimming in the pool, jogging around the reservoir, or see a movie.

_____

_____

Clichés

You also need to edit out clichés, those phrases and expressions that you've heard thousands of times. Writers try to eliminate them because they have been used so often that readers stop thinking about what they really say. Clichés produce the same effect for writers at times. Writers get caught up in the familiarity of the cliché and forget why they are using it, or they fail to see that even though it is familiar, it may not fit. For instance, in a paper in which a student writer discussed the cultural advantages of big city life over living in a rural area, these were the concluding sentences:

> What is true of Kansas City, Mo., is also true of New York. As that famous song says, "If you can make it here, you can make it anywhere."

Readers just couldn't see what the words of the song had to do with the diversity of stores, the advantages of public transportation, the variety of movies, and the number of schools in Kansas City that the writer had contrasted with their limited counterparts in a small town. So try to find your own words rather than prefabricated words. If you've heard the words a thousand times, don't use them in your writing. Avoid phrases like these:

out to lunch	a needle in a haystack
quick as a wink	through thick and thin
a drop in the bucket	up the creek without a paddle
a word to the wise	open and shut case
break the ice	calm before the storm
the more the merrier	dead as a doornail

ACTIVITY 11.6

On another piece of paper, rewrite the following passage to eliminate trite, overused expressions and to make the passage more vivid and exact.

1   Getting started when I had to write a paper was always difficult, and I felt that I was stuck in a rut. How could I compete in this dog-eat-dog world and move up the ladder of success if I could never start my term papers? I wanted to produce something that was good beyond a shadow of a doubt the first time, but I never could. I wanted to stay cool, calm, and collected when I had to produce a piece of writing.

2   Then I discovered a method that hit the nail on the head and helped me through thick and thin. I used free writing first. I realized that it can't be smooth sailing to a perfect paper the first time. Getting down my ideas first made things easier than pie. Also I realized that I didn't have to go it alone. By showing my drafts to others I could get a helping hand, and I could develop writing that was my pride and joy.

Denotation and Connotation

The literal meaning of a word is its *denotation*. A *connotation* is an association that a word has in the minds of readers. For example, *Mercedes-Benz* denotes a German-made automobile. But it also connotes luxury and wealth. The word *animal* can have positive connotations that might lead readers to think of a cuddly kitten or a faithful puppy. Or it could have negative connotations, suggesting something like ferocity or wildness. *Brute*, on the other hand, even though listed as a synonym—a word with the same meaning—for *animal* in a dictionary or thesaurus, produces an almost totally negative response.

So, in a very real way, a thesaurus or a dictionary can be your enemy if you are not sure of the connotations of a particular word. This doesn't mean that you shouldn't look up and learn new words. However, make sure you are aware of the connotations of a word. Or try out the new words you're not sure of in an early draft. Share this draft with a fellow student or coworker to see how readers respond before giving your writing to an employer or someone who will make significant judgments about your writing skills.

For example, the words *short, curt,* and *succinct* share denotations, but are very different in terms of their connotations. What images come to mind when you read each of the three italicized words in these sentences?

1. When I asked for advice, he gave me a *short* answer.

    short: _____

2. When I asked for advice, he gave me a *curt* answer.

    curt: _____

3. When I asked for advice, he gave me a *succinct* answer.

    succinct: _____

ACTIVITY 11.7

Write three sentences of your own, each using a different one of these three words—*short, curt, succinct*—in a way that shows you understand their connotations. Or choose three other words that have a similar denotation but distinctly different connotations.

1. _____

_____

2. _____

_____

3. _____

_____

Appropriateness of Diction

Diction, the choices you make about which words to use, varies with the readers you have in mind. You choose different words when you write to a friend than when you write to your boss or the head of your school. For example, writing to a friend you might say:

> Yesterday, I was tutoring that kid I work with, and she really gave me a hard time. She argued with me over which color pen to use. I thought I'd never get to the math problems.

But writing a report to your supervisor might produce this:

> On February 24, I had a tutoring session with Sue Stevens. I had some difficulty starting the session. Sue wanted to argue about what color pen to use instead of doing the math problems.

ACTIVITY 11.8

Write two brief reviews of a film or a TV show that you've seen recently, or of a book you've read or a course you're taking. Or you may write about a problem on campus or in your community. Write the first piece to a friend. Write the second for publication in your school's newspaper. When both pieces are finished, exchange the reviews with another student. Discuss the appropriateness of the word choices each of you made in the two pieces. Then edit the two pieces you've written to improve the appropriateness of the diction for each audience.

Shifts in Style and Diction

As you have just seen, different styles are appropriate for different situations. And, as a writer, you can make choices about what style and diction you want to use for a particular audience. However, readers will be disoriented if you use several different styles in one piece. For example, look at this excerpt from a student paper:

1   There are many problems that a student encounters when he or she goes to the financial aid office at this college. First, there are the long lines in which the student must stand. Second, when a student finally reaches the window, he or she is often told that he or she has been standing in the wrong line and must get in a different line.

2   When I finally get to the window, I'm faced with a sour-looking worker who sneers and says something very close to, "What kind of idiot are you? You go to college. Can't you figure out a simple form?" This guy all but throws the papers I've given him back at me and then has the nerve to announce that he is taking a break.

3   I find such behavior highly unprofessional and inappropriate for the employees in an institute of higher learning.

The writer's first paragraph is fairly formal and distant. The form and diction are very much that of a traditional academic essay. Both writer and reader are outside of the event, observing it and linked to each other within a certain kind of contract. That contract says that the writer will be very proper and will give the reader clear signals when a new point will be examined.

The second paragraph is conversational and informal in tone and diction. There are no transitions. The writer is creating a sense of immediacy. The reader is experiencing the writer's response to the rude behavior more directly, not only because of the quotations, but also because the writer is addressing the reader as a close friend.

The third paragraph is once again formal, although the voice is more personal than in the first paragraph.

Any of the three approaches the author has used could work, depending on whom he sees as his audience and what he wants to write—a formal description of a situation, an immediate firsthand account, or a formal yet personal protest. However, the writer should choose one style, rather than force the reader to jump from one kind of relationship with the writing to another, and then to yet another.

ACTIVITY 11.9

Rewrite one of the reviews you wrote in response to Activity 11.8. Pay special attention to consistency of style throughout the paper. Exchange papers with another student. Check each other's reviews for shifts in style, diction, modification, parallelism, wordiness, or oversimplicity, as well as unity, coherence, development, mechanics (spelling, punctuation, and the like), and awareness of the readers' needs. Then revise your paper.

Chapter 12

Editing Spelling

Editing for spelling involves dealing with one of the smallest details of writing. However, this is an area that writers need to pay attention to when they edit their papers. Once again, it is readers' needs that dictate this concern. If words are misspelled, readers may either get the wrong message or become impatient with what has been written.

Spelling

Misspellings can waste the reader's time. Look at this sentence:

Life in major cities is often fast paste.

The reader wonders what life in major cities has to do with fast-drying glue. Then the reader figures out that the writer meant *fast paced*, but translating what the writer meant may distract the reader from the writer's line of argument, and so the reader may misunderstand or may have to go back and reread more than just this one sentence.

Further, readers may form negative responses to the piece as a whole if the writer talks about the famous philosopher Playdough instead of Plato. Of course, the ideas you offer and arguments you make are, in a very real sense, more important than minor spelling errors, yet those errors weaken a paper. I know of one company where letters and resumes containing misspellings are passed around for the amusement of the workers in the personnel department.

Misspellings can also cause readers to laugh in places where the writer had no intention of being funny.

Once, in a restaurant near a beach, I saw a sign that stated "No bear feet allowed." I spent a hilarious few minutes imagining tourists with furry feet being turned away. If spelling mistakes of this type occur in your writing, readers will get caught up in the unintentional humor and lose track of what your message is.

In some languages, like Spanish or German, the same sounds are always spelled the same way. Unfortunately, in English this is not the case. To some extent, the fact that English vocabulary comes from Germanic as well as Romance languages creates inconsistencies in the way we spell. *Hors d'oeuvres* is spelled as it is in French. Other words retain Latin, German,

Dutch, or Danish spellings. Also, the same sound is represented by different letters in English spelling. For example, we spell the "f" sound in *fish* with an *f* but the same sound in *rough* with a *gh*. "O" can sound like a short *i* as, for example, in *women*, while "ti" can be pronounced "sh" as in *vacation*. So *fish* could logically be spelled, as one famous writer once suggested, this way— *ghoti*.

There are spelling rules, but almost all have exceptions, so they are not as helpful as they might seem at first.

For example, it is generally true that *i* comes before *e*, except after *c* or when pronounced "ay" as in *neighbor* and *weigh*. But then there are words like *foreign*, *seize*, *leisure*, *forfeit*, and others.

So, here is some spelling advice that may help you:

1. When you are writing any draft of a paper except the final version, don't worry about spelling. Remember, get your ideas down first. Create first. Polish later. Some people were successful at memorizing lists of spelling words given in grade school. Others were not. You may belong to the second group and can never remember if a word ends in *-ance* or *-ence*. If you are writing an in-class essay and can use a dictionary, look up any words you are unsure of. But do this only after you've written the whole paper. Stopping to look up words will distract you from your thoughts and may cause you more serious problems with the logic and coherence of your paper. If you are not permitted to use a dictionary, try several alternative spellings on a piece of paper, and go with the one you think looks right.

2. When misspellings are pointed out to you, write down the correct spelling in a log that you keep in your notebook or folder. If you look these words over from time to time, you will begin to remember the correct spelling. Remember, making mistakes is not a sign of failure, but rather it is an opportunity to learn.

3. Use a standard college dictionary while editing. If you're not sure about the first letter of a word, ask a friend or teacher. Of course, if you're using a computer, many word processing programs have spell checks. However, I have found that even with an aid like that I still need to use my dictionary for spelling on occasion.

4. Reading helps you improve your spelling a great deal. The more you read and the more difficult material you read, the more likely it is that you will remember what a particular word looks like. For example, seeing *fast paced* in print would probably have helped the student who wrote *fast paste* avoid that particular error.

5. Sometimes, you can employ useful memory devices (called mnemonics). I remember being told back in grammar school a way to remember that *principle* referred to an idea or belief and that *principal* was the head of a school. The word *principal* contained the word *pal*, and the *principal* was the students' *pal*. Well, I didn't believe that, but the concept has helped me to differentiate the spelling of these two words ever since. (Of course, I still had to remember that *principal* could also mean an amount of money, but the gimmick helped somewhat.)

ACTIVITY 12.1

Look over papers you've gotten back that had spelling errors. Copy down the correct spellings and next to them write a memory device.

Word	*Mnemonic*

ACTIVITY 12.2

Working individually, in pairs, or in small groups, according to your instructor's directions, correct any spelling errors you find in this unedited draft.

1   Taking a road test can be a tramatic expereince. I was extremely nervious to begin with. Then I met the person who was going to be judgeing my preformance. He looked as if he was a drill instructor in the Marines who injoyed failing people just for the fun of it. The man obveously never cracked a smile in his intrie life.

2   He said, "Let's get started." And I risponed with a "Yes, sir!" He gave me a enigmatic look, and I though that I'd blown it. But than things seemed to be preceding. I remembered all the signals, didn't run any lites, and obayed all the signs. I was beginning to feel more confedant when a child ran out from between two parked cars. The child was chaseing a ball and was totally unaware that a car was about to hit him. I slammed on the breaks, nearly throwing my judge and me out the windshield, despite the fact that we were wareing seat belts. Then I was sure it was all over. However, he complemented me on my quick response to a potentially fatal situation.

3   So dispite some rough moments, I passed an now have my liscence. However, this was one kind of test I never want to have to go throught again. I also hope I never come so near to injuring anyone while driving. I use to think driving was easy, but that was before I realized the responsebilities a driver has for the lifes of others.

Words That Are Frequently Confused

Spelling is especially difficult when two or more words are very similar in spelling or in meaning. Here is a list of some of those words; refer to it when you're in doubt:

accept/except

Accept (verb): willingness to receive

Except (verb): to exclude; or (preposition): to make an exception of

I <u>accept</u> your kind offer.

You are <u>excepted</u> from that requirement. (verb)
I like all of his movies, <u>except</u> the last one. (preposition)

adapt/adopt

Adapt (verb): to change, to make suitable

Adopt (verb): to choose as your own or choose to use

She <u>adapted</u> her car's engine to be more fuel efficient.
Harry <u>adopted</u> his friends' attitudes about clothing; in fact, he followed their example slavishly.

advice/advise

Advice (noun): information or recommendation

Advise (verb): to recommend or give counsel

You gave me good <u>advice</u> about that course.

Ann <u>advised</u> me to take earth science instead of chemistry.

affect/effect

Affect (verb): to influence

Effect (noun): a result

Effect (verb): to cause

Classic novels like *War and Peace* <u>affect</u> me more than popular romances.

The candidate's statement on raising taxes had a negative <u>effect</u> on the voters.

If you can <u>effect</u> these changes, the boss will be satisfied with the report.

all ready/already

All ready (adjective): prepared
Already (adverb): by the time that

I'm <u>all ready</u> to leave, are you?
By the time you get the letter, he will <u>already</u> be in Scotland.

bare/bear

Bare (adjective or verb): to be
   unclothed or uncovered

It takes a brave person to <u>bare</u> his
   emotions in public like that.
   (verb)
The children stomped in the puddles
   in their <u>bare</u> feet.
   (adjective)

Bear (verb): to carry a heavy load;
   or (noun): an animal

Only Paul Bunyan could <u>bear</u> a <u>bear</u>
   on his shoulders.

born/borne

Born (verb): to be brought into life
Borne (verb, past tense of bear):
   to be carried along

My sister's child was <u>born</u> last year.
The log was <u>borne</u> along by the
   current.

brake/break

Brake (noun): a mechanism for
   stopping; or (verb): to stop

The <u>brake</u> on that model is defective.
   (noun)
Always <u>brake</u> when you come to a
   stop sign. (verb)

Break (verb): to smash or fracture;
   or (noun): an opening or fracture

He did <u>break</u> his leg when he went
   skiing, but it wasn't a bad <u>break</u>.

breath/breathe

Breath (noun): the air taken into
   the body or the air exhaled

After all that work, you have to take
   a minute and catch your <u>breath</u>.
Eating raw onions can cause bad
   <u>breath</u>.

Breathe (verb): the act of
   respirating

It is difficult to <u>breathe</u> at extremely
   high elevations.

capital/capitol

Capital (noun): the administrative
   seat of a county, state, or nation
Capitol (noun): the building in
   which the legislature meets

The <u>capital</u> of Missouri is Jefferson
   City.
The <u>capitol</u> is undergoing extensive
   repairs.

choose/chose/choice

Choose (verb): to select
Chose (verb, past tense of
   choose): selected
Choice (noun): a selection

Which topic did you <u>choose</u>?
I <u>chose</u> to write about fast food
   restaurants.
That was a good <u>choice</u> you made.

cite/sight/site

Cite (verb): to quote an authority

Which experts did you <u>cite</u> in your paper on censorship?

Sight (noun): the ability to see; or (verb): to see for the first time

When I reached forty, I discovered my <u>sight</u> was not what it had once been.

That sailor was the first to <u>sight</u> land.

Site (noun): a place

Have the executives chosen a <u>site</u> for the new office yet?

complement/compliment

Complement (noun or verb): to add something, or something that is added to or completes something else

That tie really <u>complements</u> that shirt. (verb)

Those benefits really are a <u>complement</u> to the salary increases. (noun)

Compliment (verb): to say something nice; or (noun): kind words of praise

Let me <u>compliment</u> you on your tie. (verb)

A <u>compliment</u> like that about my writing makes me want to write more. (noun)

conscience/conscious

Conscience (noun): the faculty for telling right from wrong

My <u>conscience</u> would not permit me to cheat anyone.

Conscious (adjective): to be aware or awake

I am <u>conscious</u> that good writing doesn't just happen.

desert/dessert

Desert (verb): to abandon; or (noun): a dry arid region

Men who <u>desert</u> their families should be forced to pay child support.

You'd better have a lot of water if you plan to cross that <u>desert</u>.

Dessert (noun): an after-dinner course

We're having peach pie for <u>dessert</u>.

effect (see affect)

ensure/insure

Ensure (verb): to make sure something happens

Proofread to <u>ensure</u> that your reader is not confused by anything in your paper.

Insure (verb): to set aside money to cover a loss

You'd better <u>insure</u> your collection of valuable books.

except (see accept)

hole/whole

Hole (noun): an opening

The <u>hole</u> in the road caused her to lose control of her car.

Whole (adjective): complete or entire

Yes, you do have to reread the <u>whole</u> essay.

incident/incidence

Incident (noun): an event

The <u>incident</u> at the registrar's office made me really angry.

Incidence (noun): the frequency of something happening

The <u>incidence</u> of misspellings in her papers is very small.

its/it's

Its (possessive form of pronoun *it*)

The main advantage of that stereo system is <u>its</u> price.

It's (contraction formed of pronoun *it* and verb *is*)

<u>It's</u> cold today.

lead/led

Lead (noun): a metal; or (verb): to conduct

<u>Lead</u> in paint can be hazardous to one's health.
Don't <u>lead</u> me down the garden path.

Led (verb, past tense of *lead*): conducted

Recognizing the problem <u>led</u> me to the solution.

lessen/lesson

Lessen (verb): to decrease

A heavy rainfall this month will <u>lessen</u> the water shortage.

Lesson (noun): something learned

Well, I certainly learned a <u>lesson</u> about using paint remover.

loose/lose/loss

Loose (adjective): free, not secured

The <u>loose</u> screw caused the shelf to collapse.

Lose (verb): to misplace

I hope I don't <u>lose</u> my keys again.

Loss (noun): what has been lost

When that theater closed, it was a great <u>loss</u> to the town.

maybe/may be

Maybe (adverb): possibly

May be (verb): to express
   possibility

Maybe this list will be helpful.

It may be too early to plant those
   seeds.

no/know

No (adverb): the opposite of *yes*

Know (verb): to be sure of

No one I know likes to eat bologna
   and whipped cream sandwiches.

passed/past

Passed (verb, past tense of
   pass): went by

Past (noun): time gone by

The other car passed me much too
   closely.

That is in the past; I've forgotten it
   already.

precede/proceed

Precede (verb): to go before or
   in front of

Proceed (verb): to go on, to
   continue

Adjectives usually precede nouns.

When the officer tells you, you can
   proceed.

peace/piece

Peace (noun): harmony, the
   absence of war.

Piece (noun): a portion

Peace is something we all hope for.

Save me a piece of that pie.

quiet/quite

Quiet (adjective): not loud or
   noisy, silent

Quite (adverb): to a large degree

It was very quiet in the library.

Rebecca's essay was quite good.

raise/raze

Raise (verb): to lift up

Raze (verb): to tear down

Can you raise your average if you do
   really well on the next test?

The workers will raze that building
   next week.

residence/residents

Residence (noun): a dwelling

Residents (noun): tenants

I will be changing my residence next
   month.

The residents complained because
   there was no hot water.

scene/seen

Scene (noun): where an action
   occurs or occurred

The state police arrived on the
   scene of the accident within
   minutes.

Seen (verb, past participle of
   to see)

I had never seen such a funny film in
   my entire life.

than/then

Than (conjunction): used to compare and contrast two things

Then he revised his paper, making
   it more informative than it was in
   the first draft.

Then (adverb): at that time

there/they're/their

There (adverb): location

They're going to move their cars and
   park them over there.

They're (contraction formed from
   the noun *they* and verb *are*)
Their (pronoun showing third person
   plural possession)

to/too/two

To (preposition): locates something

To me, having two homes is really
   too much.

Too (adverb): in addition, or
   excess
Two (adjective or noun): number

whose/who's

Whose (pronoun, possessive form
   of *who*)

Whose idea was this anyhow?

Who's (contraction of pronoun
   who and verb *is*)

Who's going to bring the food?

your/you're

Your (pronoun): belonging to you

Is it true that you're going to bring
   your notes?

You're (contraction formed from
   pronoun *you* and verb *are*)

ACTIVITY 12.3

Working alone, in pairs, or in small groups, according to your instructor's directions, edit this passage by correcting any misspellings or misused words.

1   Throughout my academic career, I've done well accept in one area—math. I think my problems may be began back in the second grade. I had a teacher, Ms. Treglia, who was a real horror. Hers was the first time I almost didn't past a course. Whenever I didn't no an answer, she'd call on me. When I didn't answer correctly, instead of helping me, leding me to discover the solution, she'd humiliate me. She'd call me stupid and say, "Whose going to show our little problem pupil how to do it correctly?" "Come on," she'd say. "Its easy. Anyone with half a brain can get this one write." This kind of treatment made me loose any enthusiam for math.

2   In latter grades when teachers tried to give me good advise about how to study for math, I just didn't listen. I had all ready decided that math wasn't for me. I couldn't bare the idea of going to math, no matter how nice or helpful other teachers tried to be. When I was called on I'd hold my breathe and not answer. The mere site of a math book would cause fear and trembling. It was like a whole had opened up in front of me.

3   Eventually, I gained some confidence as the result of the comple-
ments my fifth grade teacher Ms. Hancock gave me. I began to see that
studying hard would insure I could pass math. But the main thing that
helped me was knowing there would be no more incidents of
humiliation when I razed my hand in class and made a mistake. Those
terribel seens were a thing of the past.

4   My experiences with those too teachers made me realize how
important it is to give people confidence. People who are going to be
teachers, or parents for that matter, need to realize that it's better to
encourage those who are trying to learn something then to criticize
them. Learners of any type need to have there efforts acknowledged as
just that—efforts. They don't need to have they're mistakes held up to
redicule. If there efforts become the basis of humiliation, they will be
unable to precede in their studies and in their growth as human beings
two.

ACTIVITY 12.4

Free write on a topic suggested by one of your journal entries or by your instructor. Find a
focus and write a draft. Rewrite and expand. Exchange papers with another student. On a
separate sheet of paper, indicate any spelling errors you find. Of course, also comment on the
unity, coherence, development, and style of the piece of writing and how well it responds to
the needs of readers. Revise your draft after reading the comments you receive.

Chapter 13

Editing for Punctuation and Capitalization

Punctuation is another of the concerns a writer must deal with as part of the editing process. Editing for punctuation is important because punctuation provides signals to readers. It shows where the writer wants them to pause, notice emphasis, and see relationships between ideas and the parts of the sentences. And, once again, the needs of readers to grasp ideas quickly and clearly govern the writer's need to edit carefully so that readers are not confused or misled. Leaving out punctuation or adding unnecessary punctuation can change the meaning of a sentence. If this happens unintentionally, readers may not get the message the writer intended in a piece of writing.

The Comma

The comma is the most frequently used mark of punctuation within the sentence. Omitted or unnecessary commas can cause difficulties for readers. Look at this example:

As you've read earlier editing is important.

Without commas, this sentence causes readers to do a double-take and readjust their thoughts. Readers first see "As you've read earlier editing . . ." as one thought. Then they realize the first four words are separate. It's: "As you've read earlier," new idea—"editing is important." However, if the sentence is properly punctuated, like this,

As you've read earlier, editing is important.

it is much easier to understand on first reading.
Similarly, extra commas can confuse readers too.

The American people, are concerned about the victims of the flood.

Because of the comma, readers think that after "The American people" there should be a pause, followed by a new idea or an interruption of some kind.

But neither is about to occur. In fact, the same idea is continued. So the sentence should be written this way, with no internal comma:

The American people are concerned about the victims of the flood.

Here are some rules for the correct usage of the comma:

1. Use a comma to mark the end of an introductory word or group of words before an independent clause. In other words, as you saw in Chapter 8, use a comma to separate a front shifter from the rest of the complete sentence (an independent clause).

While I was studying, I was distracted by my neighbor's loud radio.

The subordinate clause "While I was studying" is set off from the independent clause "I was distracted by my neighbor's loud radio." "While I was studying" is a front shifter that could be moved to the end of the sentence.

I was distracted by my neighbor's loud radio while I was studying.

Note that when the dependent clause is shifted to the end of the sentence, there is often no need for a comma to separate it from the main body of the sentence.

In the following example, the comma sets off a phrase (a group of words without a subject and verb) from the independent clause that follows.

Because of the noise, I couldn't study properly.

Again, the group of words at the beginning is a front shifter. It could be moved elsewhere in the sentence.

I couldn't study properly because of the noise.

And again, commas are often not used when the front shifter comes at the end of the sentence.

You can see how real confusion could result if the comma was omitted after the front shifter in this case:

As you've seen working two jobs can be tiring.

You naturally read the sentence this way:

As you've seen working . . .

As a result, you wonder what you've "seen working." Then you have to go back and reread the sentence from the beginning to understand it. This is avoided when the comma is added.

As you've seen, working two jobs can be tiring.

A single word coming before an independent clause may or may not be set off with a comma.

Later I will edit the paper I've put aside for the moment.

Later, I will edit the paper I've put aside for the moment.

Using the comma in the second example stresses more strongly the idea that there is a break in time. Either is acceptable.

2. Use a comma to set off a word or group of words attached to the end of a sentence that provides additional information, information that clarifies what is already in the sentence.

It snowed on the first of May, something I never expected.

I have two papers to write during the spring break, one for my history class and one for anthropology.

In each case, without the comma, the reader would be confused, thinking the ideas were:

It snowed on the first of May something . . .

I have two papers to write during the spring break one . . .

3. Use commas to set off a word or group of words that interrupts the sentence to provide an explanation.

The old library, which was about to be torn down, is being renovated.

However, use commas only if the additional information is not necessary to identify the subject of the sentence, to show that it is different from something similar. If readers need the additional information to identify the subject, don't insert any commas.

The old library which was about to be torn down is being renovated.

In the first sentence, there is only one old library. In the second, there is more than one old library, and the writer wants the readers to know that the sentence is about the library that was scheduled to be demolished, not any other library.

Look at this sentence:

All children who have not received their shots are at risk.

You would not put commas around the dependent clause—"who have not received their shots"—because it is restrictive. The sentence is not saying that all children are at risk. It is saying the risk is restricted, is limited, to those "who have not received their shots."

On the other hand, this sentence,

The Women of Brewster Place, which we read in class, was a fascinating book.

has commas around the dependent clause—"which we read in class"—because that clause is not necessary to identify the book. The writer is saying that *The Women of Brewster Place* is a fascinating book. The fact that it was read in class is additional but nonessential information and so is set off by commas.

4. Use commas to separate items in a series.

They are interested, motivated, hard-working students.

5. There is one variation you should know about punctuating a series of adjectives before a noun. Commas are used to separate adjectives before a noun if the word "and" could be inserted between them or if they can be reversed.

Sidney Reilly was a handsome, clever man.

A comma is used because you could say that Reilly was a clever, handsome man, or you could say that he was a handsome *and* clever man.
However, you'd write,

To the Soviets, he was a feared enemy agent.

You can't say that he was *an enemy feared agent*, nor would you say that he was *a feared and enemy agent*, so no comma is used here. *Enemy* is really a part of the noun *agent*. *Enemy agent* is a unit described by the adjective *feared*. As a result, you don't have a series of equal or coordinate adjectives in this case, and a comma would be incorrect.

6. Commas are used, as you saw in Chapter 8, before coordinating conjunctions (FANBOYS, see pages 158–159) when they link two independent clauses, two complete sentences.

   Witnesses are asked to tell the whole truth, but clever attorneys word their questions so that only some of the facts come out.

7. Use commas to separate names of cities from names of states or regions, states or regions from countries, and exact dates from years.

   My grandfather was born in Frankfurt, Germany, but grew up in St. Louis, Missouri, where he has lived ever since.

   He was born on March 14, 1887, during a blizzard.

ACTIVITY 13.1

Working individually, in pairs, or in small groups, according to your instructor's directions, correct any errors in comma usage (including adding omitted commas) in this draft.

Now that I am the father of two children I have learned that much

more is involved in parenting than I had, ever realized before. I now

see that I have to control my emotions, and words for those little peo-

ple have big ears, and imitate whatever I say and do something I'd

never realized. For instance I made a comment to my wife which

seemed as if it were no big deal at the time about a friend of the family,

who is single and never seemed to be able, to find a date. The next

time he visited us, my five-year-old asked him, "Joe do you have a girl-

friend yet?" Then there was the time I'll never forget just before we

moved to Toms River New Jersey when little Joanie told her aunt that

I had said she was a busybody. The date was September 12 1993 and

she hasn't spoken to us since. And of course there is the obvious pro-

blem with curse words. One day a driver cut me off and since I was
angry I let one of those words the ones you're never supposed to say
slip out. Needless to say I heard it from certain small lips soon after. So
I am trying to be more careful about what I say do and even think since
I'm sure those seemingly innocent unaware little folks can even read
my mind.

The Semicolon

1. Semicolons are used, as you saw in Chapter 8, to join two closely related independent clauses, two complete sentences, when no linking word is used.

   She is studying to be a substance abuse counselor; he wants to be a physical therapist.

2. As you also saw in Chapter 8, semicolons are used before conjunctive adverbs—words or groups of words that are not FANBOYS—when they link two closely related independent clauses, two complete sentences.

   Everyone I know liked *The Untouchables*; however, I thought it was a seriously flawed movie.

3. Use semicolons to separate main clauses if they are long and complex or if they contain commas, even if there is a coordinating conjunction (FANBOYS) that would normally take a comma.

   The group of experts, whose backgrounds included physics, astronomy, and higher mathematics, and who came from seven nations around the world, gathered on the tiny tropical island; and there they began to set up their equipment, to take notes, and, of course, to argue about their theories.

4. Writers also use semicolons to separate items in a series if they are long, complex, and/or contain commas.

   The committee was made up of Sara Forde, an expert on employee benefits; Jodi Barnett, a senior editor; and James Power, the head of the personnel department.

The Colon

1. A colon is used after a generalization to introduce a list or paragraph that illustrates that generalization. For instance, after a category, a colon would introduce a list of the items within that category.

   The archaeologist visited the sites of four ancient cities: Lagash, Umma, Kish, and Ur.

   Usually, a colon is used only if the introductory part is a complete sentence. You shouldn't use a colon in a sentence like this:

   She bought butter, eggs, and soda. (Not, She bought: butter, eggs, and soda.)

2. A colon is also used between the statement of a point and the reasons or examples that prove or explain that point.

   She had to find a job: she had to pay her tuition and support her baby.

   In each case, the colon must be preceded by an independent clause, a complete sentence.

The Dash

Dashes can be used in place of commas, semicolons, colons, and parentheses when you want to make a more emphatic break in a sentence. But they should be used sparingly—only for strong emphasis.

   Picasso's paintings during the Blue Period show his compassion for the outcasts of Paris society—the poor, the blind, and the lame.

   Picasso's paintings of the outcasts of Paris society—the poor, the blind, and the lame—show his compassion.

   English 201—that's a course I'll never forget.

Parentheses

Use parentheses to set off information that you want to share with your reader, but which is clearly secondary. When parentheses are used correctly, the sentence will make sense without the information that is set off in this way.

   Free writing (a technique popularized by Peter Elbow) will make getting started much easier.

The writer's main point is that free writing is helpful. The information about the author who popularized it is offered as an aside for those interested in writing theory, but most readers can skip over it without suffering any great loss. Of course, you could also put commas around the information instead of parentheses.

> Free writing, a technique popularized by Peter Elbow, will make getting started much easier.

But remember, parentheses are not used to set off really important information. Parentheses are used rarely. If you have a page full of parentheses, you need to revise, eliminating most of them.

The Period

1. The period is, of course, used to mark the end of sentences. The British called it a full stop, which is an accurate description of how it functions. It says stop. There is no more to this sentence.

2. Use the period after letters in abbreviations.

etc.	pp.
M.D.	Jan.
B.C.	Mr.

Periods are not necessary, however, for familiar initials or names of companies like IBM, CIA, JFK, FDR, or NATO.

The Question Mark

Use a question mark after a sentence that asks a direct question.

> Are you going straight home from the airport?

But don't use a question mark after indirect questions. An indirect question does not include the exact words of the speaker. It contains the idea of a question but is not phrased in the form of a direct question.

> He wanted to know whether Ron was going straight home from the airport.

ACTIVITY 13.2

Working individually, in pairs, or in small groups, according to your instructor's directions, edit the following passage for any errors in punctuation—including the misuse or absence of semicolons, colons, dashes, parentheses, periods, commas, and question marks.

Last night I rented a move; Kubrick's *Full Metal Jacket*. I found it is really powerful for several reasons the brutality of the boot camp scenes, the lack of any dialogue in the first part, except for the drill instructor's words and the recruits' set, required answers, and the way it tricked me into feeling the way I was condemning the characters for feeling. I was really angry at the way the recruits were insulted and humiliated: in fact I wanted to run from the room, rather than watch any longer I've seen many movies about wars and soldiers being trained but I never saw one where there were no personal conversations no expressions of feelings, wishes, resentments or outside interests only the words the men were allowed to use in responding to the sergeant. I asked myself, "How could anyone breathe, or even live, in this narrow, closed world the world of a Marine Corps training camp. Mr Kubrick, the director, tricked me too. I was thinking how horrible it was that the men were being turned into killing machines however when one went crazy and killed the cruel sergeant, I cheered. Then I realized what the film had done to me it had made me as violent, as full of the desire to see another die as the recruits. How could I feel superior anymore. He Kubrick really got to me with this film.

The Apostrophe

1. Add an apostrophe and an *s* to show possession.

   The dog's eyes were almost red in the photograph.

2. When forming the possessives of singular nouns ending in *s*, be guided by the way the word is pronounced.

   a. If a new syllable is formed when you pronounce the possessive, add an apostrophe and an *s*.

   The actress's reading of the part was convincing.

   My boss's office is really a mess.

   b. If adding another *s* to a word that ends with an *s* or an *s* sound makes the word hard to pronounce, just add an apostrophe without an additional *s*.

   Moses' leadership kept the people together.

   For her conscience' sake, she decided to turn in the wallet she found.

3. Use apostrophes alone, without the *s*, after plural nouns ending in *s*.

   The Glantzmans' German shepherd is far more likely to bite someone than my Doberman is.

   Those are the students' books. (They are the books of several students.)

   In the second example above, the *s* shows that the word is a plural as compared with:

   Those are the student's books. (They are the books of one student.)

4. Use an apostrophe with an *s* after irregular plurals that don't end in *s*.

   The women's responses to the survey were radically different from the men's.

5. Add an apostrophe and *s* to the last word in a group of words joined with hyphens or in a compound term.

   My brother-in-law's luck at cards is amazing.

   Ask for someone else's notes; I don't have mine with me.

6. Form the plural of letters, numbers, or words that are being named as words by adding an apostrophe and an *s*.

Underline all the *-ed*'s in those sentences.

How many 3's are there in the equation?

If you combine some of those short sentences, you'll get rid of some of those *and*'s.

7. Use apostrophes to indicate the omission of letters, numbers, or words in contractions.

it is	it's
the class of 1990	the class of '90
of the clock	o'clock
do not	don't
she will	she'll

A word on contractions: Many teachers and employers react negatively to contractions, so if you find yourself in a class or job where this is the case, replace all contractions with the more formal and academic forms. Write

I have completed my research.

rather than

I've completed my research.

In writing this book, I've used contractions most of the time because I wanted to talk to you as one writer to another. I didn't wish to be formal or academic, but the style I've chosen to use is not always appropriate. It all depends on the audience. If I were to write to a public official or to the president of a college or if I were creating a formal document, I wouldn't use contractions.

Quotation Marks

1. Use quotation marks to set off the exact words someone else has written or spoken.

The governor said, "I favor the death penalty."

Quotation marks are not used with indirect quotations.

The governor said that he was in favor of the death penalty.

2. Use quotes for the titles of magazine articles, short stories, and poems.

    "The Death Penalty: Deterrent or Murder?" was an interesting article.

3. Use quotes to show irony, or that you disagree with a phrase or label, or as a substitute for *so-called*.

    He is a real "genius."

4. To call attention to a word, use underlining or italics rather than quotes.

    I don't understand what the writer meant by the word *interesting* in her review.

Here are some guidelines for using other marks of punctuation with quotation marks:

1. When the attribution (who said or wrote the quote) precedes a full sentence quotation, it is followed by a comma.

    Governor Smith said, "I favor the death penalty."

2. When the quotation is a phrase that is an integral part of the sentence, don't follow the attribution with a comma.

    Representative Jones said he felt the death penalty was nothing but "murder by the state."

3. When the quote comes first in the sentence, it is followed by a comma placed inside the quotation marks, then the attribution.

    "I favor the death penalty," said Governor Smith.

    When the attribution comes in the middle of a single sentence quotation, place a comma inside the first set of quotation marks and after the attribution, before the second set of quotation marks.

    "I favor the death penalty," said the governor, "because it will act as a deterrent."

    When the attribution comes between two sentences, link it to one sentence with a comma. The other quoted sentence stands alone.

    "I totally disagree with the governor," said Representative Jones. "The death penalty is nothing but murder by the state."

4. When a quote comes at the end of a sentence, always place the period inside the quotation marks, whether you are quoting a sentence or just a few words.

    Representative Jones said he felt that the death penalty was "murder."

5. Always place colons and semicolons outside the quotation marks.

    The governor said, "I favor the death penalty"; furthermore, he said that he would " veto any bill that would ban it in the state."

6. Question marks, exclamation points, and dashes go inside the quotation marks if they are part of the quotation. They go outside if they are part of the sentence in which the quotation appears.

    The governor asked the Assembly, "Will you support the death penalty bill?"

    How can he say the death penalty is "murder by the state"?

Capitalization

1. Capitalize the first word of all sentences.

2. Capitalize the first word of all complete sentences in quotations.

    He said, "The bill will be defeated."

    But don't capitalize the first of a few quoted words that are not a complete sentence.

    He said that the bill would "never make it out of the committee."

3. Capitalize all words in a title except prepositions, articles, and other short connecting words, unless they come first. Do capitalize even the shortest verbs in a title.

    The Complete Guide to New Automobiles
    Interview with a Vampire
    "I Am Woman"

4. Capitalize the names of people, places, languages, races, and nationalities.

    John Cleese   Australia
    English   Japanese

5. Capitalize the names of the months, days of the week, and holidays, but not the seasons.

March	Columbus Day
Monday	spring
Christmas	fall

6. Capitalize proper names of particular people, titles, places, institutions, courses, etc., but not when the references are general instead of specific.

I'm taking Art History 202.	I'm taking art history.
I have to see Doctor Maher.	I have to see a doctor.
I went to Northeastern High School.	I went to high school in that part of the city.
I will visit Aunt Grace.	I will visit my aunt.
I will vacation on the West Coast.	He lives on the west coast of the island.

ACTIVITY 13.3

Working individually, in pairs, or in small groups, according to your instructor's directions, edit the following passage for errors in the use of commas, the apostrophe, capitalization, and quotation marks.

I, along with many women, find the way men speak to me, mens word choices, offensive. When I was in Biology class, last summer (I think it was in july), one man said to me Hey, baby can I borrow your notes? Im no infant; how dare he use the word baby and suggest I am less mature than he is, an intellectually undeveloped being? Can you imagine if a woman said come here little boy or hey Papa? The man would run away for fear that she belonged in a Mental Hospital. a mans ego would never allow him to accept such words. My fiance James words once embarrassed me too. This is my old lady he said to his friend at a party on campus, in johnson hall I think, "don't flirt while i go over and get her some food." After much discussion he realized what he'd done and said that "He'd never introduce me that way again." and then there are the comedians on tv who talk about broad's, cow's, and even bitches. I want to scream at the screen and ask them "where they get the nerve to talk about women that way." Like the author of the article It's time for the girls to speak up, I want to tell them you are insulting me.

ACTIVITY 13.4

Working individually, in pairs, or in small groups, according to your instructor's directions, correct any punctuation and capitalization errors in this unedited draft.

1   I believe that College teachers shouldnt take attendance because, student's have to gain a sense of responsibility at some point in their lives and College is the place to begin. Learning to show up for classes on their own without someone checking up on them I feel prepares students to be responsible adults; and will benefit them in their future lives.

2   Students dont get to demonstrate a great deal of responsibility or a chance to experience much freedom during their High School years. College is a place where students finally can exercise freedom irresponsibly or where they can show that they are responsible people. As my friend Sam said: if a teacher does'nt take attendance; I realize that its totally up to me to decide whats necessary for me to pass a

course He went on to say that "if a student can't handle the responsibility he will realize hes not ready to handle a family a job (or any other kind of situation adult's have to face on their own").

3   It's all part of taking responsibility for whether you get As Bs or Fs on your own without someone standing over you with a stick. The ability to decide how to handle college responsibilities on your own helps you grow it will help you to independently get a good performance evaluation on the job later on. And because you set your own rules and guidelines you feel a great sense of satisfaction you feel you are an adult a responsible person.

4   If teachers take attendance in College classes many students will feel they are being treated like children They will become resentful and this will cause them to do poorer quality work than they would do otherwise. If they treat me like a baby. One of my friends said. Then I am a baby: I'll want them to do everything for me to feed me to give it all to me—(I'll be less likely to earn it for myself) wont I?

5   When college instructors don't take attendance students see the results of their action's not other peoples. As Sam says: Its like knowing I have to get up at 7 o clock; not 7,30 to get there on time— because Ill miss something not because, of someone's elses rules not because Ill have a mark against me in the teachers' little green book". "Its my choice: he feels: my responsibilities; and not someone elses, right"?

ACTIVITY 13.5

Free write on the subject of a practice followed at your school that you feel is either beneficial or detrimental. You might write about required labs, or tutoring, or letter grades versus pass/fail grades. Or pick a topic you wrote about in your journal or one suggested by your instructor. Find a focus and write a draft. Rewrite and expand. Exchange papers with another student. On a separate piece of paper, indicate any errors in punctuation or spelling in addition to commenting on the unity, coherence, development, and style of the paper, and how well it meets readers' needs. Revise your draft after rereading it and looking over the editorial comments you receive.

Chapter 14

Sentence Combining

Sentence combining is a technique that many people have found useful for practicing their editing skills. In Chapter 11, you saw that combining sentences helps you edit short, simple sentences that contain a lot of repetition. You can also use sentence combining to practice setting sentence boundaries, using connecting words, transitions, and modifiers, and recognizing the logical connections between ideas. Sentence combining provides you with practice in expressing ideas in the most compact and direct manner, by providing practice in making substitutions for words and phrases. You'll have opportunities to practice parallelism. And, in some of these exercise sentences, there are passive constructions that you can make active.

This chapter consists entirely of activities in which you will be combining ideas. You'll turn each group of short sentences into one comprehensive sentence. You will cut out repeated words and add subordinators and coordinators (see Chapter 8, pages 158–163) as needed. But be sure to include all the information and ideas from the sentences. Do not omit any of these when you reduce the number of words. These activities will give you practice in making choices about the ways in which you can express your ideas. There are no single right choices; there is a range of choices in each group. And ideas within each group can be moved around. In other words, you don't have to follow the exact order of the original short sentences in creating the new, more compact, and more interesting sentence.

Your instructor will tell you whether to work individually, in pairs, or in small groups.

Before you start, here's a brief example:

1. I bought a personal computer.
2. I bought it to play computer games.
3. I bought a word processing program.
4. I used it to write.
5. I found writing was easier.
6. It was easier because I could make corrections.
7. I made them before I printed anything.
8. I didn't have to type whole pages over.
9. I didn't have to do this to make changes.

Here's one way these nine sentences could be combined into one:

Although I bought a personal computer just to play games, after I bought a word processing program, I discovered that writing was much easier because I could make corrections before I printed anything and didn't have to type whole pages over to make corrections.

ACTIVITY 14.1

Combine each group of sentences into a single sentence. Combine sentences 1 to 5, 6 to 10, 11 to 19, and so on. You will end up with a six-sentence paragraph on the topic Alternative Fuels.

ALTERNATIVE FUELS

1. There are drivers.
2. There are about 8,000 of them.
3. They are in British Columbia.
4. Their vehicles use natural gas.
5. They use it instead of gasoline.

6. The vehicles emit mostly carbon dioxide and water.
7. They are being hailed by environmentalists.
8. The environmentalists are concerned about air pollution.
9. The vehicles are hailed as a good alternative.
10. They are an alternative to gasoline-powered cars.

11. Less-polluting vehicles are in use in other programs.
12. The programs are in California.
13. The programs are in Washington.
14. The programs are in New York.
15. They illustrate how natural gas can be an alternative.
16. They illustrate how electricity can be an alternative.
17. They illustrate how methanol can be an alternative.
18. Methanol is a derivative of natural gas.
19. These things are all alternatives to gasoline.

20. Less-polluting vehicles have received more attention.
21. They have done this since 1989.
22. Southern California has adopted an air-quality program.
23. The program is stringent.
24. The program could eventually ban some cars.
25. The program could eventually ban some trucks.
26. The program could eventually ban some buses.
27. These vehicles burn gasoline.
28. These vehicles burn diesel fuel.

29. Alternative fuels could become more widespread.
30. The air quality will improve.
31. There will be some problems.
32. Fueling stops will have to be more frequent.
33. These stops will be more frequent than for gasoline-powered cars.
34. Electric vehicles will never accelerate quickly.
35. They won't do this as fast as gasoline cars.
36. This is probable.

37. Technology will advance.
38. It will advance in response to needs.
39. The needs will be created by the new fuels.
40. Many of the problems will disappear.

ACTIVITY 14.2

Combine each group of sentences into a single sentence. You will end up with a five-sentence paragraph on Nonverbal Behavior.

NONVERBAL BEHAVIOR

1. Some things convey messages.
2. One way is the way we dress.
3. One way is how close we stand to other people.
4. One way is whether we make eye contact.
5. One way is whether we touch.
6. One way is what we do with our hands.

7. These are forms of nonverbal behavior.
8. These nonverbal forms of behavior communicate something.
9. They communicate messages.
10. These messages don't employ words.
11. These messages can also enhance.
12. They enhance what our words say.
13. Sometimes, they contradict what our words say.

14. Rolling your eyes is an example.
15. It shows disapproval.
16. It shows this without words.
17. To roll your eyes and say "That's silly" does something else.
18. It reinforces your words.

19. We send other messages.
20. These messages are nonverbal.
21. These messages are about how we feel.
22. We send them at a certain time.
23. At that time we are bored.
24. At that time someone is talking.
25. We look around the room.
26. We play with our hands.
27. We play with a pencil.

28. These activities do something.
29. They send a message.
30. The message is nonverbal.
31. The message says something.
32. It says that we want to escape.
33. It says that we don't want to be there.

ACTIVITY 14.3

Combine each group of sentences into a single sentence. You will end up with a six-sentence paragraph on Learning About the Past.

LEARNING ABOUT THE PAST

1. Digging up remains can tell archaeologists a lot.
2. The remains are of old houses.
3. The houses date from the 1700s.
4. They tell about the environment.
5. They tell how people lived.
6. They tell what people ate.
7. They tell what people wore.
8. They can't answer all the questions.

9. Finding the cellar full of a jumble of bricks is an example.
10. Finding human bones is an example.
11. These examples are found together.
12. They suggest quick destruction of the building.
13. They suggest violent destruction of the building.
14. The destruction could have been from an earthquake.

15. Oyster shells were found in one spot.
16. They were 9 to 10 inches long.
17. The spot was near the Atlantic Ocean.
18. Archaeologists know what people ate.
19. Archaeologists know that animal life has changed.
20. Oysters of that size don't exist today.
21. Oysters of that size don't exist in North America.

22. Archaeologists learn about clothing.
23. The clothing was worn by people in the past.
24. Archaeologists find remnants of cloth.
25. The cloth is made in a different way.
26. Archaeologists find cloth on rare occasions.
27. Archaeologists are more likely to find buttons.
28. The buttons are made of bone.
29. The buttons are made of pearl.
30. The buttons are made of pewter.

31. Archaeologists can't always tell about the owners of the building.
32. A carefully constructed building could be a sign.
33. A carefully constructed building could have belonged to rich people.
34. A carefully constructed building could reveal high-quality workmanship.
35. High-quality workmanship could have been common.
36. High-quality workmanship could have been used in all houses built at a particular time.
37. High-quality workmanship could have been used in all houses built in a particular place.

38. Artifacts are found.
39. Artifacts could have been dumped on the site later.
40. The ground could have been turned up.
41. The ground could have been turned up at some later point in the past.

ACTIVITY 14.4

Combine each group of sentences into a single sentence. You should end up with a six-sentence paragraph on Vietnam Vets.

VIETNAM VETS

1. The Vietnam veteran has a set of problems.
2. This set of problems is different from those of other vets.
3. Those vets served in Korea.
4. Those vets served in World War II.
5. Those vets are older.

 6. The Vietnam War was unpopular.
 7. This was especially so.
 8. It was unpopular on all levels of society.
 9. This happened throughout the country.
10. It was protested on campuses.
11. It was attacked in Congress.
12. It was denounced in the media.

13. The soldiers returned home.
14. Most of them had been forced to go.
15. They had been drafted.
16. They were met with contempt.
17. They were made to feel evil.
18. Employers were reluctant to hire them.
19. The soldiers were looked upon with suspicion.
20. They were seen as bombs ready to explode.

21. The government didn't help.
22. It didn't provide enough psychological help.
23. It didn't provide enough medical help.
24. The help was needed.
25. The vets needed this help.
26. They needed the help to reenter civilian life.
27. They needed the help to do so successfully.

28. Congress didn't give them money for education.
29. This wasn't done to a degree.
30. The degree wasn't the same as for World War II veterans.
31. The degree wasn't the same as for Korean War veterans.
32. Vietnam vets get only a stipend.
33. It is monthly.
34. It is barely enough to live on.

35. There are results from this treatment.
36. The results are negative.
37. The results include an unusually high rate of alcoholism.
38. The results include an unusually high rate of divorce.
39. The results include an unusually high rate of arrests for criminal offenses.
40. Vietnam vets feel alienation.
41. Vietnam vets distrust other people.

ACTIVITY 14.5

Combine each group of sentences into a single sentence. Then combine the seven sentences into a paragraph that describes the choices two workers made.

A DIFFICULT CHOICE

1. I heard a program.
2. It was on National Public Radio.
3. It was called "Choices of the Heart."
4. It was about two men.
5. The two men worked in a plant.
6. The plant was in Connecticut.
7. The plant produced submarines.
8. The submarines were designed to carry nuclear weapons.

9. One worker said he liked his job.
10. He said it paid him a good salary.
11. He said he did good work.
12. He said the work he did made him proud.
13. He said he felt he contributed to the defense of his country.

14. Another worker was troubled.
15. He felt nuclear weapons were wrong.
16. He felt they could destroy the world.
17. He felt this could happen if either side used them.
18. He felt they were wrong even for defense.
19. He was concerned about supporting his family.

20. He had many years of experience at the plant.
21. He had received many promotions at the plant.
22. He was a supervisor at the plant.
23. He received a very high salary.
24. He couldn't make as much money.
25. He couldn't do this at another job.

26. The work he did bothered him.
27. He felt guilty.
28. He started taking his problems out on his family.
29. He realized he had to do something.

30. He thought about his dilemma.
31. He thought about it for a long time.
32. He turned it over in his mind.
33. He talked to his wife.
34. He talked to his children.
35. He made a decision.
36. This was the final step in the process.

37. He decided to quit his job.
38. This made me think.
39. I thought about what I would do.
40. I might have a job.
41. The job might involve doing something.
42. That thing might go against my values.
43. I would lose money.
44. This would happen if I quit.

ACTIVITY 14.6

Combine each group of sentences into a single sentence. You should end up with a seven-sentence paragraph about a very unusual man.

THE EMPEROR NORTON

1. Joshua Norton was born in England.
2. He immigrated to San Francisco.
3. This happened in the nineteenth century.
4. This happened in the first half of that century.
5. He was thirty years old.
6. He wanted to make a fortune.
7. He tried to corner the rice market.
8. He went bankrupt.
9. This upset his mental balance.

10. He stopped working.
11. He began to brood.
12. He brooded about the problems of the world.
13. He decided that the United States needed a monarch.
14. He believed this because of conflict between the North and South.
15. He believed a ruler could unite the nation.
16. This ruler would have absolute power.

17. He put a notice in a newspaper.
18. The newspaper was the *San Francisco Bulletin*.
19. He did this in 1859.
20. The notice said that Norton declared himself Emperor of the United States.
21. The notice said that Norton did this at the request of some citizens of the country.
22. These citizens made up the majority.

23. Norton began to dress a certain way.
24. It was the way he thought an emperor would dress.
25. He wore a long-tailed coat.
26. The coat had gold epaulets.
27. The coat was trimmed with brass buttons.
28. He wore a beaver hat.
29. The hat was tall.
30. The hat was topped by an ostrich plume.
31. The ostrich plume was green.
32. He carried a sword.
33. He carried an umbrella.

34. The people didn't mock him.
35. The people accepted him.
36. They were the people of San Francisco.
37. Tailors made uniforms for him.
38. They gave them to him for free.

39. His uniform was worn out.
40. This happened one time.
41. No tailors could be found to give him a new one.
42. Norton issued a proclamation.
43. The proclamation said that many people complained.
44. It said they complained about the state of the imperial wardrobe.
45. The city fathers voted.
46. They voted to buy him a new uniform.
47. They voted to do this at public expense.

48. Norton died.
49. This happened in 1880.
50. There was a funeral.
51. The funeral was on a grand scale.
52. The funeral was paid for.
53. Leading businessmen put up the money.
54. Ten thousand people attended the funeral.

ACTIVITY 14.7

Combine each group of sentences into a single sentence. You should end up with a seven-sentence paragraph about horror films.

HORROR FILMS

1. Stephen King wrote a book.
2. The book is called *Danse Macabre*.
3. It was written in 1981.
4. It consists of essays.
5. The essays are about films.
6. The films are about horror.
7. The essays are nonfiction.

8. King says something about art.
9. Art is a piece of work.
10. It is creative.
11. The audience gives something.
12. It gets more than it gives.
13. Horror films offer artistic value.
14. The value lies in a connection.
15. The connection is between fantasy and fear.

16. Something is true.
17. Horror films are not made with art in mind.
18. They are made to make money.
19. Art is not consciously created.
20. It is thrown off.
21. The throwing off is like radiation.
22. The radiation comes from an atomic bomb.

23. Horror films play on something.
24. They play on our fear.
25. We have a fear of death.
26. One type of death can be good.
27. One type of death can be bad.

28. Horror films give us an experience.
29. They make us experience death.
30. The kind of death is bad.
31. This scares us.
32. This is the source of the films' best effects.

33. These films play on our curiosity.
34. We want to know something.
35. It is behind a door.
36. The door is locked.
37. It is in the basement.
38. The basement is in a mortuary.
39. It happens in a graveyard.
40. It happens when the mourners have left.
41. It happens when the moon is dark.

42. King says something else.
43. The films violate taboos.
44. This has value.
45. This helps us to understand.
46. We do this better.
47. We understand what the taboos are.
48. We understand why they make us feel something.
49. We feel uneasy.

ACTIVITY 14.8

Combine each group of sentences into a single sentence. You should end up with six sentences that form a unified paragraph about black English.

BLACK ENGLISH

1. Some say black English is valuable.
2. They say it gives African Americans a sense of identity.
3. They say it is something that is unique.
4. They say it is unique to them.
5. They say it keeps them from being absorbed.
6. They say they would be absorbed by the white culture.

7. Others say black English creates problems.
8. Black English is not acceptable to employers.
9. Employers believe Standard American English is proper.
10. Employers believe black English is bad English.
11. Employers believe black English is a sign of something.
12. Employers believe black English shows a lack of education.
13. Employers believe black English shows a lack of knowledge.

14. This second group have feelings.
15. These feelings are strong.
16. Black English should not be used.
17. It should never be used.
18. Many react to it.
19. They react negatively.
20. This will cause African Americans to suffer.
21. African Americans will not get good paying jobs.
22. African Americans will not get a piece.
23. The piece they want is part of the American dream.

24. Still others believe something else.
25. They say African Americans can use two languages.
26. They say African Americans can use black English.
27. They should use it with other people.
28. These other people use it, too.
29. Using it will create a bond.
30. They say African Americans should use Standard American English.
31. They should do this in business situations.
32. They should do this in their professional capacities.
33. Standard American English is a language.
34. It is the language of money.
35. It is the language of power.
36. It will help African Americans get ahead.
37. They will get ahead in business.

38. They point out something.
39. Martin Luther King didn't use black English.
40. Malcolm X didn't use black English.
41. They didn't use it when they wrote.
42. African American newscasters don't use black English.
43. African American doctors don't use black English.
44. African American lawyers don't use black English.
45. African American executives don't use black English.
46. African American educators don't use black English.
47. They don't use it in professional situations.

48. People can have two languages.
49. They can use them in different situations.
50. These people are bilingual.
51. They have skills.
52. Other people don't have these skills.
53. Having two languages can be an advantage.

ACTIVITY 14.9

Free write on a topic suggested by the first eight activities in this chapter: eccentric characters, dialect, moral choices, and the like. Or write on a topic suggested by one of your journals. Find a focus and develop a draft. Exchange papers with another student. Do not write on the other person's paper, but on a separate piece of paper, discuss the other writer's paper in terms of unity, coherence, development, style, and mechanics. Comment on how well the paper meets the readers' needs. And, finally, make suggestions about how sentences might be more effectively combined. Or, if your instructor prefers, read over your own paper keeping in mind all the areas for possible revision listed above. In either case, rewrite your draft.

PART III
Research

Chapter 15

Doing Research

Sometimes beginning writers, and even more experienced writers, moan at the mention of research. But as you will see, the process isn't really all that difficult. In earlier chapters, you drew on your memories of your experiences, on facts you knew in a general way, on your recollection of your reading and television viewing for ideas to use in your writing. In doing research, you collect more exact and precise information from outside sources, react to it, and present it to your readers. When you do research, the only additional steps are gathering the information, integrating it into your paper, and indicating to your readers the sources you used. Beyond that, finding a focus, drafting, revising, and editing all call on skills you've already developed.

Doing research is valuable for both writers and readers. By exploring what other writers have said about a topic, you as a writer gain knowledge and can more effectively demonstrate your authority and expertise in the area you're writing about. Your readers benefit from the increased information they receive and from the service you provide them by bringing together ideas from various sources.

Interviewing to Collect Information

Let's start with a simple research project. The only way this piece of writing differs from the previous ones you've created is that you will be using direct and indirect quotations more extensively. You will have more than a few sentences like these:

> In the course of discussing his guitar playing, Tom noted that his hobby "changed his attitude toward hard work."

> "Cooking Indian food involves shopping around for spices and other ingredients and no little time," Rao told me.

> Leo said that while skiing is not an activity that is immediately mastered, the rewards, if a person sticks to it, are great.

You might want to look back at Chapter 13 to refresh your knowledge of the proper use of quotations and quotation marks.

ACTIVITY 15.1

1. Interview another student, and he or she will interview you. You might ask the other person about (a) an accomplishment that he or she is particularly proud of, or (b) a difficulty that he or she has overcome.
2. Take notes on what the person tells you.
3. Ask more questions to get specific details and to clarify anything that you do not understand clearly.
4. The other person will repeat the process with you, asking questions and taking notes.
5. Write a draft of a paper in which you discuss the accomplishment of the person you interviewed or the problem he or she overcame. Make sure you have a main idea—that is, that you make a contract with your reader—that you give details to help your reader understand the situation, and that you order those details in a way that makes the situation clear for your reader. Be sure to name the person you're writing about.
6. Exchange papers with a person other than the one you interviewed. You will read and respond to the other person's paper, and he or she will read and respond to yours. Tell the writer:
    a. What the main idea is.
    b. What the paper's strong points are.
    c. What needs to be changed in terms of unity, coherence, development, and style.
7. If your paper lacks important details, go back to the person you interviewed and get the information you need.
8. Rewrite your draft.

Or, as an alternative to the interview, try writing an oral history, described in Activity 15.2.

ACTIVITY 15.2

One valuable way to learn about another time and place is to interview someone who has had experiences that are significantly different from yours, to organize that material, and present it to readers as an oral history.

1. Interview an older relative, or a stranger for that matter, and write down what that person tells you about his or her experiences in the Depression, during the 1960s, or in some other period. You might find out about the kind of work the person did, or you might find out about customs in a different culture, a foreign country, or another part of the United States.
2. Take notes on what the person has to say.
3. After you've collected the information, look for a main idea. Then write a draft of a paper that illustrates what you feel is the central focus of the information that you've collected. Be sure to make appropriate use of direct and indirect quotations (see Chapter 13).

4. Exchange drafts with another student. You will read and respond to the other person's paper, and he or she will read and respond to yours. Tell the writer:
    a. What the main idea is.
    b. What the paper's strong points are.
    c. What needs to be changed in terms of unity, coherence, development, and style.
5. If your paper lacks important details, go back to the person you interviewed and get the information you need.
6. Rewrite your draft.

Starting Research That Involves Using the Library

Writing a Documented Essay

Whenever you are writing an essay on a topic about which you have some knowledge, but not a great deal, you may find it useful to do some research. Sometimes, you may want to use only one or two source(s). In such a case, you will not use the type of documentation or a formal Works Cited list that a formal research paper requires (see later in this chapter). For a documented essay, you just need to mention your source(s) in the body of your paper. Read ahead in this chapter to find out about locating sources (pages 269–274), quoting (pages 276–277), paraphrasing (pages 278–279), and avoiding plagiarism (pages 281–285). Also, you may want to refresh your memory on the use of quotations in Chapter 13.

In a documented essay, you can indicate a quotation from a source in this way:

> I understand that the American dream doesn't come true for everyone, but I didn't realize how frustrating working for minimum wage can be. As Mickey Kaus notes in an article in *The New Republic* of August 2, 1993, "Someone working forty hours a week, every week, at the minimum wage ($4.25 an hour) makes $8,840 a year."

Even when you restate the information from an outside source in your own words, or paraphrase, you need to tell where the idea came from. You can document a paraphrase in this way:

> Recycling is not as productive as many people think. In fact, I read that because there are so many types of plastics and they are difficult to separate, recycling is inefficient. As a result, as was stated in a *Time* magazine article called "Recycling: Stalled at the Curbside," which appeared on October 18, 1993, only 2.2 percent are recycled. Nevertheless, recycling is popular and, as *Time* notes, such programs across the country have increased in the last three years from 50 to 4,000.

ACTIVITY 15.3

1. Select a topic of your choice, one suggested by your instructor, or one from the following list:
   a. Welfare
   b. Pollution
   c. Taxes
   d. Working mothers
   e. Late-night TV shows
   f. A different culture or country
2. Free write about the topic, find a main idea, and write a draft.
3. Look up and study one or two sources related to your topic in the library.
4. Rewrite your draft, working in quotations, paraphrases, and/or pieces of information from your sources.
5. Edit and proofread your essay.

Writing a Formal Research Paper

Compared to a documented essay, a research paper is a longer piece of writing that relies on more sources. When instructors assign such papers, they usually tell you what length the paper should be and how many sources you should have. You will also use a different form of documentation than in a documented essay, and your paper will include a Works Cited page. The following sections show you how to get started, how to document, how to avoid plagiarism, and how to construct your Works Cited list. In fact, they will present all the basics about writing a research paper.

One problem that writers encounter in generating a research paper is that they collect a great deal of information on a topic about which they have never given much thought. The result is a paper that merely strings together a lot of information, without a particular focus or direction. Two approaches, both of which involve writing a preliminary paper, can help you deal with this problem.

On the one hand, if your instructor asks you to do research that involves a topic on which you already have some knowledge or about which you have some opinions, do Activity 15.4 after reading this section of text. For instance, suppose you are going to do a research paper on censorship. If you first write a paper, without doing any research, you will clarify your position on the subject. Then you can direct your research toward finding out what arguments have been made for and against that position. If you are against censorship, you will direct your research toward finding support for your position and finding the arguments that proponents of censorship use so that you can dispute them when you write the actual research paper. Of course, if your research convinces you to change your mind, that's fine too. You will be involved in the research process, and it won't be the dull job of merely collecting a lot of facts to which you are indifferent. Even if you are asked to write an objective paper in which you do not argue your opinion, you'll have a focus to your research—the pros and cons on the subject.

Perhaps you'll also find a particular area you want to explore—like censorship of school newspapers—and so have a specific area to zero in on while conducting your research.

If you are writing a paper that involves finding out what the critics have to say about a book, play, or film, write your own review without using the library first.

On the other hand, if you have to write a report for an anthropology course about family structure among the Maori of New Zealand and know nothing about that culture, write a paper first about family structure in a society you do know about, from either your personal experience or your reading in the course. This too will give you a sense of what areas to explore and may suggest a structure for your paper such as comparison/contrast.

If the subject matter is totally alien to you, do Activity 15.4 after you've looked at one or two sources.

ACTIVITY 15.4

Free write or cluster or ask yourself questions (see Chapter 1) on the research topic you've chosen or have been assigned.

Write a "pre-research" draft, as described in the text you have just read.

Read over your draft or exchange drafts with another student to get feedback on what areas require research. Ask yourself or have the other person tell you what questions need to be answered when you look up information in the library.

Using the Library

Now that you have a direction for your research, the next step is to begin collecting information.

Finding Books

Finding books is easy. You simply consult the card catalog or computer terminal, looking for the topic, author, or titles you want. Usually looking under the subject will be the most useful way to start. Books will lead you to other books and articles. Footnotes and references—lists of works that the author consulted in writing his or her book—will suggest other books and articles that might be useful. If your library has open stacks, while you're locating the books you want, you may discover other books on the same topic on the same shelf.

To find the appropriate subject headings to look under, you can play the "telephone book game." In other words, try to think up alternate ways to describe what you're looking for. A better approach is to consult a volume called *Library of Congress Subject Headings*. All libraries use the headings employed by the Library of Congress in Washington, D.C. So consulting this book, found in the reference section of your library, will show you what heading subjects are classified under. Since the book is cross-indexed, finding one heading will lead you to other headings you can check. The entry will also tell you how to break the subject down into various subdivisions. This reference work will also show you related headings, indicate broader headings that include your area of interest, and tell you which headings are dead ends—in other words, which headings are not used by the Library of Congress and therefore are not used by your library.

Censorship   *(May Subd Geog)*

    UF   Book censorship

            Books—Censorship

            Intellectual freedom

            Literature—Censorship

    BT   Church—Teaching office

            Literature, Immoral

            Literature and morals

    RT   Condemned books

            Expurgated books

            Index librorum prohibitorum

            Prohibited books

    SA   *subdivision* Censorship *under subjects,*

            individual wars, and names of

            literary authors, e.g. Radio—

            Censorship; Theater—Censorship;

            World War, 1939–1945—

            Censorship; Shakespeare, William,

            1564–1616—Censorship

    NT   Book burning

            Freedom of the press

            Libraries—Censorship

            Prior restraint

Censorship (Canon law)

Censorship (Judaism)

    [BM729.C4]

    NT   Approbations (Hebrew literature)

Censorship and the arts

    USE   Arts—Censorship

Censorship in libraries

    USE   Libraries—Censorship

Censorship of the press

    USE   Freedom of the press

            Press law

            Prohibited books

Censorship of the stage

    USE   Theater—Censorship

Figure 15.1 *Library of Congress Subject Headings* Entry for Censorship*

---

*Library of Congress Subject Headings, s.v. "censorship."

When you return to the library card catalog with your list of headings to pursue, the important information to copy down is the author's name, the complete title of the book, the city of publication, the publisher, and the copyright date. If more than one city is listed, copy down the first one. This is the information that you will include in your Works Cited. Of course, you can get this information from the title page and copyright page, once you've actually found the book. To locate the book, the most important information is the *call number,* which will enable you or the workers at the circulation desk to find it on the shelves.

Here's a typical card catalog entry for a book:

```
KF 994 4.A937                 Censorship   condemned books
                                           arts
                                           US


Ernst, Morris Leopold
Censorship: the search for the obscene
NY Macmillan 1964
```

Notice that the entry in the card catalog contains all the headings under which the book is listed in the library. This can lead you to other works on the same subject.

Many colleges now have On Line Public Access Catalogues. You use these computer programs in basically the same way as a card catalog. You can look up an author, a title, or, most likely, a subject. A computer catalog often contains a fuller list of related headings than a card catalog. There are many different types of computerized catalogs, but the information that appears on the screen or on a printout will contain the same information that you saw on the catalog card reproduced above.

Finding Articles and Reviews

The most recent information, however, is not found in books, which appear in print a year or two after they are written, but in newspapers, magazines, and journals—specialized scholarly publications in a given field.

To find out what has been published in periodicals, you can consult an index. There are bound volumes and listings on computer terminals in many libraries. In some fields, there are abstracts—summaries of articles published in the discipline.

To locate information from newspapers, refer to *The New York Times Index,* which is issued every two weeks. For papers in other major cities in the United States, use the *Newspaper Index.* There is also an index to the *London Times.*

If you want to consult magazines, the place to go is the *Readers' Guide to Periodical Literature*, which is issued twice a month. Here you will find items listed by subject, author, and individuals discussed. Movie reviews are listed under Motion Pictures.

CENSORSHIP
See also
Government and the press
Textbooks—Censorship
International aspects
At stake: the freedom to imagine [booksellers pull S. Rushdie's Satanic verses off shelves in wake of murder order issued by Khomeini] L. Shapiro. il *Newsweek* 113:36-7 F 27 '89
Thanks to protesters, a runaway best seller [S. Rushdie's Satanic verses] L. Shapiro. il *Newsweek* 113:32-3 Mr 6 '89
Great Britain
Thatcher puts a lid on. J. Atlas. il *The New York Times Magazine* p36-8+ Mr 5 '89

Figure 15.2 *Readers' Guide to Periodical Literature* Entry on Censorship*

There are also various indexes to scholarly journals in the humanities, social sciences, and literature. The reference librarian can help you identify and use these works.

Again, your institution may use CD ROM on line databases instead of bound volumes like the *Readers' Guide*. This simply means the information about the articles you are looking for is contained on a compact disc, like the kind on which you listen to music. These discs are updated regularly, just like the print sources. The computerized lists of articles (Infotrac, Wilson Data Bases, and Resource One are some of the more popular systems) are used in the same way as any printed index, but they do have certain advantages. For instance, the computerized index may indicate which periodicals and newspapers are carried by the library that you are using, may show more subtopics, may present the articles in alphabetical order or list the most recent ones first, and may even help you find key words that are not part of the title of the article. Many of these programs can print out abstracts (summaries) of the articles, and some even print out the entire article for you, thus eliminating the need for you to find the actual article either on microfilm or in the maga-

* *Readers' Guide to Periodical Literature*, s.v. "censorship." *Readers' Guide to Periodical Literature*, 1988–89. Copyright © 1989 by the H. W. Wilson Company. Material reproduced by permission of the publisher.

zine or newspaper itself. Since there are many CD ROM programs, and many are operated in slightly different ways, you should talk to the reference librarian and ask his or her assistance in using these tools.

Taking Notes

Although you can keep library books several weeks, it is difficult to keep track of which parts are important to your research, short of being selfish and marking them up. And even if you were to engage in this destructive process, finding the right pages would be difficult. Magazines and other periodicals don't circulate and are often available only on film, so they are available to you for an even shorter amount of time. When you return to the library, someone else may be using the materials you want, or they might be misshelved, or they might be in the bindery, or they might be being transferred to microfilm. Of course, you can photocopy articles or pages and chapters of books, but this is expensive and you still have to go over them again and pick out what is important. The solution is to take notes. Also, note-taking forces you to decide what is important and gives you practice in making accurate summaries.

I have found using index cards to be much more efficient than using a pad or a notebook. You need to collect two kinds of information: (a) You need the titles, authors, publishers, and dates of the works you are using for your Works Cited notes, and (b) you need the facts and arguments that comprise your research information.

The publication data (recorded on the first set of cards described above) must eventually be put in alphabetical order. It is much easier to do this if each entry is listed on a separate note card. You just move the cards around. There's no need to recopy or to cut and paste.

The ideas that you get from your sources can also be organized more easily if you use index cards. There's another advantage, too. Since the note cards are small, usually 3" x 5", you usually can't write more than one idea on each card. With a pad or notebook, it's easy to overlook or lose track of an idea you worked long and hard to find while incorporating another item on the same page into your paper. When I was young and foolish, I used to take notes on a pad. Then as I wrote the paper, I'd circle ideas that I felt fit into different places in the paper in different colors. I crossed out the ideas as I put them into the paper. What a mess! Also, I had to read the same material over and over. Take it from one who learned from sad experience. Index cards make research much easier.

Works Cited Cards

For each book you consult, create a work cited card. Include the call number, in case you want to go back to it, the author's name, the title, the place of publication, the publisher, and the date.

```
KF 9944

.A9E7

Ernst, Morris. Censorship: The Search for the Obscene.

    New York: Macmillan, 1954.
```

For each magazine or newspaper article, you want to copy onto your card the author, article title, the name of the periodical, the date, and the pages. You may also need to include the number of the volume, series, or issue.

```
Sander, James R. "Supreme Court Allows Greater

    Restriction on Student Expression." New York Teacher

    Bulletin 17 April 1989: 9.
```

Information Cards

You should only put information from one source on each card. Ideally put only one idea on each card so no material will be overlooked when you go through and use the cards.

Direct Quotes

As you read, you will find information in books and articles you want to use in your paper. When you're not sure what part of a quote you will use, are in a hurry and fear you won't get the information down accurately, or think the information is worded in a particularly impressive way, copy down the entire passage onto your note card. Make sure to enclose the material in quotation marks. In addition, so that you can identify the source of the quotation, jot down the author's last name, the key word of the title, and the page number on which the quote appears.

Here's an example of a note card containing a direct quotation. Notice that the student has placed quotation marks around it so she will remember that it contains the exact words of the source she has consulted.

```
Treiman "Constructive"

p. 14 "Studies have clearly shown that children exposed

to violence on television tend to re-enact what they see

with rougher-than-usual schoolyard play. The same

studies have shown that the greater the amount of

violent television a child views, the more predisposed

he is to becoming a criminal offender later."
```

The student has already created a work cited card for the article that looks like this:

```
Treiman, Susan.   "Constructive TV Tuning."  New York

    Daily News 25 May 1986: 14.
```

So on her information card she only needs the author's last name and the page number. This student has included a shortened form of the title, just in case she comes across another work by the same author.

Paraphrasing

When you come across a lot of useful material that would take a long time to copy, or when the original is not worded in a particularly memorable way, paraphrase it. In other words, put it into your own words.

Here's the same passage that was copied exactly on the last note card as a direct quote, this time written in the student's own words.

```
Treiman "Constructive"

p. 14 She says that studies show kids who see a lot of

violence on T.V. play rougher games at school than the

other kids. Also states that studies show that the more

violence they see the more likely it is that they will

commit crimes at some later point.
```

This student wrote down just the idea. He didn't worry about grammar or style. He can reword it again when he actually incorporates the idea into his paper. Because these are not the exact words of the article, he didn't use quotation marks, but he did make note of the author, title, and page number since paraphrases as well as direct quotes must be credited in the final paper. He didn't put down the newspaper name because he has that information on his work cited card on this source.

When you paraphrase, you want to include all the information you need to document this information. Remember, when you paraphrase you should really use your own words, not just rearrange the words of the original. You don't want to duplicate the rhythm or style of the original or you may, even though you document it, end up with unintentional plagiarism. I've found that the most useful method is to cover or turn over the passage that I'm paraphrasing and then put it in my own words. After that, I look back at the original to make sure that my paraphrase is accurate and complete.

Here's an example of a paraphrase that is too close to the style of the original. If you compare the exact quote on the first note card with this supposed paraphrase, you see that the writer is just shifting words around or changing a few words. As a result, the writer will end up with unintentional plagiarism in the body of her paper.

```
Treiman "Constructive"

p. 14 Studies have shown that children who see a great

deal of TV violence tend to re-enact what they've seen

in rougher-than-usual school-yard play. These studies

also show that the larger the amount of violent shows

the child watches, the more he is predisposed to become

a law breaker later.
```

This writer should have either quoted directly or looked away from the original and tried to reconstruct it in her own words as a paraphrase, and then checked back with the original to make sure she got all the ideas down accurately.

ACTIVITY 15.5

Read the following note cards that contain direct quotes. Then change them into note cards that contain paraphrases. Make sure that your paraphrases are accurate and that your language doesn't duplicate the wording and style of the originals. (Notice on the first card that quoted material within the direct quote is placed in single quotes.)

Exchange paraphrases with another student. Then check each other's paraphrases for accuracy and originality. Your instructor may ask you to do this as a whole group activity or to hand in your paraphrases.

Edwards "Censorship in the School"

p. 39 "Heading the list of favorite books to be censored, however, is the classic story of a teenager's quest for maturity, J. D. Salinger's <u>The Catcher in the Rye</u>. 'Obscene' is the usual cry, based on the four-letter words. 'Blasphemous' claim the protesters over the caustic comments about religious hypocrisy. <u>Catcher</u> has become the symbol for critics of what they perceive to be a vile, ungodly plot on the part of the schools to undermine the morals of American school children."

Bruwhelheide "Reasons"

p. 416 "Parents have a traditional, legal and moral part to play in their children's education. They have the right and responsibility to control certain aspects of their individual child's educational experience. However, parents do not have the right to censor the education of other children in a community. Would-be censors question materials, actions, and methods that do not conform to a particular, narrow view of the world. These people seem to want public schools to ensure preservation of their specific values, even if these values belong to a minority."

Documenting Your Sources

After you've looked up your information and taken notes, you can begin to write the actual paper. The main difference between this paper and the others you've written is that you will document your sources in a formal way. You do this for a number of reasons. For one thing, citing your sources gives you credit for all the work that you've done. Further, giving credit to your sources adds to your authority. It shows your reader that you know what has been written about your topic. You can use the sources to support what you believe. Or you can cite sources and then show, with your own arguments and insights or by citing other sources, why they are wrong. In either case the presence of sources makes your paper more effective and more convincing. Acknowledging sources also helps any reader who wants to explore the subject in more depth. He or she knows where to go to find out more.

Beyond that, you want to show where you got your information to avoid plagiarism, a form of theft and something you want to avoid for ethical reasons. Some students fail to realize that plagiarism is wrong. Unfortunately, in many high schools it seems to be acceptable to copy encyclopedia entries and book jacket blurbs without giving credit or using quotation marks. Others feel if they paraphrase ideas that are not their own, because those ideas are now in their own words, they don't have to give credit to the source. However, both of these activities constitute plagiarism and are more than unacceptable.

Another form of plagiarism, buying term papers, is not only dishonest but deprives students of the opportunity to develop their research skills, of the opportunity to learn how to support their opinions and to challenge printed material.

What to Acknowledge

Anything that is common knowledge does not need to be documented. For example, if you know that the Watergate scandal was instrumental in forcing President Nixon to resign, you can say so without any documentation. However, if your reading provided you with specifics, regardless of whether you quote or merely report the ideas, you do need to document. If you repeat judgments of writers you've read, again, whether you quote them or just summarize them, you need to document them.

Source Citation

Formerly, research papers required an elaborate footnote system, which involved placing a number after the last word of a quote or paraphrase and a corresponding number on the bottom of the page. The number on the bottom of the page was followed by the author, title, pages, and other information that identified the source of the information. However, this not only duplicated information in the Works Cited list, but also was difficult for anyone who was not a professional typist because a great deal of skill was involved in deciding how much space to leave at the bottom of the page for the footnotes.

True, some of the better word processing programs can calculate the space for footnotes, but information is still unnecessarily duplicated.

Gradually, this system was replaced by endnotes. The list of notations that corresponded to the reference numbers in the text was placed at the end of the paper. This eliminated the writer's problems with spacing, but still duplicated the information found in the list of Works Cited.

The parenthetical citation form is now generally preferred. It involves merely placing the author's last name, or the title of the article if there is no author, and the page number in parentheses after the last word of the quote or paraphrase. For example:

```
The court said that the "school acted unconstitution-
ally when it suspended students for wearing black
armbands to class in protest against the Vietnam War"
(Lacoyo 54).
```

A fuller description of the source will be found in the list of Works Cited at the end of the whole paper (pages 290–292). It will look like this:

```
Lacoyo, Richard. "Stop the Student Presses." Time 25
     Jan. 1988: 54.
```

Before practicing using this form, there are a few more points to know about working quotes smoothly into your paper.

Introducing Your Quotes

If you name the author in your text, you need to put only the page number in the parentheses.

```
As Brown says, "This kind of censorship is intolera-
ble in a free society" (69).
```

Making the Language of the Quotes Fit

Sometimes, when writers integrate quotes or parts of quotes into their papers, they omit too much, and as a result, the quote and the material around it don't make sense. For example, look at this sentence from a research paper:

```
"Records should be rated," says Hammer. The public
has a right to know "adult material in the lyrics
before they spend money" (12).
```

This is confusing. How does a rating system give people the right to "know adult material" before they purchase a disc? When the student rewrote this section, things became a lot clearer.

```
"Records should be rated," says Hammer. The public
has a right to "know if there is adult material in
the lyrics, before they spend money" (12).
```

Square Brackets

At other times quotes may contain pronouns whose references aren't clear or other words that can confuse the reader. In such cases, you can use square brackets [ ], not parentheses ( ), to show that you've made a change in the original quote. For example, if the surrounding sentences do not make clear who *they* is in this quote

```
Lovitt claims, "They are not mature enough to decide
what is responsible journalism and what is not" (46).
```

the passage can be rewritten this way:

```
Lovitt claims, "[High school students] are not mature
enough to decide what is responsible journalism and
what is not" (46).
```

Ellipses

If you leave out some words from a quote, use ellipses (three spaced dots) to show that some words are missing. Here's a passage as it appeared in an original source:

```
"The stories were too controversial for the conser-
vative administrators--even though they elicited only
yawns when the now-defunct St. Louis Globe Democrat
published them in response to community curiosity."
--Steve Visser, "A Civics Lesson at Hazelwood East,"
The Nation 24 Oct. 1987: 441.
```

In writing her paper, this student decided that the fact that the newspaper that reprinted the stories in question was out of business was not important for her purposes. So she used the quote this way:

```
"The stories were too controversial for the conserva-
tive administrators--even though they elicited only
yawns when the . . . St. Louis Globe Democrat pub-
lished them in response to community curiosity"
(Visser 441).
```

If you leave out part of a quote that goes to the end of a sentence, there are four dots—. . . . The last one is the period.

```
"The stories were too controversial for the conserva-
tive administrators—even though they elicited only
yawns when the now-defunct St. Louis Globe Democrat
published them. . . ." (Visser 441)
```

Obviously, when you leave something out of a quote, you don't want to change the meaning of the passage as is sometimes done in unethical movie ads. The original review may read: "This film is a stunning example of stupidity." The ad, however, says ". . . stunning. . . ."

Longer Quotes

If you are incorporating a quote of three or more sentences into your paper, it may be hard for your reader to keep track of the beginning and end of the material. So instead of using quotation marks, reduce the margins like this:

```
    Censorship not only affects the immediate mate-
rial school officials, parents, and particular groups
don't like, it also has an effect on forms of expres-
sion that are not yet available to the public.
```

```
The chilling effect can also be seen at work
among textbook publishers who have omitted the
word "evolution" from high school biology texts
to avoid offending proponents of creationism.
Critics of the movie rating system point out that
filmmakers have on several occasions deleted
scenes to avoid an X rating. School librarians
are increasingly wary about ordering books and
magazines that might draw protests from parents.
(Meville and Mitchell 26)
```

Note that when this form is used, the citation is *not* included before the final period, but is outside the sentence altogether.

Quotes Within Quotes

If you quote a passage that already has quotation marks within it, the quotes in the original become single quotes. If the original says,

> Many people felt a sense of "deep outrage."

the quote in the body of your paper would look like this:

```
Jones said in his article, "Many people felt a sense
of 'deep outrage' " (123).
```

ACTIVITY 15.6

Here are several note cards and a page of a research paper. Read over the cards and the page of text. Then insert the parenthetical citations (author's name and page number) after each quote or paraphrase. Hint: There are seven statements that need documentation.

```
"Court to Student"
_____

p. 10 Critics say that as a result of the court ruling

"school officials will clamp down on any articles that

cause a stir."
_____

_____

_____

_____

_____
```

Seligman and Namuth

p. 56 Justice William Brennan who dissented from the
majority ruling said the decision will "strangle the
free mind at its source."

Visser "Civics"

p. 442 Principal didn't want faculty advisor to allow
any controversial articles after ones on women coaches
getting less money and grading practices that were seen
as unfair.

Visser "Civics"

p. 442 praises students who sued with aid of ACLU. "To city reporters and to me, the administrators spouted platitudes about responsible journalism and irresponsible students. The kids, they implied, weren't mature enough for First Amendment freedom; school authorities should judge what information was fit to print. But the three students, Kuhlmeir, Smart, and Tippert-West, were the only ones who acted responsibly. They stood up for their rights, the action that gives meaning to the Constitution."

Taylor "Court, 5 to 3"

p. 1A Court says school can censor newspapers, plays and other "school-sponsored activities" because they seem to carry approval from the school authorities.

```
Taylor "Court"

p. 1A The principal at Hazelwood high in Mo. deleted

articles about divorce and student pregnancies from

student newspaper. Said they were "inappropriate."


p. 27A Principal Robert A. Reynolds said he did it to

protect the identity of unnamed students who talked

about their pregnancies in an article and because he

felt references to sexual activity and birth control

methods were not fit for younger students to read.
```

Text

1   A principal in Hazelwood, Missouri, deleted
articles from a high school newspaper in 1983
because he felt the subject matter--divorce and
teen pregnancy--was "inappropriate." He said he
censored the paper to protect the identity of the
unnamed students whose pregnancies were the subject
of one of the articles. He also felt that the
younger students should not read discussion of
sexual activity and birth control.

2   . The Supreme Court, in January 1988, agreed that
he had acted correctly. The Court said in a 5-to-3
decision that school newspapers, plays, and other

"school-sponsored activities" could be censored
because they might seem to convey the school's
approval.

3   Justice William Brennan, who disagreed with the
majority ruling, said that the court's position
would "strangle the free mind at its source." And
others upset by the ruling believe that, as a
result, school officials will "clamp down on any
articles that might cause a stir."

4   Steve Visser, writing about the situation in
Hazelwood before the court reached its decision,
lends support to this view. He notes that after
articles appeared in the school paper discussing
unfair grading and the fact that female coaches
were paid less than their male counterparts, the
principal told the paper's faculty advisor not to
permit any more controversial subjects to appear in
print.

5   Visser further writes of the three students who
brought suit with the help of the American Civil
Liberties Union:

To city reporters and to me, the administrators
spouted platitudes about responsible journalism
and irresponsible students. The kids, they
implied, weren't mature enough for First Amendment freedom; school authorities should judge
what information was fit to print. But the three
students . . . were the only ones who acted responsibly. They stood up for their rights, the
action that gives meaning to the Constitution.

Works Cited

After you've completed your paper, you need to include a list of the works you've used. This list gives fuller information about the sources you mentioned in the body of your paper. The works are listed in alphabetical order by the author's last name, or by title if there is no author.

Here's a Works Cited list for the items in Activity 15.6:

"Court to Student Editors: Teacher Knows Best." U.S.
News & World Report 25 Jan. 1988: 10.

Seligman, Jean, and Tessa Namuth. "A Limit on the
Student Press." Newsweek 25 Jan. 1988: 56.

Taylor, Stuart Jr. "Court, 5 to 3, Widens Powers of
Schools to Act as Censors." New York Times 14 Jan.
1988: 1A, 27A.

Visser, Steve. "A Civics Lesson at Hazelwood East."
The Nation 24 Oct. 1987: 441-442.

Here are some examples of the forms this information should take:

1. A book with one author is cited like this:

Lacquer, Walter. The Terrible Secret. London: Weiden-
feld and Nicolson, 1980.

2. Citation of a book with two authors follows this form:

   ```
   Peters, Thomas J., and Robert H. Waterman, Jr. In
        Search of Excellence. New York: Warner Books, 1984.
   ```

   Only the first author's name is reversed. There's no need to put the second author's last name first because it has no effect on the alphabetical order.

3. If a book has more than three authors, list just the first one, and replace the names of all the others with the abbreviation *et al.* (which means *and others*).

   ```
   Cutlip, Scott M., et al. Effective Public Relations.
        6th ed. Englewood Cliffs, N.J.: Prentice-Hall, 1985.
   ```

   Notice in this entry "6th ed." tells the reader that this is a particular edition of this book. This is important since different editions contain different information and identical information may appear on different pages.

4. If you are citing a collection of essays or stories or poems, the volume's editor's name comes first.

   ```
   Abrahams, William, ed. Prize Stories: The O. Henry
        Awards 1985. Garden City: Anchor Books, 1985.
   ```

5. If you are citing more than one work by the same author, arrange them alphabetically by title. After the first entry, replace the author's name with a dash (typed as three hyphens) and a period.

   ```
   Tyler, Anne. Dinner at the Homesick Restaurant. New
        York: Berkley Books, 1983.

   ---. Morgan's Passing. New York: Berkley Books, 1983.
   ```

6. If there's a translator, list him or her after the title.

   ```
   Susskind, Patrick. Perfume. Trans. John E. Woods. New
        York: Alfred A. Knopf, 1986.
   ```

7. For an article in a weekly periodical, use this form:

   ```
   Shapiro, Walter, and Kim Willenson. "Pentagon Versus
        Press." Newsweek 31 Dec. 1984: 54.
   ```

8. If there's no author, just start with the title.

    ```
    "Court to Student Editors: Teacher Knows Best." U.S.
        News & World Report 25 Jan. 1988: 10.
    ```

9. With a scholarly journal, include the volume and number before the date.

    ```
    Benda, Susan R., and Morton H. Halpren. "Forbidden
        Writers--The Foreign Threat in Literary Garb."
        College English 47:7 (Nov. 1985): 690-97.
    ```

10. For an article reproduced in a collection of essays, list under the last name of the author of the article.

    ```
    Smith, Vicki. "Censoring Students." Censorship in
        America, Ed. Mary Wing. Boston: Newbury Co., 1993.
    ```

11. With a newspaper article, if the paper has more than one section, include the section with the page.

    ```
    "U.S. Cuts Off All Bank Funds of Japanese." St. Louis
        Star-Times 8 Dec. 1941, sec. 1:8.
    ```

12. With an encyclopedia article, you needn't give the pages or volume since all the entries are in alphabetical order.

    ```
    "Censorship." The World Book Encyclopedia. 1982.
    ```

13. For a film, start with the underlined title, then include the director, main actors, company, and date.

    ```
    Citizen Kane. Dir. Orson Wells. With Orson Wells,
        Joseph Cotton, and Everett Sloane. RKO, 1941.
    ```

14. For a television show, you want to include the title, episode, network, local station, and date of broadcast. Add writers or actors if useful.

    ```
    The Story of English. "Black on White." Writ. Robert
        MacNeil. National Educational Television. WNET, New
        York. 15 Aug. 1989.
    ```

ACTIVITY 15.7

Create a list of Works Cited for the four print sources mentioned in the following passage. All the information you need is provided, but you will need to dig out the important details from the passage. Remember to list the sources in alphabetical order, to indent the second line of each entry, and to skip a line between entries.

> Bloodbath City, a new horror film, opened locally
> last week. The critic of The New York Times, Floyd
> Smith, writing on page 25 of section C in an article
> entitled "More Slash and Trash" on Friday, November
> 1, 1994, said it was a film that made one grateful
> for the rating system. However, Rex Jones, on page 5
> of Newsday on the next Monday, found it "creative"
> and "exciting." His review was called "A New Cut."
> Time magazine's critic on November 5th, in a piece
> entitled "More Repulsion," which appeared on pages 15
> and 16, said it was the kind of film parents needed
> to keep their children away from. Finally, Joe Blow
> in the Village Voice of Thursday, November 7th, in a
> review entitled "Juicy New Wave Killings," wrote that
> the film was "fashionably warped." He stated on page
> 65 that the murder committed with a television set
> was a vivid commentary on the evils of the media.

ACTIVITY 15.8

Write a draft of a research paper on the topic you picked for Activity 15.4. Include parenthetical citations and prepare a list of Works Cited at the end.

ACTIVITY 15.9

Exchange research papers with another student and read each other's drafts. Each reader will write to the other, answering the following questions:

1. Does the paper have a clear main idea?
2. What are the strengths of the paper?
3. Does the paper need any work in the areas of unity, coherence, development, and/or style?
4. Does the writer need to document any quotes or paraphrases? In other words, are there places where you wonder where the writer got his or her information?

5. Do all the quotations fit into the flow of the paper?
6. Are the proper forms of documentation used in the text and in the Works Cited?

ACTIVITY 15.10

Rewrite your paper in response to the comments you received, and submit it to your instructor.

Index

Instructor's Guide for

A Writer's Journey
SECOND EDITION

GEOFFREY PLATT
Orange County Community College

D. C. Heath and Company
Lexington, Massachusetts   Toronto

Address editorial correspondence to:

D. C. Heath and Company
125 Spring Street
Lexington, MA 02173

Published simultaneously in Canada.

Printed in the United States of America.

International Standard Book Number: 0-669-35479-1

10 9 8 7 6 5 4 3 2 1

Preface

This expanded guide presents solutions to many of the Activities found in the text. It also offers sample syllabi and some suggestions for presenting the materials based on my experiences using them in the classroom.

The text is obviously designed for use in a collaborative learning environment. I have found this setting, as have many others, to be highly productive in helping writers discover what they have to say and how to say it. And so I strongly recommend using the text as a basis for creating collaborative learning. However, instructors can certainly use the Activities for individual work, especially in Part II of the book, to reinforce editing skills as needed. The writing assignments and other Activities can also be used as the basis of individual or whole class work, depending on the instructor's preference or the need to move through the material more quickly.

When using the Activities in a collaborative setting, particularly those Activities in which the students generate writing rather than edit material in the text, I've found that I must remind students not to make either positive or negative judgments about each other's writing. Readers should simply say what they see or hear. Writers should listen and take notes, but never defend or say what they intended to write but didn't. Writers accept or reject what readers have to say when they rewrite. As they move from group to group or pair to pair, instructors can contribute their observations too, but should save any evaluative comments until they mark the papers.

It is my practice to write "rewrite" on a paper that is unsuccessful, and add questions and suggestions to encourage further revision. Only after the student has revised and/or edited do I assign a grade.

Contents

Preliminary Activity

One strategy that I have found useful on the first or second day, depending on whether a diagnostic or other procedures are needed on the first day, is to have the students interview each other in pairs. Each person spends five minutes collecting information about the other person and writing it down. I ask them to find out the following information about the interviewee:

His or her name

His or her major

His or her interests, in school and out

Then they obtain answers to the six questions in the Preliminary Activity found in "To the Student" on text page x.

After the 10 minutes of interviewing, each partner introduces the other to the whole class, and I comment briefly on their responses.

I find this exercise to be valuable in several ways. First, it is a mini-writing activity in which the students collect information, write it down, if only in an abbreviated form, and present it to an audience. Second, I tell them I'm doing this because they need to know their readers, develop a sense of audience, and meet their editors and fellow writers. Third, it gives me a chance to talk about the content of the course as the issues—getting started, grammar, and so on—arise naturally from the students, instead of my merely talking at them for a long time without interaction. Fourth, the students begin to see writing as less private and isolated, more as interaction with others. And finally, students get to hear the concerns of others, which usually makes them realize they are not facing unique obstacles.

PART I

*Discovering and Organizing Ideas
for Your Readers*

Chapter 1

"Every Journey of a Thousand Miles Begins with One Step"

The purpose of this chapter is to help students overcome their fear of writing, to help them deal with the difficult task of getting started, and to help them avoid the dangers of premature editing.

You can cover the various techniques for getting started—free writing, asking questions, and clustering—in order, or you may wish to return to Chapter 1 to introduce a new tactic each time the students are going to write a paper. Of course, given time limitations, you might use only a few of the many techniques presented for getting started.

Free Writing

ACTIVITY 1.1

As is suggested in the text, you may choose to write along with your students. This strategy is useful for giving them a sense of not being alone in the writing process. However, since this may be the first time many of them are doing free writing, you should look up periodically and encourage the students to keep writing, to repeat the last word, to write "I'm stuck," whatever. Some students will pause and think and try to plan ahead, thus defeating the liberating potential of free writing. I incorporate statements of my own frustration about what to write next and my wish to pause in my free writing. This reinforces the spontaneous nature of free writing and encourages the class to do nonstop writing when I read my sample aloud in Activity 1.2.

ACTIVITY 1.2

It is my practice to read my own unfocused free writing first, not as a model of how it should be done, but to reinforce the students' sense of being part of a community of writers. And the moment of anxiety I feel, even after all these years, serves to increase my awareness of and empathy with the students and their fear of sharing a difficult but fundamental part of the writing process. It is important to keep this situation nonjudgmental. Ideally, students should be asked to volunteer to read their free writing, and no comments should be made, positive or negative, about what they have written. Also students should not editorialize—apologize for or defend their attempts. They should just share what they have written and see what getting started is like for various writers in the class.

ACTIVITY 1.3

Keeping a daily journal gives students training in getting started and so helps them face essay exams, whether in writing courses or other classes. It also reinforces, on a daily basis, writing in their own voices. And so it serves to limit the kind of overinflated writing students believe college instructors expect.

Free writing should not be graded or judged in any way, but I *do* recommend collecting the journals once a week to ensure that students are writing. I put a check on each entry and limit my comments to occasionally responding to their remarks about the course or their writing process, to encouraging them to write more if they have written only a few sentences and obviously *not* done free writing, or to suggesting that they explore some aspect of their journal writing in greater depth another time. I do not read every word of the journals.

At some point in the semester, students may say they are running out of things to write. At that point, I suggest they write about ideas from other courses, news items, or that they write from the point of view of another person—their parents, their children, a public figure, movie star, famous athlete, or the like.

ACTIVITY 1.4

Responses will vary.

ACTIVITY 1.5

During this group activity, your main concern should be to make sure that the ground rules laid down in the activity are followed. You can do this by moving from group to group and listening to student interaction. I have found that I need to intervene mainly to keep the writers from adding ideas not contained in their writing, and to remind listeners not to make judgments or other comments not called for in the activity. And writers need to be reminded to *write down* the feedback they get, not to argue with it.

ACTIVITY 1.6

Before students begin to write, remind them that readers' responses are valuable and should influence what they write, but that they themselves make the decision about what was most valuable, that they need not follow all the comments slavishly.

Asking Questions to Get Started

The activities in this section (1.7 to 1.10) are self-explanatory and will result in a variety of individual responses.

Clustering

Before students create individual clusters, they may find it useful to work together as a class. I ask my students to agree on a topic, and I write down on the board the various ideas that they contribute, thus producing a group cluster.

Again there will be a variety of responses to Activities 1.11 and 1.12.

Chapter 2

Making Contracts with Your Reader

All the tactics introduced in Chapter 1 for getting started—free writing, asking questions, and clustering—can be repeated in the setting of the whole class, in addition to the activities contained in this chapter, as the basis for discussions on finding the main idea and making a contract with readers.

ACTIVITY 2.1

Wordings will vary, but answers should basically

1. Restate the first sentence.

2. Restate the last sentence.

3. Express the idea that the writer's first job was difficult.

4. Contain the idea that opinion on the polar explorers has changed and that Amundsen is now seen in a more positive light than Scott.

ACTIVITY 2.2

Individual responses will vary.

ACTIVITY 2.3

1. Ideas the writer should cut are:

   Sentences 5, about wanting to pass the course.

   Sentences 7 and 8, about friends and loneliness.

   The next to last sentence, about the weather.

2. Ideas the writer should cut are:

The first two sentences.

Sentences 4, 5, and 6, which compare different kinds of transportation.

Sentence 7 as it stands doesn't really fit either, but it could be expanded if the writer were to show how the romance of railroads contributes to the specialness of the atmosphere of the old building. However, if this notion cannot be developed, the sentence is not part of the contract.

ACTIVITY 2.4

Answers will vary, depending on the main idea a student finds. The important thing is that students are clear about why they choose to include or omit particular details. However, it seems to me that the main idea in the first selection is the student's response to the book, not the nature of the antiutopia. Pointing out where the student has written the most can be useful in leading her to see the difference between the topic, here the terrible society, and the potential contract, her *feelings* about the society. Students need to see that if they pick a main idea centered on the nature of the society, they will need to cut all their responses to it and so lose a lot. Understanding this is extremely valuable because many students, for reasons unknown to me, feel they should not offer their own opinions in a paper, a belief that restricts what they have to say in writing situations.

ACTIVITY 2.5

Answers will vary. The important concern here is that whatever students decide to include clearly illustrates their main idea. I think, however, the last sentence contains the potential main idea.

ACTIVITY 2.6

Answers will vary.

ACTIVITY 2.7

New Main Idea: Responses will vary, but this is an opportunity to talk, in a preliminary way, about paraphrasing and the effects of different word choices on readers. I urge the students not to copy the exact words found in the body of the text.

Evidence from   This should include the underlined material on pages 29–31.
Free Writing:

New Evidence: This should include the following:

The number of trials she could attend (paragraph 2).

The specifics about locations (paragraph 2).

All of paragraph 5 after the first two sentences.

All of paragraph 6.

ACTIVITY 2.8

Individual responses will vary.

EDITING ACTIVITY

This is the first of the Editing Activities that you will find at or near the end of each chapter in Part I. At this point, you can either go to the chapter in Part II that is mentioned in these activities and cover the material, doing some or all of the activities with the class, or you can refer students to the chapter for individual work. Of course, you could use a combination of the two approaches. In any case, you can locate the answers to the activities in the editing and sentence-combining chapters in Part II of this guide.

ACTIVITY 2.9

This is the first of a series of final writing and exchange activities, each of which will build on the previous skills and will add another aspect of writing for the reader to check. Here the emphasis is on main idea. The next chapter will ask the student editor to check for development as well as main idea. And the chapter after that adds coherence, and so on. The end-of-the-chapter activities in Part II each add a particular mechanical skill to the checklist.

Whenever students exchange papers, they should work with a different partner.

When I read these activities, I read over the first draft primarily to see what changes the student has made for the second version, but I rarely make any comments on it. I reserve major comments and suggestions for revision on the second draft. I also comment on the editor's work and the writer's responses. If there is time, it is useful for the editor to read the writer's comments on his or her editing.

One valuable result of this type of activity, in addition to making writers aware of a larger audience and their needs and showing how writers can benefit from feedback before producing a final draft, is that most of the time the second drafts are better, even if the editor's comments are a bit off. Student writers frequently state that their editors were not helpful, but then produce a much stronger second draft anyway because of their awareness of the presence of a reader.

Peer editing also makes students aware that the concerns of the instructor are not idiosyncratic, that they are not just writing to please one person—the teacher. Peer editing and revision make the writing process clearer to the writer, too.

My experience is that editors' comments are often too broad or vague. Calling their attention to this—and asking them to be more specific— reinforces the theme of the next and later chapters: that writers need to think about what readers need to know.

Whole Class Work on Sample Papers

Once students begin to produce drafts, paragraphs, and finally essays, I find it productive periodically to spend a class session looking at copies of their work, photocopied but with the names covered up, in the setting of the whole class.

This provides an opportunity to discuss a paper's strengths and areas for improvement in greater detail than can be done with comments in the margins. It is also another setting in which writers can get feedback from many editors. There is great value in moving to a larger audience and seeing that many people find the same strength or weakness in a particular area or aspect of a piece of writing.

I usually make enough copies so two students must share each one. This not only saves trees and the institution's budget, but also forces the students to work together first in pairs, and then as a whole class.

I ask them to read the piece of writing once to get the general idea. After a second reading, students write down answers to specific questions. Then we discuss those answers as a class.

Readers always answer this question first:

1. What do you like about the paper?

   This positive feedback is necessary because the person whose paper is being edited in this way needs to be put at ease. Although there are no names on the papers, I refer to the writer as "he" and "she" at different times to further protect that person's identity. Also, I throw out reminders at various points in the process that we are talking about writing, not writers, and that the purpose is to aid the writer in his or her revision, to offer options for improvement, not to criticize or say what he or she should have done.

2. They state the main idea.

3. After Chapter 3, students can suggest where they want or need to hear more.

4. Later I add questions on organization and coherence.

5. The last question, after or without items 2 and 3, depending on the point in the semester, relates to editing: what can the writer do to improve the work at the sentence level? As always, we suggest options rather than definitive answers. Be sure to remind students that here they are thinking about specific editing and proofreading skills, but that a rewrite that adds details and changes organization, topic sentence, or main idea may no longer contain the particular sentences we are looking at right now.

Chapter 3

Developing and Supporting Your Contract

ACTIVITY 3.1

Answers will vary, but here are some guidelines that show what questions should be answered by the students' revised statements:

1. Which movie? In what ways was it "good"?

2. Which chair? What's wrong with it?

3. Why do you have a more difficult time? In what ways, particularly?

4. What actions or words might they imitate? How might they get into trouble? What kind of trouble?

5. Which course? How did it help? For which other courses did it provide help?

6. Which diets? How can they be dangerous? What are the dangers?

7. What "things"? In what ways are they confusing?

8. What kinds of problems? Why? Which writer? What was the writer trying to say?

9. Which car? What features in particular?

10. Who? In what way is she talented? To what degree?

ACTIVITY 3.2

The writing and how the small group responds to it will vary. You may want to move from group to group to hear responses and to add your own as well.

ACTIVITY 3.3

Responses will vary, but the major concern is that the students use specific details and examples to support the value judgments and other generalizations. Changes should provide answers to questions the reader may have, such as the following (only paragraphs 1 and 2 are covered here):

1. What kind of independence? How is it helpful? Why do women especially need it? Why and how will it help children? What financial benefits will they get?

2. Who influences the child outside the home? In what ways? How exactly might these influences be harmful? How exactly does the loneliness manifest itself? How is the resentment shown?

ACTIVITY 3.4

A wide range of responses is possible.

ACTIVITY 3.5

Answers will vary. For question 1, they should be extremely specific; for question 2, the selected main idea should express support for these workers going on strike.

ACTIVITY 3.6

Responses will vary.

ACTIVITY 3.7

Responses will vary.

ACTIVITY 3.8

Answers will vary, but they probably will be similar to these:

1. Tokyo in particular and Japan in general offer a high degree of personal safety and freedom from crime, but there is a price to pay—a loss of personal freedom.

2. The details about the park create a sense of calm, security, and safety. Then the mood shifts to a feeling of isolation. Perhaps the reader expects danger or a continuation of the atmosphere of peace and quiet. In any case, the appearance of the police officer is a surprise and an intrusion. The writer wants the reader to feel uncomfortable at that point.

3. The details about Franco's Spain are used for comparison/contrast. (You may have to elicit facts or tell students about Franco.) In both cases the writer felt bad, but in Japan the officer is not making a show of his power; he is polite. He is not a symbol of a dictatorship; he is a symbol of the lack of personal freedom and privacy.

4. Examples might include being able to sit alone in a park at night in perfect safety, losing a wallet in one city and having it returned in another, and being able to carry and display large sums of money without fear.

5. They create a sense of safety and security by harsh punishments, but also by the lack of privacy. Japan is a society in which who you are, where you were born, where you live, and what you do is public knowledge.

6. Responses will vary.

7. Specifics may include the writer's statement at the end that he felt he'd suffered some essential loss, his discomfort at being asked for his passport, the reference to the "old Japan hand's" "joyless" laugh, and the sense that there is nowhere to turn.

8. Responses will vary.

ACTIVITIES 3.9, 3.10, 3.11, AND 3.12

These four activities will produce a variety of papers, responses to them, and revisions.

EDITING ACTIVITY

See the comments at the end of Chapter 2 in this guide, page 8.

Chapter 4

Using Your Reader's Needs to Organize Paragraphs

Students will respond in various ways to the questions at the end of the paper on being a returning student (pages 70–71). The exact wording will of course vary, but the ideas should be similar to these:

Paragraph 3   I worry about leaving my son with other people.

Paragraph 4   My responsibilities at home leave me little time for my studies.

Paragraph 5   Compared to her fellow students, she cares more about her work, appreciates more the value of education, and has a greater sense of accomplishment because of the odds she faces.

Paragraph 6   Restates the writer's main idea.

ACTIVITY 4.1

Paragraph 2   "Once I was on my own . . ."

Paragraph 3   "I knew how to work a washing machine . . ."

Paragraph 4   "The first time I cleaned the bathroom . . ."

ACTIVITY 4.2

Main Idea: My height makes me feel like an outsider.

Sections: There will be one on the writer's experiences in grade school, one on high school, and one on the present.

Details:

1. What happened on the first day of school. (You might ask the students to speculate here, and in the next two sections as well, about what specifically might have happened—he was made fun of, left out of games, and so on.)

2. A range of specifics about what happened at high school dances.

3. A range of specifics about how he feels uncomfortable today.

ACTIVITIES 4.3, 4.4, AND 4.5

Varied writing and individual responses.

ACTIVITY 4.6

The wording will vary, but this is an opportunity to review complete sentences if necessary. Here's one possible order for the sentences:

i, b, d, f, g, c, a, e, h, j

ACTIVITIES 4.7, 4.8, AND 4.9

Individual paragraphs and responses.

ACTIVITY 4.10

Main Idea: I enjoyed my trip to Maine.

Major Points: I enjoyed the biking because of the terrain and scenery, the ocean, which was clean and cool, and the really special Fourth of July display.

ACTIVITY 4.11

Main Idea: Not stated directly in a topic sentence, but implied, is the idea that the pass/fail system is less than ideal.

The main categories expressed the ideas that pass/fail grades:

don't motivate poor students.

discourage good ones from trying as hard as the otherwise might.

don't show employers and other schools what students can really do.

New Idea: It is time for a change to letter grades.

ACTIVITY 4.12

Individual writing and responses.

EDITING ACTIVITY

See the comments in the Editing Activity section of Chapter 2, page 8.

ACTIVITY 4.13

Individual responses and writing. The students *do* need to recognize that the cartoon is saying that employers do not trust their workers and that the final panel is ironic.

Chapter 5

Organizing the Whole Paper to Meet Your Reader's Needs

ACTIVITIES 5.1, 5.2, AND 5.3

These activities will produce individualized responses. You will probably have to remind the students that their retroactive outlines should focus on how the parts of their papers work, not just on what they contain.

ACTIVITY 5.4

The suggested comparison/contrast topics are deliberately broad to allow for a wide range of possible responses; however, some students will benefit from a narrower focus. For those students you can easily amend these topics to, say, two types of buildings used for the same purpose, or two types of jobs available near campus.

ACTIVITY 5.5

Main Idea: Having an auto accident is one experience I'd never want to repeat.

Main Categories: The location, the suddenness, the actual event, and the writer's feelings afterward are the main sections that are forecast by the introduction.

Organizational Principles: Overall, the writer used time order for the body paragraphs of the paper.

Paragraph 1, the introductory paragraph, provides a generalized frame related to the issue of experiences people would hate to repeat. It then moves to the specific event the writer is going to examine. In doing so, it does set up a contrast. After the main idea is stated, the paragraph concludes with a forecast of what the body of the paper will show.

Paragraph 2 uses spatial order to describe the location and time order to advance the narrative.

Paragraph 3 uses time order. (You might want to point out the shift in style to shorter, more abrupt sentences here, paralleling the tension of the situation.)

Paragraph 4 continues with time order. (You might ask the students to identify the transition at the beginning of the paragraph and to note the change to longer sentences to present a situation that, no doubt, seemed to last a long time for the writer.)

Paragraph 5 opens with a brief transition and continues with time order.

Paragraph 6, the conclusion, restates the main idea and goes further, stating a result of the worst day in the writer's life.

ACTIVITY 5.6

Individual responses will vary.

EDITING ACTIVITY

See the comments in Chapter 2, page 8.

ACTIVITY 5.7

1. Main idea: A pair of hoaxers tricked scientists and researchers into believing circles and other designs in fields they themselves had made were created by nonhuman forces. (Wording will vary.)

2. Some thought the patterns were nonhuman in origin, proof of "superior intelligence," made by UFOs, weather, and ball lightning.

3. Students should paraphrase details from paragraph 9.

4. Students need to look again at the last paragraph and speculate about why people still want to believe in supernatural causes for the circles. These might include not being willing to admit error, wishing there to be supernatural events to make life more interesting, and wanting to be able to discover the new and unusual.

ACTIVITY 5.8

Individual responses will vary.

Chapter 6

Getting to Know Your Readers

ACTIVITY 6.1

A. The first passage might be addressed to the citizens of the town in a letter to the editor of a newspaper with the expectation that it will be reprinted in the paper. The language is fairly formal, and the writer assumes that the readers are concerned with the environment and the tax base of the town. (So perhaps business owners and government officials are also assumed to be part of the potential audience, along with public-minded citizens.)

B. The second passage is less formal and addresses the reader directly. Students might point to the use of "Let's" as an appeal directly to the reader and as an attempt to associate the writer with the reader. This is in contrast to the respectful distance maintained in passage A. Passage B seems to be aimed at an average person concerned with the quality of life and the well-being of his or her family.

ACTIVITY 6.2

Responses will vary.

ACTIVITY 6.3

Responses will vary, but students should keep in mind the questions at the end of Activity 6.2 as they develop their drafts.

ACTIVITY 6.4

Responses will vary.

ACTIVITY 6.5

Responses will vary. Again, it is important to remind students to *listen* to feedback, not to respond to it by talking about what they *intended* to write.

ACTIVITY 6.6

1. The writer begins by acknowledging three reasons why people oppose the use of computers before she starts to undercut those arguments.

2. She shows, in paragraph 2, that "computer errors" are really human errors. (Ask the students to support this generalization with specifics from the paragraph.)

3. In paragraph 3, the writer shows how computers, in fact, create more jobs. (Again, ask for specific examples supporting this argument.)

4. Paragraph 5 begins with a concession to the other side, then moves to the argument that we master other difficult tasks, and finally shows that learning to use a computer is not as hard as some think. (Elicit the specifics that support these points.)

5. Answers may vary, but one explanation could be that readers first need to be shown that computers are useful. Once readers agree that computers help some people, they can be shown that computers don't harm people. At this point readers may be thinking, "That's fine for others, but I can't use them." So the next logical step is to show them that they *can* learn to use them.

6. The company's decision was probably based on the ideas in the preceding paragraph, so starting with this provides a link between the two. Also, the decision comes before the results. Finally, it makes sense to first show that you understand what the readers fear before you show that the results won't be so bad. In other words, giving what seems to be bad news first not only brings the writer and readers into seeming agreement, but it makes the readers more likely to accept the good news because it calms their fears. They want to accept it.

ACTIVITY 6.7

1. The writer establishes a common ground with phrases like "As we know," "Those of us who use computers daily," and "our faithful

machines" (paragraph 2). Students can find additional examples in the paper.

2. The writer uses the beliefs of those who disagree to underscore the common ground between herself and her friendly readers. This cements writer and readers. "It's hard to believe, but some people are still resisting the use of computers in the workplace" (paragraph 1). This implies we're smart and they're not. This is reinforced by the last paragraph. Creating an "us versus them" situation involves the readers. They want to read on and find out more ways in which they are in the know.

3. The writer has omitted negative points about computers. She doesn't say they do sometimes mess up or that some people may lose their jobs. There's no reason to for this audience. They're on her side, and she doesn't want to suggest reasons why they shouldn't be. Besides, she has used some objections to strengthen her position by showing how unfounded they are.

4. She includes shared experiences about dealing with the difficulties of learning (getting pickles out of a jar in the next to last paragraph) and the shared judgment about typewriters. Again, the bond between writer and readers is being strengthened.

ACTIVITY 6.8

Responses will vary.

ACTIVITY 6.9

1. Elbow assumes his readers may react negatively to the idea of free writing: "I find free writing offends some people" (paragraph 1) and the long quotation in paragraph 3.

2. He seems to agree—"Yes, it produces garbage" (paragraph 3) and then undercuts the agreement—"But that's all right." Or in paragraph 5, he agrees there is a negative kind of "carelessness" before showing there is a positive kind. So he moves from stating objections and showing why they are wrong, one at a time, to making his case most strongly in the final paragraph.

3. He says those readers would be right if his approach were carried to an extreme, if people did nothing but free write.

4. He turns around the point about writing "garbage" by saying the "garbage" is there, but not in the writing. Rather, he says, it is in our heads. And then he goes on to show that free writing solves the very concern his readers might have. Free writing helps get rid of "garbage."

5. In the last paragraph, as well as restating his "garbage" argument, Elbow anticipates that his readers may assume that free writing is just therapy, a natural response to his argument in the previous paragraph. But he shows that because it takes the focus off writing better and puts it on personal issues, free writing ends up producing better writing.

ACTIVITY 6.10

1. Vonnegut assumes that his readers agree with him, and, perhaps somewhat arrogantly, that those who don't aren't worth writing to.

2. He doesn't have to acknowledge that the opposition has any valid points, and he can engage in name calling—"lunks," "dimwitted," "orangutans," and worse. He can be emotional and outrageous rather than rational and logical. Since he doesn't have to convince, he can simply express his emotions, and in the final paragraphs, enjoy the triumph of his position.

3. The readers are not eager to be associated with the "illiterates," so this kind of attack makes them identify even more strongly with the writer and his position.

4. He does assume that those who share his point of view might try to convince others to change their minds. However, he feels the attempt is a waste of time. At this one point in the piece in which he knows he may be at odds with his readers, he does present their side first.

5. Vonnegut starts the piece by narrating an incident, then discusses its significance, proposes a half-serious solution, rejects another solution, and, finally, celebrates the victory of his side.

6. He is answering questions from his readers. "What do you think about that situation?" He vents his anger. "What can we do about it?" He offers an unrealistic, but meaningful solution. "But seriously what can we do?" Here readers are expecting him to call for protests, letter writing, and so on. But he tells them not to bother. "So what should we do?" The answer: Don't worry. We'll win.

ACTIVITIES 6.11, 6.12, 6.13, 6.14, AND 6.15

There will be a wide range of responses to these activities.

EDITING ACTIVITY

See the comments in Chapter 2, page 8.

Chapter 7

Creating Coherence

ACTIVITY 7.1

1. However . . . today: Sets up the contrast between society's attitude toward women in the present and in the past.

2. Consequently: Shows cause (both parents are working) and effect (women are not home all day).

3. And so: Also shows cause (women are not home all day) and effect (mothers have less time to spend with their children).

4. Therefore: Shows the result of women not having time to spend with their children (both parents are involved in raising the children).

5. Now: Emphasizes, once again, the contrast between the past and the current situation.

6. More than before: Shows a greater number of opportunities for men now than in the past.

7. Too: Shows addition (men as well as women).

8. So: Indicates result (change in the decisions of courts) of previous sentence (men have had a chance to show that they can raise children).

ACTIVITY 7.2

Answers may vary, but here is one possible solution:

Paragraph 1   In other words . . . For example . . . However . . . At the same time . . . Also . . . Furthermore . . .

Paragraph 2   For instance . . . On the one hand . . . On the other hand . . . Still . . . Ultimately . . . Indeed . . .

ACTIVITY 7.3

Paragraph 1   <u>Both women</u> in sentences 3 and 4

Paragraph 2   <u>Husbands</u> in sentence 1
(back to <u>husbands</u> in sentence 4, paragraph 1, and ahead to sentence 2, paragraph 2)

<u>wives</u> in sentences 1 and 2

<u>"Yellow Wallpaper"</u> in sentence 2 (back to that title in the first line of paragraph 1)

<u>writing</u> in sentences 3 and 4

<u>John</u> in sentences 3 and 4

<u>"Really, Doesn't Crime Pay?"</u> in sentence 5 (back to the same title in paragraph 1)

<u>writings</u> in sentence 5 (back to <u>writing</u> in sentences 3 and 4)

<u>fear</u> in sentence 5 (repeats the idea of <u>afraid</u> in sentence 4)

ACTIVITY 7.4

In the period of which we speak, there reigned in the cities a <u>stench</u> barely conceivable to us modern men and women. The streets <u>stank</u> of manure, the courtyards of urine, the stairwells <u>stank</u> of moldering wood and rat droppings, the kitchens of spoiled cabbage and mutton fat; the unaired parlors <u>stank</u> of stale dust, the bedrooms of greasy sheets, damp feather beds, and the pungently sweet aroma of chamber pots. The <u>stench</u> of sulfur rose from the chimneys, the <u>stench</u> of caustic lyes from the tanneries, and from the slaughterhouses came the <u>stench</u> of congealed blood. People <u>stank</u> of sweat and unwashed clothes; from their mouths came the <u>stench</u> of rotting teeth, from their bellies that of onions, and from their bodies, if they were no longer very young, came the <u>stench</u> of rancid cheese and sour milk and tumorous disease. The river <u>stank</u>, the marketplaces <u>stank</u>, the churches <u>stank</u>, it <u>stank</u> beneath the bridges and in the palaces. The peasant <u>stank</u> as did the priest, the apprentice as did his master's wife, the whole of the aristocracy <u>stank</u>, even the king himself <u>stank</u>, <u>stank</u> like a rank lion, and the queen like an old goat, summer and winter. For in the eighteenth century there was nothing to hinder bacteria busy at decomposition, and so there was no human activity, either constructive or destructive, no manifestation of germinating or decaying life that was not accompanied by <u>stench</u>.

ACTIVITY 7.5

Here's one solution:

I oppose gun control because it is against the Constitution, which guarantees us the right to own firearms. Thus, I oppose this unconstitutional ban that violates our rights.

ACTIVITY 7.6

Sometimes a person has to support his family by doing something that goes against <u>his</u> morals like working at a plant that builds nuclear weapons. And there's no way <u>he</u> can support <u>them</u> on an unemployment check. However, in other cases the person realizes that money isn't everything. <u>He</u> realizes that <u>it</u> can't buy happiness and earning <u>it</u> in a particular way can cost him <u>his</u> family. If an individual quits <u>his</u> job, there are ways <u>he</u> can find another job. It may not pay as much as the first job, but <u>he</u> and <u>his</u> family can cut back on some little extras. But if <u>he</u> stays on a job that involves doing something immoral, <u>he</u> will be eaten up inside. This emotional state will affect the family as a whole. What happens on the job may fill <u>him</u> with guilt and anger at <u>himself</u>. He will bring these feelings home and <u>he</u> might take <u>them</u> out on those near and dear to <u>him</u>.

ACTIVITY 7.7

Here are some of the ways in which the ideas are connected:

1. Murray links paragraph 3 to paragraph 2 by using the word *need* in the first line of paragraph 3, which takes the reader back to *need* at the end of paragraph 2. Paragraph 3 develops examples of the *needs* writers have.

2. Many sentences being with *We* which is used as a unifying device.

3. Paragraph 3 ends with a statement that in all of the cases he mentioned, information is necessary. This idea serves as a link to the next paragraph.

4. Paragraph 4 continues dealing with the idea of the *need* for information and expands on it, providing illustrations.

5. There is a repetition of *we*, which links paragraph 4 not only to the preceding one but to the first two paragraphs as well.

6. The series of examples in these later paragraphs echoes the list of reasons in the first paragraph.

7. And, finally, paragraph 4 ends with a summary statement that ties up the ideas it contains and reminds the reader of the importance of the audience, mentioned in paragraph 2.

ACTIVITY 7.8

1. No response called for.

2. The wording can vary (or perhaps students will find a different main idea); most likely, they will come up with something like this:

   It's too bad that we neglect older people, because they have a lot to offer to us.

3. If students use the main idea given above, the sentences could be ordered this way:

(1) b	(7) c
(2) j	(8) g
(3) k	(9) i
(4) a	(10) h
(5) f	(11) d
(6) e	

4. Answers will vary.

5. Answers will vary, but if students are following the main idea and sentence order listed above, their writing will need to show contrast between how we neglect older people and why this is a mistake. They will also need to signal the shifts between the different examples of what older people have to offer.

ACTIVITY 7.9

Responses will vary.

ACTIVITY 7.10

Responses will vary, but here is one model:

Paragraph 3

Reader	So what do the teachers know?
Writer	A teacher who is knowledgeable in the subject . . . can teach them about the development of their bodies. . . .
Reader	Will that help them with the problems you mentioned earlier?
Writer	They can teach the children about . . . diseases. . . .
Reader	Oh, but don't they present just scientific facts?
Writer	They can talk about the emotional side too.
Reader	But couldn't parents do that?
Writer	Sure . . . but a lot of them [don't].

Paragraph 4

Reader	Won't talking about sex cause promiscuity?

Writer	Some people might argue that . . . but promiscuity does not come about as a result. . .
Reader	Are you sure?
Writer	The knowledge does not make them run out and have sex.
Reader	So what does having the knowledge do?
Writer	[It] makes them think twice before they act.
Reader	And if they do have sex?
Writer	They are less likely to have unwanted pregnancies [and] to catch diseases.

Paragraph 5

Reader	I'd still like to keep kids away from sex.
Writer	[But] sex is discussed everywhere, and parents are not doing their jobs. . . . Some responsible person . . . must teach the children. . . .
Reader	Yes, but why a teacher?
Writer	The greatest number of children will be reached.

ACTIVITY 7.11

Wording will vary, but answers should include these ideas:

1. Multiple choice tests are harmful for teaching and learning.

2. a. Students don't learn.
   b. These tests lead students to think in terms of isolated facts, not to think about the significance of the facts (paragraph 8).
   c. Many subjects require more than just knowing facts and information (paragraph 9).
   d. The tests stress knowing disconnected facts (paragraph 10).

3. The piece is organized by first catching the reader's interest (paragraphs 1 and 2), showing major problems, and then moving to a cause that perhaps the reader hadn't thought about (paragraph 2).

    The writer acknowledges the claims of multiple-choice proponents (paragraph 4) and then refutes them. This helps him to decide how to order his arguments. He says if those who favor multiple-choice tests are right, it must be a good approach (paragraph 5), but then he goes on to illustrate why they are not right.

    Near the end, the author cites an expert in education to add authority to his point of view.

4. Coherence is created in many ways. For example, Barzun seduces the reader with the point about Valley Forge. He seems to be showing what multiple-choice tests can do, and the reader who holds that they are useful tools reads along comfortably. But then the writer surprises the reader, showing how the knowledge of this particular isolated fact is really not helpful at all.

5. The students could point to *But* (paragraphs 2 and 5) as an example of a transition. They could point to the repetitions of the words *test* and *tests*. They could illustrate pronoun use with *They* (paragraph 4) or *this* (paragraph 7). They could illustrate having a conversation with the reader by pointing to the section in paragraph 7 in which Barzun actually states a question he anticipates from the reader and goes on to answer it. Of course, there are many other possibilities.

ACTIVITIES 7.12, 7.13, 7.14, 7.15, AND 7.16

These activities will lead to a variety of responses.

EDITING ACTIVITY

See the comments in Chapter 2, page 8.

PART II

Editing and Proofreading

Chapter 8

Sentence Boundaries

ACTIVITY 8.1

The sentence subjects and verb parts are marked below. Sentences 1, 2, 5, 7, 8, and 10 were complete. The fragments may be corrected in several different ways.

1. <u>My little brother</u> <u>plays</u> . . .

2. <u>I</u> <u>used to be addicted</u> . . .

3. <u>I</u> <u>spent</u> hours . . . (subject missing)
   <u>Spending</u> hours . . . <u>was</u> my idea of fun. (verb part missing)

4. <u>I</u> <u>saved</u> . . . (verb part missing)

5. <u>Playing</u> <u>was</u> . . .

6. <u>It</u> <u>took</u> away all the tension . . . (subject missing)

7. <u>These machines</u> <u>were</u> . . .

8. At home, <u>I</u> also <u>played</u> . . .

9. <u>Games</u> like . . . <u>were</u> my favorites. (verb part missing)

10. . . . <u>these games</u> <u>were</u> . . .

ACTIVITY 8.2

The wording of the explanations of why we are left hanging—and the student corrections—will vary. Here is one version of the corrected passage:

1   I love horror films because I liked being scared. Of course, I
     wouldn't like being in a terrifying situation in real life. However, these

33

movies get my pulse racing. At the same time, knowing that I will be safe when the scene is over and knowing that I can close my eyes if the blood and gore get to be too much are fun. Although I don't want to face physical harm, there is a part of me that wants to feel the thrill of danger and enjoys coming through a horrifying experience and living to tell about it.

2   The special effects are a turn-on too. I like figuring out how they are done, and I admire the skill that is involved in creating them. On the other hand, poorly done effects are fun too. Even though we know the monster is stepping on toy cars and cardboard buildings, my friends and I have fun screaming out loud. I remember one film in which a killer baby attacked people. It was so funny watching the rubber baby being thrown through the air.

ACTIVITY 8.3

As stated in the instructions, there are a variety of solutions. The following is just one possibility:

The Shakers were noted for their fine furniture and their beautiful architecture, which were constructed with perfect proportions and balance. The Shakers felt that work was a form of prayer, so everything that they did was done the best way they knew how, with total dedication, and no rough edges. There were no short cuts, no unfinished corners. Their buildings reflected their beliefs in a way. Since men and women lived separately, for the Shakers did not permit sexual intercourse among members of their sect, they constructed dwellings with separate doors outside and separate staircases inside for use by members of each sex. Because they had few personal possessions, their rooms were empty and bare. Reflecting the simplicity of their lives, their architecture, furniture, and even their utensils had simple lines and no trim or fancy designs or carvings of any kind whatsoever. You can see Shaker villages in several states, for instance, in Massachusetts, New Hampshire, Maine, and Kentucky.

ACTIVITY 8.4

There are often several ways to correct the errors. For instance, students could change the second sentence to "Every household gadget that comes on the market is fair game to me. I have had . . ." or "Every household gadget is fair game to me; for example, I have had . . ." "Whenever I hear of a new toy, I have to get it; however, . . ." could also read "Whenever I hear of a new toy, I have to get it. However, . . ." The following are suggested corrections:

Paragraph 1   See above.

Paragraph 2   My initial reaction was that I didn't need one. Then some close friends bought one. At their house I played a game . . . I was fascinated, but I felt . . . I pondered this for about two months; meanwhile, I recalled . . . She said to me, "That's great. However, it's nothing compared to a word processor. . ."

Paragraph 3   Some friends helped me set up the computer. They put . . . They then told me . . . BASIC. When they left, I was left with two tomes . . . Anyone . . . knows how I felt. I couldn't understand . . .

ACTIVITY 8.5

As in Activity 8.4, several solutions are possible. What follows is just one set of corrections:

Paragraph 1   Terror set in, and fear came with every breath. . . . Then I made daily phone calls to friends for help and instructions. Sometimes, they were quite patient; other times, they told me, "Read the book. It's in there. Look it up in the index."

Paragraph 2   I found a book on DOS while visiting a bookstore. I bought it, and it made sense. . . After I made it halfway through this book, suddenly all the instructions made sense. . . I played Dungeons . . . morning and played with the word processor. I even bought some new games, becoming hooked . . .

ACTIVITY 8.6

Responses will vary.

Chapter 9

Editing Verb Usage

ACTIVITY 9.1

1   I <u>have</u> mixed feelings about TV talk shows. In some ways they <u>are</u> good. After all, they <u>enlighten</u> the public about injustices, unfair laws, corrupt practices in government and business, and environmental issues. They <u>may change</u> peoples' attitudes about sex roles, members of various ethnic groups, and people who <u>think</u> or <u>act</u> differently than the majority of viewers.

2   However, these shows <u>are</u> often silly and <u>deal</u> with unimportant issues like the lives of celebrities or <u>offer</u> empty, unrealistic solutions to serious problems. For example, a talk show host <u>asks</u> a guest or a member of the audience how a situation like drug use <u>can be</u> corrected. The answer nine times out of ten <u>will be</u> "We all <u>have to work</u> together." That really <u>tells</u> the viewer a lot. Many people <u>watch</u> these shows just <u>to see</u> what kind of outrageous thing <u>will happen</u>. <u>Will</u> Donahue <u>wear</u> a skirt again? <u>Will</u> someone <u>punch</u> Geraldo in the nose, or <u>will</u> he <u>go</u> to a nudist colony? For these reasons, I often <u>think</u> that it <u>is</u> a waste of time <u>to watch</u> these shows.

ACTIVITY 9.2

Here is one solution:

What does an employee do when the company she works for <u>decides</u> to move to another location? I guess it <u>depends</u> on whether the worker <u>wants</u> to move to another town. Making this decision <u>involves</u> thinking about the wishes of members of the family. What the new location has to offer also <u>is</u> a factor. A person who <u>likes</u> to go to the theater, for example, would be miserable if she <u>moves</u> to a location far from a major city. If the worker <u>owns</u> a home, how much can she get for her house and what homes cost in the new community <u>become</u> major concerns. If she rents, then she is concerned with rents in the new location. Sometimes, companies <u>pay</u> bonuses to workers who go with them to the new location. This <u>helps</u> some people to make the move while the offer of extra money only <u>makes</u> things harder for others. Still other employees <u>have</u> to decide whether the disadvantages of a long commute <u>are</u> outweighed by the advantages of staying with a company where they <u>have</u> accumulated retirement and where their chances for advancement <u>are</u> good. All of these concerns <u>make</u> the decision to stay with the company or to look for work elsewhere very difficult.

ACTIVITY 9.3

Subject-verb agreement errors can be corrected as follows:

1   There <u>are</u> different ways of studying. Some students, like my friend Janet, <u>prefer</u> to study while watching television or listening to the stereo. However, other students, including another friend, Joan, <u>feel</u> that studying in a quiet place with no distractions is best. And I agree with Joan.

2   Janet says that distracting noises <u>are</u> not a problem for her. She claims that music and TV shows <u>relax</u> her so she can do a better job on her assignments and papers. Behind her claims <u>is</u> just an excuse for not wanting to concentrate on her work. At least that's what I think. Janet is getting low grades. Here <u>is</u> the cause—she can't give her full attention to what she is doing. She, as well as many other students, <u>doesn't</u> realize how distracted she is by what's going on around her.

ACTIVITY 9.4

A. Joan and I <u>agree</u> about the best kind of environment in which to study. Each of us <u>finds</u> that distractions cause problems. For example, Joan says that if she hears a song on the radio while she is writing a paper, she finds that words from the song <u>end</u> up on her page. I, too, have discovered that either words or an idea from a TV show <u>finds</u> its way into my thoughts if I try to study with the TV on in the same room. As a result, I misunderstand what I am reading, or many hours of my limited time after work in the evening <u>are</u> wasted because I have to read the chapter or section all over again. Everyone <u>has</u> the right to his or her own opinion, but as a result of our experiences, Joan and I always <u>study</u> in a quiet place.

B. Attending college classes regularly <u>is</u> very important. Economics <u>is</u> one class many students feel they can cut if they follow the syllabus and read the chapters. They feel that the three hours a week spent in a class <u>is</u> a waste of time. Students who cut regularly don't realize what they are missing. In class, there are discussions about points that are not covered in the text. In many of these classes that students feel they can cut, the instructor gives examples that help students understand ideas that aren't clear in the text. For example, *Microeconomic Practices* is a difficult textbook. Grasping its ideas is difficult without having them illustrated by an instructor.

ACTIVITY 9.5

Subject-verb agreement errors can be corrected this way:

A number of people feel they write best early in the morning. Others like to work later in the evening. Some people write best after drinking coffee; others need to meditate and calm themselves down first. Some of these approaches work for some people, some work for others. There is no one right way for all writers. My class has widely differing opinions about the best way to write and the best time to write.

ACTIVITIES 9.6, 9.7, 9.8, 9.9, AND 9.10

Responses will vary.

ACTIVITY 9.11

Tense shifts can be corrected as shown below:

1   In Maxine Hong Kingston's book, *The Woman Warrior*, I read a horrifying description of what happened to the author's aunt back in China. Her aunt was married to a man who migrated to America to earn more money than he could in China. He left his wife alone for many years, and she forgot what he even looked like. The aunt lived with her parents. After several years, she became pregnant. When the villagers found out, they broke into the family home and destroyed everything. They killed farm animals and destroyed the furniture. They stole food and various items from the kitchen. They did this to show their disapproval of what she had done, having committed adultery and having had an illegitimate child.

2   The aunt was forced to leave her family's house because of the disgrace and to give birth to her child in a pigsty. It was horribly filthy. She killed herself and her baby by drowning in a well. The worst thing was that her family denied her existence. They would never speak her name. And the belief in Chinese society was that offerings of food must be made to the dead. So the aunt is forever doomed to be a nameless and hungry ghost.

ACTIVITY 9.12

Responses will vary.

Chapter 10

Editing Pronoun Usage

ACTIVITY 10.1

Pronoun agreement errors have been corrected in the following paragraphs:

1   Teachers should not be blamed if <u>their</u> students fail because high
school students have a mind of <u>their</u> own. They are the ones who
decide if they want to be educated or not. <u>They make</u> the decisions for
<u>themselves</u> when they don't pay attention in class or decide to cut.
Teachers can only do so much with unwilling students. <u>They</u> can't
teach a student if <u>he or she</u> is always acting up and disturbing the class.
Giving extra work and shouting at troublemakers will not make a
student learn; it will not change <u>his or her</u> mind if <u>he or she</u> doesn't
want to learn.

2   The school boards are also to blame. <u>They have</u> rules and regulations that prevent the teachers from doing the best job possible. For
instance, the board may say that the teacher must spend six weeks
teaching his or her class about probability theory, but the students
know all about that part of the curriculum. <u>They need</u> help in
percentages or some other area. So valuable time is wasted. <u>It</u> could
have been used more profitably, giving the student what <u>he or she</u>
really <u>needs</u>.

ACTIVITY 10.2

In addition to correcting pronoun agreement errors as shown below, students
should also catch the tense shifts in the verb *interpret*.

Doing research for my African history class made me realize how true
the saying is that there is no history, only the opinions of historians. Many
of the books I read about Ethiopia contained the same facts, but <u>they</u>
offered different opinions about what these facts meant. The one group of
writers interprets the facts from its socialist, leftist perspective. The writers
who were members of another group <u>interpret</u> [students should catch the
shift in verb tense here] the facts to fit <u>their</u> conservative beliefs. Either the

virtues of nationalism or an attempt to find value in colonialism <u>was</u> secretly being fed to the reader. Somebody who wasn't aware of the particular beliefs held by the writer might believe <u>he or she was</u> reading objective information. For example, each of the books I read about Menelik II presented <u>its</u> own point of view about this ruler. Anybody could be confused in <u>his or her</u> reading. Was Menelik II a great figure who freed his country from foreign domination, or was he a cruel ruler who tortured prisoners and created the system of land ownership that has caused famine and the deaths of so many in the past few years? I guess everybody who reads more than one book on a historical topic has to decide what is true for <u>himself or herself</u>.

ACTIVITY 10.3

Pronoun usage errors can be corrected as follows:

Have you ever been disoriented when you visited a place you haven't seen for a long time? My friend Kim and <u>I</u> paid a visit to our favorite teacher back at our junior high school. Everything in the building had changed size and shape. I was surprised how small and narrow the hall seemed. Kim felt this even more strongly than <u>I</u>. The classrooms were so tiny; <u>they were</u> much larger in our memories. The desks were so close together that we couldn't believe there had once been room for <u>us</u> to walk between <u>them</u>. They were tiny, too. Had we really sat in <u>them</u>? And the blackboard was so low that <u>we</u> couldn't imagine that we had had to stretch to write on <u>it</u>. Of course, Ms. Coles looked much older. Kim and <u>I</u> remember <u>her</u> as being a young woman. We hoped she didn't notice the looks that passed between <u>us</u> two.

ACTIVITY 10.4

Ambiguous reference and other pronoun usage errors can be corrected as follows:

Virgil remembers his grandfather well even though he died ten years ago. <u>Virgil</u> would always watch baseball games with him. Grandpa would say, "It's hard to tell the difference between a ball and a strike on the TV screen." <u>The boy</u> said he didn't understand how this could be. The cameras, which were positioned in different places around the park, always showed <u>the pitches</u> clearly. But <u>Grandpa</u> disagreed. He said the cameras distorted everything. For example, Grandpa said the distance between the bases looked different on the screen. But he said everything looked different in the ballpark, too, depending on where he sat. Anyhow, he would disagree with what the umpire said. <u>Grandpa</u> was sure <u>the umpire</u> couldn't see either. At the time, <u>the arguments</u> seemed silly and annoying. Now <u>Virgil</u> misses those arguments with <u>his Grandpa</u>. He recalls those arguments now and realizes how lonely he feels not being able to argue with <u>his Grandpa</u> anymore. <u>Those arguments</u> brought <u>him</u> and his grandfather together in many ways.

ACTIVITY 10.5

Pronoun usage errors and sexist language can be corrected as follows:

1   A friend told me that when she was in high school <u>some students</u> would make fun of her because she wore a certain brand of jeans. At first thought, it seems foolish for <u>people</u> to be so concerned about their clothes. <u>Students</u>, especially <u>ones</u> who <u>don't</u> have a lot of money, shouldn't have to spend more of <u>their</u> money, or <u>their</u> parents', to buy a particular brand. And <u>students</u> are being insensitive and tyrannical in forcing <u>others</u> to conform to the group's standards.

2   But there's another way to look at this situation. <u>Individuals</u> in their teenage years <u>are</u> learning behavior they will need as adults. When <u>they graduate</u> and <u>find</u> a job, <u>they</u> often must dress in a particular way. A businessman must wear a suit and tie. A businesswoman wears suits, too. And not only <u>do they</u> have to wear certain types of clothes, but they can't wear certain colors and materials if they don't want the people they deal with to form negative judgments about <u>them</u> and <u>their</u> company.

3   I've noticed that teachers, too, conform to peer pressure when it comes to what <u>they wear</u>. If the head of the department and other powerful members of the staff dress casually, the newer employees will follow the same pattern after a few weeks. Also, many other workers, like salespersons in stores, have to follow dress codes. My cousin works in a clothing store, and her boss said that she always had to wear dark, conservative colors. Thus we can say that the pressure teenagers put on <u>their</u> friends to dress in a particular way is not harmful to <u>them</u>, but trains them to adapt to rules they will have to follow as adults.

ACTIVITY 10.6

Pronoun voice shifts can be corrected as follows:

1   Whether peer pressure is harmful or beneficial depends on <u>one's</u> peers. After high school, I had no plans to attend college, but several of my friends from high school went immediately. When we got together, they would talk about ideas and books <u>I'd</u> never heard of. <u>I</u> felt left out of the conversation, and even worse I felt inferior. So, following their example, I enrolled. And I'm glad I did. Now <u>I'm</u> a part of their conversations and I already have gotten the chance to have a better-paying job.

2   At other times, peers can have a negative influence. If they feel that a course is a waste of time, <u>a person</u> may begin to feel that way too. As a result, a student misses classes, his or her grades drop, and the grade point average goes down. When <u>a student has</u> friends like this, <u>he or she</u> will stop striving to reach his or her goals, and <u>he or she</u> will regret it later.

ACTIVITY 10.7

Responses will vary.

Chapter 11

Editing Style, Syntax, and Diction

ACTIVITY 11.1

Obviously, your students can rewrite the draft in any of a number of ways. What follows is just one solution:

1   In our country, the time spent on education is extended to an extreme degree. We accept that pre-college schooling takes more years than necessary to provide students with the information required for the jobs they want. As a result, large amounts of time are wasted and colossal amounts of money spent.

2   My final high school years were, in my opinion, an example of the wasteful nature of an overly extended education. These years mainly consisted of a review of the materials I learned in previous years. At that point I could have easily slept through hours of classroom instruction and still have obtained a decent grade point average. As a result, I did not learn any new material, and these years, as a consequence, were a total waste.

ACTIVITY 11.2

Here is one way to make the passage more active:

1   Left-handed people encounter many problems. For example, in a typical college classroom, there are very few desks designed for the left-handed. This means that left-handed people have to sit in desks made for the right-handed. Lefties must twist their bodies and reach across their chests so they can write. Many of them find this extremely uncomfortable.

2   Left-handed people also encounter another problem. When right-handed people write with a pen or pencil, their hand moves across the page in front of what they have written. However, lefties move their writing hand across what they have already written. So, often, they smear and smudge their writing. When I was in grammar school, the teachers insisted that I use a fountain pen. You can imagine what a

horrible mess a lefty like me made. Ballpoint pens made life much more pleasant for people like me. And typewriters and computers really improved my life.

ACTIVITY 11.3

The following shows one way to combine sentences and rewrite the paper.

It was really about how a scientist like Feynman thought and dealt with a non-scientific problem.

1　For example, when Feynman was a young boy and collected stamps, he got some from Tuva, formerly an independent country in Central Asia but at that time it was a part of the Soviet Union.
2　He was fascinated by this place that almost no one ever heard of, so after he became an adult, he wrote a letter to the Soviet Travel Bureau, which wasn't in Tuva but in Moscow, requesting permission to visit Tuva. The answer he received stated that there were no tours there, and since in the U.S.S.R. travelers could only visit places with a tour, he was denied permission to visit Tuva.
3　However, he didn't give up, but instead read all he could about Tuva, learning some of the language from a book that contained phrases and sentences in two languages—Tuvan and Russian. So Feynman had to translate the Russian into English to learn to say some things in Tuvan, because he wanted to write another letter to someone in Tuva.
4　After a long time passed, he got an answer written in Tuvan, which he didn't understand, so he translated it into Russian and then into English. The answer told him about Tuva and a special kind of singing done there that sounds like a voice and a flute but is really made by one person.
5　More time passed before Feynman learned there was going to be a contest in Tuva for people who sing this way. He tried to get invited, but the contest was cancelled.
6　Then there was an art exhibit in Sweden containing art from Tuva, so Feynman and a friend contacted the people in charge of the exhibit saying, "We want to bring this show to America," and they succeeded. A Russian expert on art from Tuva came to America with the exhibit, and Feynman talked to him and said, "I need to go to Tuva to see the places the art came from," and finally got permission to go there.
7　This TV show didn't tell me about a problem in physics but rather about how one scientist worked on a problem. He became interested

in something, tried different ways to find out about it, studied different fields, used different tactics, and didn't give up.

ACTIVITY 11.4

The rewordings offered below, of course, represent only one set of choices:

Paragraph 1   In the past, adoption was the only option for infertile couples who wanted to have a baby of their own. . .

Paragraph 2   Being paid $10,000 or more, a surrogate mother carries the child for a woman who cannot have a child. Artificially inseminated with the husband's or another man's sperm, the surrogate carries the child for nine months until it is born.

Paragraph 3   . . . I would rather provide a home for some poor child who is unwanted than . . . Also, after having carried the baby for nine months, the surrogate mother and the woman who hired the surrogate end up in the middle of a custody fight over some of these children. I know from reading the newspapers of one surrogate mother who sued to keep the baby. Then too, the surrogate who is picked may smoke, drink . . .

Paragraph 4   By using an adoption agency, the would-be parents can pick a child according to the sex and appearance they want. In the case of adoption, health records are available . . .

ACTIVITY 11.5

Other alternatives than the following are possible for correcting errors in parallelism:

1. . . . go to the shelves, and see what is available on my topic.

2. . . . in other times, and the way other cultures see the world.

3. . . . of her own body, and to be tyrannical.

4. . . . selfish, cruel, and murderous act.

5. . . . and not feel alone when I write.

6. . . . coordination, increase alertness, and improve reflexes.

7. . . . find the house, and buy it.

8. . . . friendly neighbors, and many trees.

9. . . . write a draft, and edit her paper by Monday.

10. We will swim in the pool, jog around the reservoir, or see a movie.

ACTIVITY 11.6

Other rewordings are possible in your students' rewriting to eliminate trite language.

1   Getting started when I had to write a paper was always difficult, and I felt that I was immobilized. How could I survive in this competitive world and become successful if I could never start my term papers? I wanted to produce something that was clearly right the first time, but I never could. I wanted to be relaxed and in control when I had to produce a piece of writing.

2   Then I discovered a method that solved the problem perfectly and helped in all situations. I used free writing first. I realized that I couldn't write a perfect paper the first time, but getting down my ideas first was easy. Also I realized that I didn't have to write alone. By showing my drafts to others I could get help and could develop writing that I was proud of.

ACTIVITIES 11.7, 11.8, AND 11.9

Responses will vary.

Chapter 12

Editing Spelling

ACTIVITY 12.1

The lists of student spelling errors, and the memory devices they invent, will vary.

ACTIVITY 12.2

The underscored words were spelled incorrectly in the text version:

1   Taking a road test can be a <u>traumatic experience</u>. I was extremely <u>nervous</u> to begin with. Then I met the person who was going to be <u>judging</u> my <u>performance</u>. He looked as if he was a drill instructor in the Marines who <u>enjoyed</u> failing people just for the fun of it. The man <u>obviously</u> never cracked a smile in his <u>entire</u> life.

2   He said, "Let's get started." And I <u>responded</u> with a "Yes, sir!" He gave me <u>an</u> enigmatic look, and I <u>thought</u> that I'd blown it. But <u>then</u> things seemed to be <u>proceeding</u>. I remembered all the signals, didn't run any <u>lights</u>, and <u>obeyed</u> all the signs. I was beginning to feel more <u>confident</u> when a child ran out from between two parked cars. The child was <u>chasing</u> a ball and was totally unaware that a car was about to hit him. I slammed on the <u>brakes</u>, nearly throwing my judge and me out the windshield, despite the fact that we were <u>wearing</u> seat belts. Then I was sure it was all over. However, he <u>complimented</u> me on my quick response to a potentially fatal situation.

3   So <u>despite</u> some rough moments, I passed <u>and</u> now have my <u>license</u>. However, this was one kind of road test I never want to have to go <u>through</u> again. I also hope I never come so near to injuring anyone while driving. I <u>used</u> to think driving was easy, but that was before I realized the <u>responsibilities</u> a driver has for the <u>lives</u> of others.

ACTIVITY 12.3

Misspellings and misused words can be corrected as follows:

1   Throughout my academic career, I've done well <u>except</u> in one area—math. I think my problems <u>maybe</u> began back in the second grade. I had a teacher, Ms. Treglia, who was a real horror. <u>Her class was the first I almost didn't pass.</u> Whenever I didn't <u>know</u> an answer, she'd call on me. When I didn't answer correctly, instead of helping me, <u>leading</u> me to discover the solution, she'd humiliate me. She'd call me stupid and say, "<u>Who's</u> going to show our little problem pupil how to do it correctly<u>?</u>" "Come on," she'd say. "<u>It's</u> easy. Anyone with half a brain can get this one <u>right</u>." This kind of treatment made me <u>lose</u> any enthusiasm for math.

2   In <u>later</u> grades when teachers tried to give me good <u>advice</u> about how to study for math, I just didn't listen. I had <u>already</u> decided that math wasn't for me. I couldn't <u>bear</u> the idea of going to math, no matter how nice or helpful other teachers tried to be. When I was called on I'd hold my <u>breath</u> and not answer. The mere <u>sight</u> of a math book would cause fear and trembling. It was like a <u>hole</u> had opened up in front of me.

3   Eventually, I gained some confidence as the result of the <u>compliments</u> my fifth grade teacher<u>,</u> Ms. Hancock<u>,</u> gave me. I began to see that studying hard would <u>ensure</u> I could pass math. But the main thing that helped me was knowing there would be no more incidents of humiliation when I <u>raised</u> my hand in class and made a mistake. Those <u>terrible scenes</u> were a thing of the past.

4   My experiences with those <u>two</u> teachers made me realize how important it is to give people confidence. People who are going to be teachers, or parents for that matter, need to realize that it's better to encourage those who are trying to learn something <u>than</u> to criticize them. Learners of any type need to have <u>their</u> efforts acknowledged as just that—efforts. They don't need to have <u>their</u> mistakes held up to <u>ridicule</u>. If <u>their</u> efforts become the basis of humiliation, they will be unable to <u>proceed</u> in their studies and in their growth as human beings <u>too</u>.

ACTIVITY 12.4

Responses will vary.

Chapter 13

Editing for Punctuation and Capitalization

ACTIVITY 13.1

The comma usage errors can be corrected as follows:

Now that I am the father of two children, I have learned that much more is involved in parenting than I had (**omit comma**) ever realized before. I now see that I have to control my emotions (**omit comma**) and words, for those little people have big ears (**omit comma**) and imitate whatever I say and do, something I'd never realized. For instance, I made a comment to my wife, which seemed as if it were no big deal at the time, about a friend of the family (**omit comma**) who is single and never seemed to be able (**omit comma**) to find a date. The next time he visited us, my five-year-old asked him, "Joe, do you have a girlfriend yet?" Then there was the time I'll never forget, just before we moved to Toms River, New Jersey, when little Joanie told her aunt that I had said she was a busybody. The date was September 12, 1993, and she hasn't spoken to us since. And of course, there is the obvious problem with curse words. One day, a driver cut me off, and since I was angry, I let one of those words, the ones you're never supposed to say, slip out. Needless to say, I heard it from certain small lips soon after. So I am trying to be more careful about what I say, do, and even think since I'm sure those seemingly innocent, unaware little folks can even read my mind.

ACTIVITY 13.2

Punctuation errors can be corrected as follows:

Last night I rented a movie, Kubrick's *Full Metal Jacket*. I found it is really powerful for several reasons—[or :] the brutality of the boot camp scenes; the lack of any dialogue in the first part, except for the drill instructor's words and the recruits' set, required answers; and the way it tricked me into feeling the way I was condemning the characters for feeling. I was

really angry at the way the recruits were insulted and humiliated; in fact, I
wanted to run from the room, rather than watch any longer. I've seen many
movies about wars and soldiers being trained, but I never saw one where
there were no personal conversations, no expressions of feelings, wishes,
resentments, or outside interests, only the words the men were allowed to
use in responding to the sergeant. I asked myself, "How could anyone
breathe, or even live, in this narrow, closed world, the world of a Marine
Corps training camp?" Mr. Kubrick, the director, tricked me too. I was
thinking how horrible it was that the men were being turned into killing
machines; however, when one went crazy and killed the cruel sergeant, I
cheered. Then I realized what the film had done to me; it had made me as
violent, as full of the desire to see another die, as the recruits. How could I
feel superior anymore? He (Kubrick) really got to me with this film.

ACTIVITY 13.3

The following draft has been edited for punctuation and capitalization:

I, along with many women, find the way men speak to me, men's word
choices, offensive. When I was in biology class, last summer (I think it was
in July), one man said to me, "Hey (**omit comma**) baby, can I borrow your
notes?" I'm no infant; how dare he use the word *baby* and suggest I am less
mature than he is, a intellectually undeveloped being? Can you imagine if a
woman said, "Come here little boy," or "Hey Papa?" The man would run
away for fear that she belonged in a mental hospital. A man's ego would
never allow him to accept such words. My fiance James' words once
embarrassed me too. "This is my old lady," he said to his friend at a party
on campus, in Johnson Hall I think, "Don't flirt while I go over and get her
some food." After much discussion, he realized what he'd done and said
that (**omit quotes**) he'd never introduce me that way again (**omit quotes**).
And then there are the comedians on TV who talk about broads, cows, and
even bitches. I want to scream at the screen and ask them where they get
the nerve to talk about women that way. Like the author of the article "It's
Time for the Girls to Speak Up," I want to tell them, "You are insulting
me."

ACTIVITY 13.4

The following paragraphs show the corrected punctuation and capitalization
errors:

1   I believe that college teachers shouldn't take attendance because
     (**no comma**) students have to gain a sense of responsibility at some

point in their lives, and <u>c</u>ollege is the place to begin. Learning to show up for classes on their own, without someone checking up on them, I feel, prepares students to be responsible adults (**no semicolon**) and will benefit them in their future lives.

2   Students <u>don't</u> get to demonstrate a great deal of responsibility or a chance to experience much freedom during their <u>h</u>igh <u>s</u>chool years. College is a place where students finally can exercise freedom irresponsibly, or where they can show that they are responsible people. As my friend Sam said, <u>"If</u> a teacher <u>doesn't</u> take attendance, I realize that <u>it's</u> totally up to me to decide <u>what's</u> necessary for me to pass a course<u>."</u> He went on to say that (**no quotation mark**) if a student can't handle the responsibility, he will realize <u>he's</u> not ready to handle a family, a job, (**no parentheses**) or any other kind of situation <u>adults</u> have to face on their own<u>.</u> (**no quotation mark; no parentheses**)

3   It's all part of taking responsibility for whether you get <u>A's, B's,</u> or <u>F's</u> on your own, without someone standing over you with a stick. The ability to decide how to handle college responsibilities on your own helps you grow<u>. It</u> will help you to independently get a good performance evaluation on the job later on. And because you set your own rules and guidelines, you feel a great sense of satisfaction<u>. You</u> feel you are an adult, a responsible person.

4   If teachers take attendance in <u>c</u>ollege classes, many students will feel they are being treated like children<u>.</u> They will become resentful, and this will cause them to do poorer quality work than they would do otherwise. <u>"If</u> they treat me like a baby," one of my friends said, <u>"</u>then I am a baby<u>.</u> I'll want them to do everything for me, to feed me, to give it all to me<u>.</u> (**no dash; no parentheses**) I'll be less likely to earn it for myself, (**no parentheses**) <u>won't</u> I?"

5   When college instructors don't take attendance, students see the results of their <u>actions,</u> not other <u>people's.</u> As Sam says, "It's like knowing I have to get up at 7 <u>o'clock,</u> not <u>7:30,</u> to get there on time (**no dash**) because <u>I'll</u> miss something, not because (**no comma**) of <u>someone else's</u> rules, not because <u>I'll</u> have marks against me in the <u>teacher's</u> little green book<u>."</u> "<u>It's</u> my choice<u>,"</u> he feels, <u>"</u>my responsibilities, and not someone <u>else's,</u> right<u>?"</u>

ACTIVITY 13.5

Responses will vary.

Chapter 14

Sentence Combining

I have found it useful to have students write completed combined sentences on the board and then check them in the setting of the whole class.

The combination solutions that follow are, of course, not the only ones that are possible.

ACTIVITY 14.1

Alternative Fuels

1–5   About 8,000 drivers in British Columbia use natural gas instead of gasoline in their vehicles.

6–10   Because the vehicles emit mostly carbon dioxide and water, they are being hailed by environmentalists who are concerned about air pollution as a good alternative to gasoline-powered cars.

11–19   Less-polluting vehicles are in use in other programs in California, Washington, and New York, and show how electricity, natural gas, and methanol—a derivative of natural gas—can serve as alternatives.

20–28   Less-polluting vehicles have received more attention since 1989, when Southern California adopted a stringent air-quality program that could eventually ban some cars, trucks, and buses that burn gasoline or diesel fuel.

29–36   As alternatives become more widespread, the air quality will improve, but there will be some problems such as the fact that fueling stops will be more frequent than for gasoline-powered cars and electric vehicles will never accelerate as quickly as gasoline cars.

37–41   However, as technology advances in response to needs created by new fuels, many of the problems will disappear.

ACTIVITY 14.2

Nonverbal Behavior

1–6   The way we dress, how close we stand to other people, whether we make eye contact, whether we touch, and what we do with our hands all convey messages.

7–13   These nonverbal forms of behavior communicate messages without employing words, by enhancing what our words say or by contradicting what they say.

14–18   For example, rolling your eyes shows disapproval without words while rolling your eyes and saying, "That's silly," reinforces your words.

19–27   In addition, we send other nonverbal messages about how we feel; for instance, we send one when we are bored with what someone is saying by looking around the room and playing with our hands or a pencil.

28–33   These activities send a nonverbal message that says we want to escape, that we don't want to be there.

ACTIVITY 14.3

Learning about the Past

1–8   Digging up the remains of old houses from the 1700s can tell archaeologists a lot about the environment, how people lived and what they ate and wore, but questions may still remain.

9–14   For example, finding a cellar full of a jumble of bricks and human bones together suggests quick, violent destruction of a building in an earthquake.

15–21   When oyster shells 9 to 10 inches long were found in one spot near the Atlantic Ocean, archaeologists knew what people ate and, furthermore, that animal life has changed since oysters of that size don't exist in North America today.

22–30   Archaeologists learn about clothing when, on rare occasions, they find remnants of cloth that was made in a different way, or, more likely, when they find buttons made of bone, pearl, or pewter.

31–37   Archaeologists can't always tell about the owners of the building because, while a carefully constructed building could be a sign that it belonged to rich people, careful construction could indicate that high-quality workmanship was common in all houses built in a particular time and place.

38–41   Artifacts that are found could have been dumped on the site later, and the ground could have been turned up at some later date.

ACTIVITY 14.4

Vietnam Vets

1–5   The Vietnam veteran has a set of problems different from those of other older vets who served in Korea or World War II.

6–12   The Vietnam War was especially unpopular on all levels of society, and throughout the country, it was protested on campuses, attacked in Congress, and denounced in the media.

13–20   The soldiers, most of whom had been drafted and forced to go, were met with contempt and made to feel evil by employers who were reluctant to hire them, looking on them with suspicion, seeing them as bombs ready to explode.

21–27   And the government didn't provide enough of the psychological or medical help needed to assist the vets to successfully reenter civilian life.

28–34   Congress didn't give them money for education to the same degree as it did for World War II and Korean War vets, giving the Vietnam vets only a monthly stipend that was barely enough to live on.

35–41   The negative results of this treatment include unusually high rates of alcoholism, divorce, and arrests for criminal offenses; in addition, the vets feel alienation and they distrust other people.

ACTIVITY 14.5

A Difficult Choice

1–8   I heard a program on National Public Radio called "Choices of the Heart" about two men who worked in a plant in Connecticut that produced submarines designed to carry nuclear weapons.

9–13   One worker said that he liked his job, which paid him a good salary and made him proud because he did good work that contributed to the defense of his country.

14–19   Another was troubled and felt nuclear weapons, even if only used for defense, were wrong, since if either side used them, they could destroy the world; yet he was worried about supporting his family.

20–25   He had many years of experience at the plant, had received many promotions, had become a supervisor, and received a very high salary; in addition, he knew he couldn't make as much money at another job.

26–29   Because the work he did bothered him, he felt guilty, but when he started taking his problems out on his family, he realized he had to do something.

30–36   He thought about his dilemma for a long time, turning it over in his mind, and after talking to his wife and children, he took the final step in the process, making a decision.

37–44   He decided to quit, and that made me think about what I would do if I had a job that involved doing something that went against my values, but quitting meant I would lose money.

ACTIVITY 14.6

The Emperor Norton

1–9   Joshua Norton was born in England but immigrated in the first half of the nineteenth century, when he was thirty years old, to San Francisco to make a fortune; he tried to corner the rice market but went bankrupt, and as a result, lost his mental balance.

10–16	He stopped working and began to brood about the problems of the world, and finally came to the conclusion that the United States, because of conflict between the North and South, needed a monarch with absolute power to unite the nation.
17–22	He put a notice in the *San Francisco Bulletin* in 1859, declaring himself Emperor of the United States at the request of the majority of citizens.
23–33	Norton began to dress the way he thought an emperor should, wearing a long-tailed coat with gold epaulets and brass buttons, wearing a tall beaver hat, topped with a green ostrich plume, and carrying a sword and an umbrella.
34–38	The people of San Francisco didn't mock him but accepted him, and tailors made uniforms for him—for free.
39–47	Once, when his uniform was worn out and no tailors could be found to give him a new one, Norton issued a proclamation stating that many people complained about the state of the imperial wardrobe, so the city fathers voted to buy him a new uniform at public expense.
48–54	When Norton died in 1880, his funeral was on a grand scale, attended by ten thousand people and paid for by leading businessmen.

ACTIVITY 14.7

Horror Films

1–7	In 1981, Stephen King wrote a book called *Danse Macabre*, a collection of nonfiction essays about horror films.
8–15	King says art is a creative piece of work to which the audience gives something, but from which it gets more than it gives, and he also says horror films offer artistic value in the connection between fantasy and fear.
16–22	It is true that horror films are made to make money, not with art in mind, yet while they do not consciously create art, it is thrown off like radiation from an atomic bomb.
23–27	Horror films play on our fear of death and the fact that certain types of death can be good or bad.
28–32	These films make us experience the bad kind of death, which scares us, and that is the source of the films' best effects.

33–41   These movies play on our curiosity to know what is behind a door, what is in the basement of the mortuary, and what happens in a graveyard when the mourners have left and the moon is dark.

42–47   King also says that the films violate taboos, which is valuable because by doing so they help us to better understand what the taboos are and why they make us feel uneasy.

ACTIVITY 14.8

Black English

1–6   Some say black English is valuable because it gives African Americans a sense of a unique identity and keeps them from being absorbed by the white culture.

7–13   Others say black English creates problems since it is not accepted by employers, who believe Standard American English is proper and that black English is bad English, a sign of a lack of knowledge and education.

14–23   This second group have strong feelings that black English should never be used because many react to it negatively, and this will cause African Americans to suffer by not getting good paying jobs or a piece of the American dream.

24–37   Still others believe that African Americans can use two languages, using black English with others who use it to create a bond, and using Standard American English in business situations and in their professional roles since, as the language of money and power, it will help them get ahead in business.

38–48   These people point out that neither Martin Luther King nor Malcolm X used black English when they wrote, nor do African-American newscasters, doctors, lawyers, executives, or educators in professional situations.

49–54   People who speak two languages—that is, who are bilingual—have an advantage over people who don't; bilinguals can use different languages in different situations.

ACTIVITY 14.9

Responses will vary.

PART III

Doing Research

Chapter 15

Doing Research

ACTIVITIES 15.1, 15.2, 15.3, AND 15.4

Responses will vary.

I believe it is extremely valuable to have students write about a topic *before* they do research on it. This involves them and their ideas from the start and helps eliminate the kind of research paper that is merely a series of glued-together quotations and paraphrases.

ACTIVITY 15.5

Responses will vary, but the important concern is that students do not repeat the wording or the rhythm of the originals. The process of paraphrasing is tricky, and so students may need several tries at this activity.

ACTIVITY 15.6

1. . . . was "inappropriate" (Taylor 1A). [paragraph 1]

2. . . . and birth control (Taylor 27A). [paragraph 1]

3. . . . seem to convey the school's approval (Taylor 1A). [paragraph 2]

4. . . . "strangle the free mind at its source" (quoted in Seligman and Namuth 56). [paragraph 3]

5. ". . . articles that might cause a stir" ("Court to Student Editors" 10). [paragraph 3]

6. . . . more controversial subjects to appear in print
   (442). [paragraph 4]

7. . . . gives meaning to the Constitution (442).
   [paragraph 5, extract]

ACTIVITY 15.7

Works Cited

Blow, Joe. "Juicy New Wave Killings." <u>Village Voice</u> 7 Nov.
1989: 65.

Jones, Rex. "A New Cut." <u>Newsday</u> 4 Nov. 1989: 5.

"More Repulsion." <u>Time</u> 5 Nov. 1989: 15-16.

Smith, Floyd. "More Slash and Trash." <u>The New York Times</u>
1 Nov. 1994: C25.

ACTIVITIES 15.8, 15.9, AND 15.10

Responses will vary.

Sample Syllabi

Here are two ways to organize your course around this text. These are not intended as prescriptions but are merely suggestions.

TEN-WEEK SYLLABUS

Week 1 Students interview and introduce each other, using writing questionnaire in "To the Student."

Chapter 1 Free writing and journal keeping
Chapter 2 Up to and including Activity 2.1; more free writing and finding a main idea

Week 2 Chapter 1 Getting help from others and asking questions
Chapter 2 Up to Activity 2.8

Week 3 Chapter 2 Rest of the chapter
Chapter 8 Sentence boundaries, readings and activities as needed
Chapter 14 Activity 14.1

Week 4 Chapter 1 Clustering
Chapter 3 Entire chapter on developing contracts
Chapter 9 Verb usage, readings and activities as needed
Chapter 14 Activity 14.2

Week 5 Chapter 4 Entire chapter on paragraphing
Chapter 10 Pronouns, readings and activities as needed
Chapter 14 Activity 14.3

Week 6 Chapter 5 Entire chapter on essays
Chapter 11 Style, syntax, and diction, readings and activities as needed
Chapter 14 Activity 14.4

Week 7 Chapter 6 Up to Editing Activity

Week 8 Chapter 12 Editing spelling, activities as needed
Chapter 14 Activity 14.5
Chapter 6 Finish chapter
Sample essays

Week 9 Chapter 7 Up to 7.10
Sample second drafts

Week 10	Chapter 7	Finish chapter
	Chapter 13	Punctuation and capitalization, readings and activities as needed
	Chapter 14	Activity 14.6

FIFTEEN-WEEK SYLLABUS

Week 1	Students interview and introduce each other, using writing questionnaire in "To the Student."
	Chapter 1	Free writing and journal keeping
	Chapter 2	Up to and including Activity 2.1; more free writing and finding a main idea

| Week 2 | Chapter 1 | Getting help from others and asking questions |
| | Chapter 2 | Up to Activity 2.8 |

Week 3	Chapter 2	Rest of the chapter
	Chapter 8	Sentence boundaries, readings and activities as needed
	Chapter 14	Activity 14.1

Week 4	Chapter 1	Clustering
	Chapter 3	Developing details, up to "Safest City"
	Chapter 8	Additional work if needed

Week 5	Chapter 3	Finish chapter
	Chapter 9	Verb usage, readings and activities as needed
	Chapter 14	Activity 14.2

| Week 6 | Chapter 4 | Paragraphing, up to final writing assignment on cartoon |

Week 7	Chapter 4	Finish chapter
	Chapter 10	Pronouns, readings and activities as needed
	Chapter 14	Activity 14.3
	Chapter 5	Up to Activity 5.2

Week 8	Chapter 5	Rest of chapter
	Chapter 11	Style, syntax, and diction, readings and activities as needed
	Chapter 14	Activity 14.4

| Week 9 | Chapter 6 | Up to Editing Activity |

Week 10	Chapter 12	Editing spelling, activities as needed
	Chapter 14	Activity 14.5
	Chapter 6	Finish chapter
		Sample essays

| *Week 11* | Chapter 7 | Up to Activity 7.10 |

Week 12	Chapter 7	Finish chapter
	Chapter 13	Punctuation and capitalization, readings and activities as needed
	Chapter 14	Activity 14.6

| *Week 13* | Chapter 15 | First two or three activities |

| *Week 14* | Chapter 14 | Final activities in chapter |
| | Chapter 15 | Finish chapter |

| *Week 15* | | In-class essay, sample papers, review for final, and revision of research paper |

Note: If there is no research component to the course or if you are doing only a brief documented paper, you can give more time to Chapters 5, 6, and 7 in the final weeks.